IF A WICKED MAN

IF A WICKED MAN

The True Story of JOHN LAWSON

Written by
JOHN SEALEY

BRIDGE LOGOS

Newberry, FL 32669

Bridge-Logos
Newberry, FL 32669

If A Wicked Man: True Freedom Behind Bars
by John Sealey

Library of Congress Catalog Card Number: 2018949492

International Standard Book Number: 978-1-61036-212-2

International Standard Book Number Hardcover: 978-1-61036-225-2

International Standard Book Number Large Print: 978-1-61036-237-5

Editing services by ChristianEditingServices.com

Cover design by Esther Kotecha, ekdesigns.co.uk

Front cover photo copyright 2018 Luke Robinson, londonluke@gmail.com

Interior design by Kent Jensen, knail.com

DEDICATION

"To my Mother Josephine, thank you for never giving up on me"

—John Lawson

"To Shelley, the wind beneath my wings"

—John Sealey

CONTENTS

PROLOGUE

GOING DOWN

1989

'The defendant will rise,' the clerk of the court ordered. A murmur buzzed around the courtroom as the judge was about to pass sentence. John Lawson, dressed in a smart tailored suit, slowly got to his feet. At twenty one, John was a handsome man with a square face and strong nose. He had an athlete's build, with broad shoulders and not an ounce of fat on his body. His gingery hair was cut short, giving his face an added fierceness.

He looked around the courtroom with an expression of casual arrogance. The members of the jury appeared satisfied with the outcome of the trial, which surprised John, as Cecil Watkins, his solicitor, seemed to be smiling too. He also noticed Inspector Ronald Atwell slouching back in his seat with an 'I said I'd get you and I'm here to see you go down,' look on his face.

None of this fazed John, for he still felt bullish as he stood in the dock at Southwark Crown Court. The judge gave a little cough as if to draw attention to the seriousness of the pronouncement he was about to make.

'John Lawson,' the judge began, his face implacable. 'It is my opinion that you are a violent man. An innocent tourist came here seeking our culture, hoping to take home good memories, but he was not given this opportunity. Instead, he was forced to pay you an extortionate amount of money, whilst terrified and fearful. In this country everyone has the right to walk the streets and enter our establishments without fear or menace. We will not tolerate this kind of behaviour, and for this you will be punished with a custodial sentence. I sincerely hope that this case will help to warn people of the unscrupulous methods you and others employ to rob unsuspecting tourists. The fact that you have changed your plea to guilty has been taken into account. However, that does not diminish the gravity and impact of your behaviour, so I am sentencing you accordingly. You will serve nine months' imprisonment. Take him down.'

John fought to suppress a grin, a mixture of relief and guilt sweeping over him as the two prison officers cuffed him and led him down the steep stairwell, their boots echoing all the way to the holding cells.

'I don't know what you're smiling about, you've just been given nine months,' one of the prison officers remarked.

'I'm grinning because I was expecting to get at least two years,' John wanted to say, but decided not to. This was his first conviction and he had no idea what he was in for.

'Your solicitor will come and see you as soon as he's finished his other cases,' the first officer said, removing John's handcuffs before marching out and slamming the cell door behind him.

John slumped down on the bench and looked around at the miserable surroundings. He thought about the lengths the Crown Prosecution Service had gone to—flying the American tourist all the way from the States—to make sure Inspector Atwell 'got him', as he had sworn he would.

The cell door opened and a prison officer announced, 'Right, your solicitor is ready to see you. Get to your feet and put your hands out.'

'Well, we didn't do too badly, did we?' Cecil Watkins said cheerfully, as soon as John was seated on the other side of the table.

'Yeah, I thought I was going to get longer,' John said with an air of relief.

'You would have, if we hadn't changed your plea to guilty and said a few words in the right ears'. Cecil Watkins' paunch bulged over the top of his waistband, pressing against the table.

'The right ears?'

'I never thought they would fly the witness in from the States. With his statement you were going to be looking at more than two years if I hadn't done a deal with the prosecuting counsel,' he said, dandruff falling on his crumpled suit as he scratched his head. 'You have to understand, the rule of law is about money. Money makes the law and the law protects the money that makes the law. The law has been after the Lawsons for a long time, without managing to nail them. But they managed to nail you. You're the first and you only got nine months. With good behaviour you'll do no more than four and a half, which won't please the likes of Inspector Atwell. Keep your nose clean and you'll be out before you know it. Don't worry, your uncles and I will take care of everything and see your mother and Daniel are taken care of.' Watkins got to his feet, crossed to the door and tapped on it.

The sweat box was aptly named, John thought as his broad shoulders pressed against either side of the confined space, the only light in the van coming from a small blacked out window next to his head. The stop-start of the prison van through the evening traffic made him feel sick, and he threw up into a plastic bag the guard had shoved under the door. When the van came to a stop, John craned his neck to look through the dark window and saw the large wooden gate and surrounding stone walls of Her Majesty's Brixton Prison.

An acrid smell pervaded the air as the prisoners were let out of the van. Filled with uncertainty, John looked around at the ancient walls topped with barbed wire. A sense of dread washed over him as he looked up at the rows and rows of barred windows that had dirty brown streaks running down from them. A group of prisoners were walking around with shovels, picking up newspaper wrappings, plastic bags and what looked like socks littered about the ground.

'What are they doing?' he asked one of the prisoners standing with him.

'That's the bomb squad.'

'What do you mean, the bomb squad?'

'Obviously your first time in here,' the prisoner remarked capriciously. 'When you need a crap at night, you don't want it lying around stinking the cell out, so you do it on some newspaper or in whatever else you can find, wrap it up and toss it out the window. These poor buggers have the job of cleaning it up. It's the worst job in the prison. Some of the real nasty pieces of work up there try to throw parcels at them while they're cleaning up the mess. Whatever you do, make sure you don't get yourself on the bomb squad.'

The induction area was a large cell that could accommodate up to about forty prisoners, with another half a dozen single cells for those likely to cause trouble. The room stank of sweat and stale tobacco, which made John want to puke again.

'Right Lawson, you're next,' a prison officer called out.

John followed him to a desk where another official took his photograph, checked his details, handed him a prison rule book and instructed him on the basics of how to behave while serving his sentence and the consequences of failing to obey the rules. Yet another prison officer guided him over to a counter where he was issued with the prison uniform—two blue and white striped shirts, a pair of jeans, two vests, two underpants, two pairs of socks and a pair of black boots. He also received a pack containing a toothbrush, toothpaste, towel, soap, disposable razor and a set of eating implements consisting of a blue plastic mug, bowl, plate, knife, fork and spoon.

'Right, bring that lot with you, move over to that cubicle, empty your pockets and place everything in the brown envelope inside the cardboard box. Then remove all your clothes,' the prison officer ordered. There were no doors on the cubicle and the prison officer watched as John slowly emptied his pockets into the envelope, which was then sealed. 'Hurry up, we haven't got all day,' the man barked, as John started to undress. 'Hand me each article of clothing as soon as you've removed it,' he added.

John watched as the prison officer searched through every pocket and lining of his brand new suit. 'You've just seen me remove everything,' he said.

'Just checking you haven't got any illegal substance sewn into the linings or pockets,' the prison officer said, handing the suit back to John. 'Now put it in that box.'

John carefully folded his clothes, placed them in the box and reached for the underwear he had been issued with.

'Right, before you do that, I want you to squat and give me a loud cough,' the prison officer ordered.

'What?' John exclaimed, indignation brimming in his voice.

'Just want to make sure you're not concealing any illegal substances in unusual places,' the officer explained.

'I don't use drugs,' John said assertively.

'Yeah, that's what they all say. Just do as I say and cut the chat,' the officer said gruffly.

John squatted and gave a loud cough, feeling anger at being treated like a common criminal; but then he smiled to himself, realising that he was in fact just a common criminal.

'I don't know what that smile is about, Lawson, but I tell you, it won't be there for long,' the officer said with a cruel grin. 'Right, put on your prison gear and line up for the doctor's examination.'

John inspected the underpants, wondering how many previous prisoners had worn them. But they looked reasonably clean, so he slipped into them and put on the rest of the prison issue.

'Do up the top button of your shirt and keep it buttoned. That is a strict rule and you'll find yourself in trouble if you don't,' the prison officer snapped.

John fastened the top button of the shirt, picked up his pack and followed the officer out of the cubicle.

The doctor gave him a perfunctory once over and announced him fit and healthy. The prisoners were then marched off to their various allotted wings. As John entered B Wing, he was struck by the enormity of it, a sense of foreboding tightening in his chest. There were four landings with rows of cells. Wire netting suspended across each landing like a trapeze artiste's safety net. The noise was deafening—a cacophony of mugs banging on cell bars, prisoners yelling to each other, music from portable radios blaring out. Some prisoners were leaning over the rails to see the new inmates being led to their cells.

They were guided to a caged staircase that led up to the fourth landing, and from there John was led to a cell that had been turned into a storeroom stacked with bedding, mops, buckets, brushes and other cleaning materials.

'Right, this is where you pick up your bedding.' John watched as an inmate gathered up two sheets, two blankets and a pillow, and handed them to him.

'Don't we get a pillow case?' John asked, already guessing the answer. The inmate just glared at him and turned away.

'Let's get you to your cell,' and John was ushered to the last cell at the end of the landing.

'Bates, here's your new cellmate,' the officer announced with a mischievous grin, shoving John into the cell before stepping out and slamming the door. Bates looked at John impassively, waiting until he heard the officer's footsteps fading before saying anything.

'Me name's Alfie. This yer first time in prison, boy?' he asked, in a broad cockney accent. There was a brooding intensity about him as he slowly swung his legs off the bunk and took a good look at John.

'Yes, first time,' John answered nervously, looking around the cell, which was no more than ten feet by eight. Two single beds were placed on either side, with a barred window high up on the rear wall. The walls had originally been painted cream, but were now a dirty yellowish brown. There was a rectangular board above each bed for pictures and photos. In the left corner stood a small table with a jug of water on it.

'That's yer bed over there, boy,' Alfie indicated, as though there was a choice. John put his belongings down on the bare mattress.

'So what yer in fer, boy?' Alfie asked, his eyes sweeping over him, dark and assessing.

'Robbery,' John said with a hint of pride.

'And what did yer get fer that?'

'Nine months.'

'Bleedin eck, only nine munfs, what did yer rob, a bleedin piggy bank? There are blokes in ere that got five years fer robbery. Yer must av ad a bleedin good brief or a bent judge.'

'I think I had a good solicitor.'

'Well, give me his address, e sounds a lot better'an the idiot I ad, didn't know his arse from his elbow. Did yer av to pay fer yer brief or did yer get legal aid?'

'No, his fees were taken care of by my family.'

'There yer go, yer know what they say? It's not ow guilty yer are, but ow much money yer got. Yer won't even av done yer apprenticeship by the time yer get out. Yer not inta drugs are yer, boy?' Alfie asked, searching John's face for any signs of drug abuse.

'I don't have anything to do with that stuff. Never have, never will,' John assured him.

'I bleedin ope so, cos I can't stand those crack'eads, junkies, bleedin morons. Yer can ear the bleedin idiots screaming their bleedin eads off and kickin the bleedin cell doors. Can't get no sleep sometimes.'

John could see the doubt on his face and was anxious to reassure him.

'Anyone that mucks around with drugs is a fool, a dangerous fool. It's something I've never been tempted to try, I don't even smoke.'

'Ah well, baccy, that's anuvver fing. Baccy's a valuable currency in ere. So when yer eventually get yer canteen money, make sure yer buy some baccy, because yer can use it ta trade for somefink yer really want.'

'What about you, what are you in for?' John asked. By Alfie's appearance he was in his late fifties, worn down by prison life, but there seemed a brutish masculinity about him. He was of average height and appeared to have a slight stoop. Otherwise he seemed in reasonably good shape. He had a rugged weather-beaten face with piercing green eyes that seemed to watch one's every move. His thinning black hair was greased straight back.

'Burglary, fraud, bit of tea leafing, nuffink too eavy, just enuff ta earn a living as it were, nuffink violent. I've been in and out of prison fer most of the last seventeen years. I mean yer av ta keep working uvverwise yer bleedin starve, yer know ow it is. The trouble wiv money is yer never av enuff, and when yer do get enuff, there's always some bleedin nutter trying ta take it off yer. Doin a twelve munf stretch this time,' Alfie said with a nonchalant air.

John felt a sense of admiration for him and became a little more at ease.

'I guess you know your way around the prison,' he said, meaning it as a compliment.

'Yeah, bin in enuff of em, and one fing I've learnt is, yer av ta try not ta fink of what's appenin on the outside. Yer world for the next four and alf munfs is prison, and the bleedin day ta day routines yer just av ta get used ta. Yer start finkin about anyfink else and it'll start ta drive yer bleedin crazy. Keep yer ead down and do yer bird and that way yer survive. That's ow I've always got frew it, which brings me ta the point. As yer can see, toilet facilities in ere are at a bare minimal. That's yer slop bucket there, but if yer av ta av a crap in the middle of the night, don't use the bleedin bucket. Get a coupla sheets of newspaper, lay em on the floor, crap on'em, then wrap it up in a parcel and frow it out the window. That way the cell don't stink all bleedin night,' Alfie explained.

'Yeah, I was told about it when we came in and saw the poor guys going around with shovels picking the parcels up.'

'Yeah well, make sure yer don't get put on the bomb squad. Anyway, the best fing, of course, is ta train yer bowels, as I don't wanna be woken up in the middle of the bleedin night and see yer squatting wiff yer trousers round yer bleedin ankles.'

Just then the cell door was unlocked and the prison officer shouted, 'Right, come and get your meals!'

'We have to take these with us?' John asked as Alfie gathered up his plastic bowl and plate.

Alfie gave him one of his long-suffering looks. 'Unless yer wanna carry the food back in yer bleedin ands.'

'You mean they don't have a canteen where we sit down and eat?'

'Sure, wiff waiter service as well. Where do yer fink yer are boy, the bleedin Ritz?'

John took his plate and bowl and followed Alfie along the landing to the staircase, the clanging of heavy boots on the metal steps intensifying as the prisoners from other levels joined and filed down to the ground floor.

'Bleedin joke, really. The ones on the lower landings get theirs before us and by the time we get ours and carry it back up ta the cell, it's bleedin cold,' Alfie shouted above the noise.

Having got their food, they made their way back to the staircase.

'Make sure yer don't spill anyfink off yer plate as yer carries it up, as they'll av yer scrubbin the bleedin stairs from top ta bottom,' Alfie warned him.

'You're right, the food is cold,' John said, taking his first mouthful as soon as they got back to their cell.

'Never mind, yer get used to it,' Alfie said, dolefully.

'Don't you ever complain?'

Alfie looked at him, his eyes narrowing. 'Listen boy, the first fing yer learn in prison is yer don't complain, unless of course yer wanna finish up on the bomb squad or on some uvver equally unpleasant jobs like cleanin the bogs. The screws will take great pleasure in findin nasty jobs for yer to do. So keep yer mouf shut and answer, yes sir, no sir, free bags full sir, when asked or told to do somefink. If yer see someone being beaten up or worse, yer say nuffink, and if yer asked, yer tell'em yer eard nuffink and saw nuffink. That way boy, yer'll manage ta survive,' he said, letting the words hang for a moment. 'So eat up boy, I know it tastes like slop, but try and imagine it's the best meal yer ever ad and breakfast tomorrow will be even better. That's how yer survive in this place. Let it get yer down, and yer struggle to survive,' Alfie said, taking another mouthful and chewing as if he was really enjoying it.

'Wouldn't be so bad if we had something to wash it down with,' John said, forcing himself to eat what was left on his plate.

'Don't worry, the tea bucket'll be round a bit later. In the meantime, make yer bed up and get yerself ready, it's almost time to be let out to use the toilets, and let's hope yer can do a crap then. That's what I've trained meself to do.'

'I'll do my best,' John said worriedly.

'Let's hope yer do, saves all the messin about.'

As John entered the toilets he was hit by an overpowering smell of urine, stale tobacco and body odour. Cockroaches and other insects scurried around in corners and crevices. Alfie saw the changing expression on his face. 'Wait till yer slop out in the morning, yer see rats runnin all over the bleedin place. But yer get used to it like we all do,' Alfie said with a slight smile.

'Did yer manage to knock one out?' Alfie asked on their way back to the cell.

'Yes, as it happens I was dying to go, so you don't have to worry tonight,' John said, shooting an expression of triumph at him, at the same time feeling rather strange about discussing his bowel movements with a complete stranger.

'Fank eavens. And if yer av ta pee in the middle of the night, make sure yer aim for the side of the bucket; that way it don't make so much noise.'

John slumped down wearily on his bed.

'Av yer mug ready, tea'll be ere any moment after they've done the ead count. Not that I'm planning on goin anywhere,' Alfie said with a wry smile.

The tea arrived in a large steel bucket. John watched as the trolley was wheeled to the cell door and Alfie eagerly dipped his mug in and filled it with the lukewarm tea. The inmate pushing the tea trolley then offered him a biscuit.

'Don't yer want any tea?' Alfie asked.

'I was just wondering how many filthy mugs had been dipped into that bucket before it got to us,' John said.

Alfie took a sip of his tea and looked at him over the rim of the mug. 'Like I said, this aint a bleedin five star otel. If yer don't bleedin want it, then I'll bleedin av it. Ere, give us yer mug.'

'Sorry, it just takes some getting used to,' John said, holding onto his mug, dipping it into the bucket and taking a biscuit.

The inmate turned the trolley around and the prison officer slammed the cell door shut, followed by a series of loud clicks as the lock turned and secured the cell door.

'That's it for the night. Now yer know why they're called turnkeys or screws, as we call em these days.' Alfie said, chewing on his biscuit. 'Yer wanna listen ta the radio, boy?'

'Have you got a radio?' John asked, without thinking.

'Would I bleedin ask yer if I adn't?' Alfie put his mug down, got onto his knees, reached under the bed and pulled out a portable radio. He placed it on the table.

'What yer fink of that beauty then?'

'Yeah, looks alright,' John said, wondering what was so special about it.

'All bleedin' right? Is that all yer got ta bleedin say? This is a Roberts Rambler, my son, it's the dog's bollocks, the Rolls Royce of radios. Yer won't see many of these around, especially in this bleedin place.' Alfie reached back under the bed and pulled out a length of electric wire, connected one end to the radio and turned to John. 'Steady the bleedin table,' he said, as he clambered onto it, reached up to the neon light fitting, removed the white guard cap, fiddled with the wires, and expertly connected the radio to the power supply.

'There yer are, all courtesy of er Majesty, except she don't bleedin know about it,' Alfie said with a conspiratorial smile as he scrambled off the table.

'What do you usually listen to?' John asked.

'I like listenin to the oldies, more my kind of music. At least yer can understand the bleedin words. I mean these days yer can't understand a bleedin word any of em are singin. That's if yer can call it singin, I mean all this bleedin pop nonsense, any idiot can do that,' Alfie said, tuning in to Radio Two.

'Welcome to the Adrian Love show! Have I got some real good chilled out classics for you lovely listeners tonight,' the DJ announced.

'There yer are, bleedin perfect, what better way to spend an evenin,' Alfie stretched out on his bunk with a satisfied grin on his face.

'I could think of some places I'd rather be than here,' John said.

'Yeah well, yer bleedin well ere and yer better get bleedin used to it.'

The music was soothing, and as John lay back on his bed he began to think of Daniel and his mother. 'When can I get to make a phone call? I noticed there are phones at the end of the landing,' he asked.

'Phone calls? It was only letters allowed when I was first banged up. What yer av to do is go down and see one of the POs and before yer ask, a PO is a senior prison officer, e'll give yer a chit, yer fill it out wiff five numbers yer want ta call, security then check the numbers ta make sure yer ain't planning an escape or somefink. It all takes forever, by which time yer av got yer canteen money and yer be able to buy yerself a phone card,' Alfie explained. 'Now will yer bleedin well shut up, I want ta listen to the music.'

John placed his hands behind his head and began to feel more relaxed. *At least I'm not sharing a cell with a nutter*, he thought as he closed his eyes and listened to the music.

A few days after filling out the forms, John got his canteen money and was able to buy a phone card. He couldn't wait to call home. As soon as the cell door was opened for the evening meal he rushed for the phone, picked up the receiver, inserted the phone card and heard a recorded voice message instructing him to enter his prison number. Then the voice instructed him to enter the number he wished to call. His hand holding the receiver began to shake. This was the first time he was going to speak to his mother since he'd been sentenced, and he was not sure how she was going to react.

He heard his mother's voice, 'Hello, hello,' but as John said hello, another recorded voice announced, 'The phone call you are about to receive is from an inmate of Her Majesty's Prison, Brixton. Please hang up now if you do not wish to receive this call.'

John's mother took a deep breath and said, 'Hello.'

'Hi, it's me.'

'So good to hear your voice, darling. I can't believe it's going to be nine months before we see you again,' her voice was warm, tinged with sadness.

'No, it's only going to be four and a half months as long as I don't do anything stupid,' he quickly assured her.

'Four and half months is still a long time for Daniel. What am I going to tell him?' John could hear the tension in her voice.

'Tell Daniel I'm working away and I'll buy him a nice present when I come home,' he said.

'Okay. I just hope he doesn't get to hear the truth from someone else. Since it got in the newspapers all the family are talking about it. Fortunately they don't know you're in prison, but I shudder to think what the reaction will be when they find out.'

'I can't talk long, Mum. How's Alex?' John asked, wanting to change the subject.

'Oh, he's doing well. He's still working at the engineering firm and he's met a lovely girl called Samantha.'

'That's great Ma, I've got to go because if I don't I won't get any dinner. So I'll call again as soon as I get a chance. I love you Mum, and tell Daniel I love him too. Bye.'

John replaced the receiver and hurried down the staircase, but was stopped halfway by a prison officer. 'You're too late Lawson, get back to your cell, NOW!'

John turned and trundled wearily back up the staircase, hungry, but pleased he'd spoken to his mother.

'I ope it was worf it missin tonight's specialty of greasy sausage and stodgy smashed potatoes, followed by rock ard cake and lumpy custard,' Alfie said when he saw John walk in with empty plates.

'I wasn't long on the phone. I even cut it short to get down there in time. It's not fair.'

'Anyone who expects fairness in this place as been seriously misinformed,' Alfie quipped. 'Like I said, this ain't no oliday camp. Anyway, did yer get ta talk ta who yer wanted ta?'

John gave a thin smile and took a long beat before saying, 'It was great talking to my mother, but when she asked me what to tell my son, well I...'

Alfie saw the confusion on his face.

'That's the bleedin problem. It's not what just appens ta yer in ere, it's ow the uvvers on the outside deal wiv it. They've got ta carry on trying to live a normal life, which ain't easy, given the circs. But I'm sure she was pleased ta ear from yer.'

John felt his eyes well up, thinking of Daniel, deserted yet again, wondering how he was going to react when his Nan tells him his dad is going to be working away for a few months more. And what if he finds out the truth? He gave an involuntary shiver, and his face clouded over.

'Yer alright?' Alfie asked.

'Sorry Alfie, it's just that, speaking to her for the first time since...'

'I know, I know, and it don't get any easier. Yer just av ta get used to it. Yer banged up twenty free ours a day, so yer going to av ta toughen it out like I've ad ta, boy,'

'Yeah, I know, it's just a bit hard at the moment.'

'Tell yer what, I'll put some bleedin music on as soon as the tea bucket's been round,' Alfie said, trying to cheer him up.

'Yeah, better than listening to the numpties out there,' John said, forcing a smile.

After they had had their tea, John watched as Alfie went through the actions of connecting the radio again.

'Get off yer arse and steady the bleedin table, yer want me ta break me bleedin neck?' Alfie said, in his usual gruff manner.

John got to his feet and gripped the table as Alfie clambered on and stretched up to connect the wires. After helping Alfie down, he lay back on his bunk, hands behind his head, and listened to the soft music. Some of the tension started lifting. He was slowly coming to terms with being in prison, and the fact that there was nothing he or anyone else could do about it.

Alfie kept the volume low so as not to attract attention, and the gentle rhythm combining with the weariness of the day slowly began to overcome John. He reached down, pulled the blankets up over his head and curled up in the foetal position, blackness engulfing him. Losing all sense of his surroundings, he felt himself drifting down a long tunnel, until he came up against a solid door. He tried to open it, but it was locked. He began to panic and hammer at the door and cry out, 'Dad, where are you? Please! Let me out!' But there was no Dad, nobody to let him out.

Suddenly he heard a voice on the other side of the door. 'Dad, is that you?' he called out. Then another voice, and heavy banging on the door. The sound was frightening. He rushed over to the far corner, away from the door and curled up, tucking his knees tightly under his chin, frightened that his father might be angry with him. Had he done something terrible to make his dad so angry he wanted break the door down? He started to shake with fear as the pounding on the door became louder and louder. He stared at the door as splinters began to appear in the panelling, until finally the door burst open. As the light flooded in, two shadowy figures rushed towards him.

'No Dad, please! I haven't done anything, honest!' he cried. 'Please don't hurt me!'

'Shush, it's alright John, darling, you're safe now,' he heard a woman's voice say. The woman leaned over and took hold of him. She started to shake him, and for a moment he thought she was angry with him.

He pulled the blanket tighter around him as he heard a man's voice saying, 'What the bleedin eck's goin on? Can't bleedin sleep wiv yer making all that racket!' Alfie was bristling with annoyance.

John slowly opened one eye, then the other, blinked several times before he looked up and saw the face staring down at him. He shook his head to clear his brain, trying to work out where he was and who it was shouting at him.

'Sorry, I must have been dreaming,' he said, as he realised it was Alfie's face staring down at him.

'Dreamin? More like a bleedin nightmare if yer ask me. Yer were calling fer yer dad not to urt yer. What the ell was that all about?'

John's mind raced as he tried to compose himself. 'I think it was the sound of the jangling keys turning in the lock that set me off.'

'Yeah, they can set yer off, they used ta me at the beginnin, but after yer bin inside as many times as I av, yer kinda get used to em,' Alfie said, consolingly.

'I was dreaming of my father turning the key in the lock and leaving me alone in our flat. I was ten,' John finally managed to say.

'Bleedin eck, ten years old, a bleedin kid, what kind of farver would lock is bleedin kid up?'

The memories flooded back. Much as he tried to fight them, they never really went away. He lived with them, like an incurable cancer. Now the anguish of being locked up again pressed the air out of his lungs.

'It's a long story,' he said to Alfie. 'It all started in 1969, when my dad took me and my mum from Glasgow to start a new life in South Africa.'

CHAPTER 1

DURBAN, SOUTH AFRICA

1970-1977

The tropical climate of the south coast of Natal in South Africa was what attracted Alexander Lawson—Lex, as he was commonly known—to Durban. The dream of starting a new life in this vibrant and exciting country was born when he visited South Africa while serving in the Merchant Navy. The cold and dreary streets of his native Glasgow, the dirty sandstone buildings and the uncontrolled gang culture made the thought of emigrating to a better place irresistible.

After leaving the navy Lex got a job as a bus driver and it was there that he met the bus conductor Josephine Curtis, a smouldering beauty with dark hair that cascaded over her shoulders. She was smitten with Lex's rugged good looks, and soon a romance blossomed. They got married in March 1966 and Josephine gave birth to John in October of that year.

Some time later Lex's best friend, Ronnie McGregor, surprised him by announcing that he and his wife Mary were emigrating to South Africa. That was all Lex needed to make up his mind too, and early in 1970 the Lawson family set sail for South Africa. John was three years old.

Once settled in Durban, Lex got a job with the City Police and soon established a reputation as a crack shot in the force. To little John he was a hero who could do nothing wrong. He loved riding in the police car with his dad and going to the shooting range with him. Lex taught him all he knew about weapons and even allowed him to fire his revolver and pistol.

Josephine had found a job as saleslady at Woolworths, and the family settled in the lush green area of Umbilo, where they rented a charming two-bedroomed apartment. John loved the outdoor lifestyle and ran around barefoot and climbed trees with the monkeys that roamed freely around the area.

In May 1972 Jose gave birth to Alexander Curtis Lawson and she and Lex felt that their family was now complete. They had become part of the local ex-pat community and were active in the social activities of the police force such as weekend barbecues and beach picnics. John loved the role of big brother, and life could not have been better for the Lawsons. But a message from England that Jose's father was desperately ill changed their lives dramatically. Jose and little Alex flew back to England and John had to stay behind with his father, as by now he was of school going age.

It was the beginning of the Christmas holidays and there was the usual buzz of excitement as the bell announcing the end of term echoed through the corridors and classrooms of Penzance Primary School in Umbilo. John grabbed his satchel and rushed out of the gates, eager to see his father who he knew would be waiting for him in his police car.

'Hey son, I'm going to have to drop you off at the flat. I have to get back to work and I might be away for the rest of the day and maybe even tonight. I want you to be a brave boy and look after the place for us.'

John's dad was his idol and he trusted him completely, so he tried to shrug off the twinge of worry that crept up on him, and looked admiringly over his shoulder at the shotgun and the array of police gadgets laid out on the back seat.

He kissed his dad goodbye with a brave smile, but when he heard the key turning in the lock, a sad look spread across his face, and he wondered what time his father would be back...

Scared and alone John waited patiently for his dad, he missed his mum and even missed his little brother. That first night John climbed into his parents' bed and cried himself to sleep. As the days went by John grew increasingly upset and weary as there was nothing to eat in the fridge and the cupboards were bare. On the fourth day, weak from starvation John collapsed on the rug in the living room. Hours went by as he drifted in and out of consciousness until he heard the sound of banging on the front door. Just when he wanted to drift off again, he heard a woman's voice, 'John! John, are you in there? Oh Les, he's not responding, you're going to have to break down the door!'

He fell asleep as the door flew open and awoke to find himself lying in a bed, tucked into soft clean sheets, with the sun streaming in through the open window. He had no idea whose bedroom it was and why he was there. He moved his hand to his stomach, which was aching with hunger. He swung his feet over the side of the bed, stifled a yawn and eased himself onto his feet. His heart drumming in his chest, legs shaky, he made his way to the door. As he slowly opened it he heard a woman's loud and angry voice. She sounded Scottish, like his dad.

'You're a disgrace! How could you do this? How could you just lock him up and go off for days with that woman?' There were a few moments' silence, and she continued, 'You'd damn well better!' followed by a telephone receiver being slammed down, which made him quickly shut the door and retreat back to the bed. Feeling totally perplexed, he sat staring aimlessly around the room until his eyes fell on a selection box in the far corner. He jumped up, pulled a chocolate bar from the box and sank to his knees while shoving pieces of the bar into his mouth.

'John darling, what are you doing?' the woman asked as she walked into the room. John looked up at her, a sheepish look on his face, which was smeared with chocolate. 'I'm sorry, I was hungry,' he mumbled. For a brief moment he stared at the woman while fragments of memory started flooding his mind. He shivered and his eyes filled with tears.

'It's all right, darling, it's all right. But let's go get you some proper food,' she said, anxious to dispel his distress. 'I've run you a bath, and by the time you're dressed, we'll have a nice hot meal ready for you.'

'Where am I?' His voice was tentative, his eyes trying to tell his brain that he knew this lady. He somehow recognised the oversized glasses she was wearing. She was dressed in a floral blouse and black slacks. She had dark curly hair and a chubby face.

'I'm your Auntie Marion,' she told him. 'Remember me?'

'Auntie!' he exclaimed happily. 'Where's my dad? I heard you speak on the phone. Were you talking to him? Why were you so angry?'

She felt the colour rising in her cheeks. What should she say to this poor child? 'Have your bath, darling. We'll talk about it when you've had something to eat,' she said, pulling him to his feet and leading him off to the bathroom.

'Hello John,' Uncle Les greeted him as he entered the kitchen. 'Come, sit down, let's fill your belly. You must be starving, poor lad.'

Uncle Les was tall, with buck teeth that showed when he smiled, and his head of black hair was neatly combed and parted to one side. John gave a half smile as he nervously shuffled to the table and sat down.

'Feeling better now you've had a good sleep and a nice bath?'

'Yes, thank you Uncle,' John answered politely.

'That's good, my lad, maybe you can go out and play with Graham and Lorraine after your meal if you're feeling up to it?'

Marion put a plate of sliced ham and two fried eggs in front of him. 'There, this will make you feel even better.' John smiled a thank you, and they both watched anxiously as he cut off a tiny piece of ham and slowly started chewing on it. With a surprised expression Uncle Les asked, 'What's the matter John, you alright?'

'Sorry Uncle, I ate a whole selection box in the bedroom.'

'Don't worry about it, John darling. I'm not surprised you were starving,' his aunt said.

'Where's my dad? Has something happened to him?' John asked, putting the knife and fork down.

His aunt and uncle exchanged glances. Finally Auntie Marion said, 'Your dad is fine, darling. He'll be coming to see you tomorrow.'

'He hasn't been shot, has he?'

'Shot?' Les exclaimed, seeing the tears well up in John's eyes. 'Why would he be shot?'

'He's a policeman and policemen get shot and he's been shot at before. He's killed people and they've tried to kill him,' John said, fighting hard not to start sobbing.

'No, it's nothing like that... it's just that...' Marion hesitated. 'Look, he'll explain everything when he sees you tomorrow,' she added consolingly.

The following morning John would not eat breakfast or play with Graham and Lorraine. He stood at the bedroom window, as he had been since getting up, waiting for his father's Volkswagen Beetle to come up the driveway. *He's going to come, he won't let me down. He won't just leave me, because he loves me as much as I love him*, he kept telling himself, but the thought became less convincing as time wore on.

He heard the familiar sound of the Beetle engine before he saw it pull up at the bungalow. 'Dad!' he screamed and rushed to the door, pulling it open, then hesitating and slamming it shut again. *Suppose he doesn't want to see me. Suppose he's mad at me*, he thought as he hurried back to the window and looked out. His aunt and uncle were walking towards his father. His aunt was waving her finger at him angrily. He opened the window to try to hear what she was saying, but he only managed to pick up some of it.

'... abandoning your son... that floozy, while poor Josephine... sick father. What were you thinking? He could have died!' Then she held up her hand. '... don't answer... sordid details. What kind of a man...?'

Then he clearly heard his father say, 'I came here to see my son, not to have an argument with you, Marion.'

Uncle Les came into the bedroom. 'Come on lad,' he said, taking hold of John's hand. 'Your dad's here.'

As soon as John saw his father, all his worries seemed to fall from his shoulders, and he ran towards him. He was a handsome man—fair-skinned, with a muscular body and short salt-and-pepper coloured hair. He was dressed in flared jeans with a denim shirt hanging over his waistband and concealing a 9mm Browning pistol strapped to his belt. He spoke with a broad Glaswegian accent. Lex Lawson dropped to his knees and scooped his son up into his strong arms. 'I'm sorry, my boy, I'm really sorry,' he said, as he held him tight.

'What are you sorry about, Dad?'

'It's difficult to explain, son,' he began, with a twisted smile. 'Listen, you're going to have to stay here for a while with your aunt and uncle until I can get you onto a plane to go to your mum. And I'll come and join you as soon as I can.'

'Why can't you come with me?'

'I can't, son. I've got work to do and I can't look after you at the same time, so you have to stay here with your aunt and uncle. I'll come and take you to the airport and I promise I'll be with you very soon.'

A few days later John looked out from his window seat as the plane lifted off the runway in Johannesburg. As they soared towards the drifting clouds, obliterating the view of the land below, he wondered if he would ever see his father again.

CHAPTER 2

BIRKENHEAD

It had been a long, lonely journey and as the plane began its approach to Heathrow airport, John looked down at the clusters of buildings below, still not understanding why his father had not come with him. They touched down around lunchtime, and his whole family was there to meet him—his mother, his little brother Alex, Granny Curtis, Auntie Ruby, Auntie Cath, Auntie Chris, Auntie Rita and several cousins.

By the time they got back to Birkenhead, near Liverpool in the north-west of England, the skies had turned a dark grey. John got out of the minibus his mother had hired and was immediately struck by the drabness of the narrow streets and the rows of terraced houses squeezed tightly together. It was in such contrast to what he was used to, with chimney stacks jutting out of the slated roofs, spewing trails of black smoke. He was still in his summer clothes and started shivering as he stepped onto the pavement of the cobbled street.

'Come on John, come inside, you look frozen,' his mother said, taking hold of his hand.

Number 4 Halcyon Road was a late Victorian terraced house. It consisted of a large front room with a bay window, which was kept shut and only used for special occasions. Children were not allowed to go in there without permission. In the hallway a coin operated electricity meter sat high up on the wall above the front door, with a cotton thread hanging down from it. Attached to the end of the thread hung a metal bolt, rather like a pendulum.

Under the stairs a storage cupboard housed the gas meter and an assortment of shoes, coats and cardboard boxes. The kitchen/dining room was at the end of the hallway. It was cold, with an unfamiliar smell of food, stale tobacco and fumes from the gas fire. The three bedrooms were upstairs. Everything was in such stark contrast to the modern apartment in Durban.

They all squeezed in around the dining room table and tucked into a meaty stew they called scouse. It was the same Scottish dish that John's mother had often cooked back in South Africa, where she called it stovies.

As the meal came to an end, John looked around and started to wonder where everybody was going to sleep. As though reading his thoughts, his mother said, 'Right, since we now have John with us, there's going to have to be a change in the sleeping arrangements. I'll be sharing the main bedroom with Gran. Auntie Ruby will have the small bedroom and you children will share the double bed in the back room.' John had never shared a bedroom before, let alone a bed. Back home he had his own bed in his own room. Now he was going to have to share a bed with his four-year old brother as well as his cousins, Donna and Louise.

As his mother and Auntie Ruby prepared them for bed, John took out some money he had in his back pocket. 'Mum, when we were at the airport, Dad told me to give you this,' he said, handing her a wad of notes held together with a paperclip.

'Thank you, darling' she said smiling, pleased to have her son with her.

'Oh, and I have a letter from Auntie Marion for you. She told me it was for you only and nobody else must see it,' he whispered. 'It's in the bottom of my satchel.'

'Right, you make sure you go to the toilet, clean your teeth and get into bed, and tomorrow you can tell me all about your dad and everything,' she said, giving him a kiss on the cheek.

No matter how he tried to sleep, he would be woken every time one of the others moved or turned over. As the night wore on it got colder, until John lay shivering on the edge of the bed. He quietly slipped out to look for something to keep him warm. As he crept down the stairs he heard voices coming from the front room. It sounded as if someone was crying. Stopping halfway down, his heart jumped when he realised it was his mother. He heard Auntie Ruby saying, 'The cheating git! How could he do this to you?'

'We don't know for sure, Ruby. It's only what Marion says in the letter,' his mother said.

'Why would she write such a thing if it wasn't true?' Ruby replied.

'She says he told her the affair is over, and he's going to sort everything out when he gets here,' his mother said. John's heart skipped a beat. He could put up with anything if he knew for certain his father was coming back.

Next he heard Ruby say, 'Have you read what it says on the back?'

There was a moment's silence before John heard Josephine's voice. 'It says, "I've just seen that woman. She had the gall to come to the airport with Lex.' Although not understanding much of what had been said, John started shivering again, reached up, grabbed hold of a coat hanging from a hook, and took it back to bed with him.

The following morning John was woken by his mother. 'Okay John, darling, let's get you going. It's a new day, a new term and a new start for you. We're going to get you enrolled at Christchurch Primary. You'll like it there, I promise. Hurry up and get ready.' As he got out of bed she spotted her coat. 'What's my coat doing here?'

'I was cold and I couldn't find anything else,' John said, suddenly worried that his mother might be angry.

'Oh my darling, I should have realised you're not used to the cold. I'll get you an extra blanket or something,' she said, giving him a reassuring hug.

As he hurried along the hallway to the kitchen, his mother noticed his bare feet and shook her head reproachfully. 'You're in England now John, go back upstairs and put on your socks and shoes. Then come down and have some breakfast.'

School in England was tough. There seemed to be a total lack of discipline, with bullies ruling the playgrounds. As the months went by, John kept wondering when his father would arrive, until he came home from school one day to find his mother awaiting him with a broad smile. She pressed him to her and said, 'Your dad is coming to see us. I got the letter today!'

At last! His eyes filled with tears. 'When is he coming?' he managed to utter.

'In two weeks' time, but he's not coming here, we're going to meet him in Scotland. Isn't that wonderful?' she said, giving him a big hug.

'I knew Dad would come. I knew he wouldn't let us down,' he said, his eyes shining.

CHAPTER 3

THE END OF THE BEGINNING

John was pleased to see his Grandmother Lawson in Scotland. Being her eldest grandchild, he had a special place in her heart. She was sixty now, a stocky woman with a friendly face and a large pair of glasses perched on the end of her nose. Her hair was white and very curly. She was dressed in her usual blouse, matching tweed waistcoat and skirt and heavy brogue shoes.

There were two sofas in the lounge, one of which opened up into a bed. John and Alex slept there, while their mother slept on the other sofa.

In the morning John and Alex heard a car draw up, rushed to the front door and threw themselves into their father's arms, while their mother stood back hesitantly at the end of the hallway.

'I suppose you'd better come into the living room,' Gran said with an air of resignation. Lex followed his mother into the living room. Josephine came up and gave him a perfunctory kiss on the cheek.

'When are we going back home, Dad?' John asked as soon as everybody had sat down. 'Did you bring me any presents?' For a moment Lex looked puzzled.

'You do know it was his birthday last weekend?' John's mother said with a hint of sarcasm.

'Of course I know it was his birthday,' he said defensively. 'It's just that with everything that's happened I forgot to bring the presents with me. I'll bring them next time, I promise, John. Now, why don't you and Alex go and play while Mum and I have a chat?' Lex looked at his wife, the tension between them tangible, even to the children.

'No Dad, I want to be here with you,' John protested, clearly upset by the suggestion. Just then the bells of an ice cream van could be heard coming down the street. 'Come on you two, I'll buy you both an ice cream,' Gran volunteered.

Lex turned to the window and watched them join the queue of children outside, then sat down beside his wife and gently took her hand. 'Jose, I'm sorry for what happened,' he began nervously. 'It was a mistake, but it's over now. I want us to go back to South Africa and start over again.' Josephine said nothing, just continued to look into his eyes, waiting for him to say more. 'Can you forgive me? I want to put the past behind us,' he said, squeezing her hand.

Her demeanour started changing. 'Are you sure it's really over? Do you promise it will never happen again?'

'Yes, I've told her it's over. I told Marion as well.'

'Yes, and she told me you had allowed that woman to come to the airport when you packed John off to me,' she said. The accusation caught him by surprise, leaving him unsure how to respond. He saw the anguish in her face as she continued. 'I love you Lex, but if we're going to get back together, you have to be completely honest with me.'

There was a moment's awkward silence before he leaned across, put his arms around her and kissed her. 'I love you too, and I never want us to be apart again,' he said passionately.

Tears began to trickle down her face. 'So when should we go back?' she asked, wiping away the tears with the back of her hand.

'The problem is,' he hesitated, 'as you know from all the calls Ma has had from the Durban police, I'm needed back there as a witness. They're sending over some papers about that rioting trial, when I shot one of the rioters, so I'm going to have to...'

'You shot someone? Is that why they want you back? Are you being accused of murder?' Josephine felt a stab of panic.

'No, of course not, it was all in the line of duty,' he said.

'Are you going to tell the boys?' she said, not wanting to hear more.

'What, about the shooting?' he asked surprised.

'No, you can keep that to yourself. That we're going back to South Africa,' she said.

'Why don't we tell them together?' he suggested with a warm smile.

When Gran came back with John and Alex, Josephine announced with a happy smile, 'We've got some good news for you, boys. We're all going back home to South Africa.' John leapt into the air and rushed to his father, nearly knocking him over.

'When are we going Dad, when are we going?'

'Steady on son, don't get too excited. There's a lot of planning to be done, so it will take some time. In the meantime you'll stay here with your mum and gran until I've got everything organised, then I'll come and get you,' Lex explained.

Gran was staring at him, surprised yet relieved at the apparent happy outcome.

'I've got to go now, so you behave yourself and look after Alex. It won't be long before we're all together again.'

It seemed like a long week, John reflected as he walked back briskly from the shops, eager to get to Gran's, hoping as always his father would be there. But he wasn't. As he rushed into the house, the smile disappeared from his face at the sound of his mother's voice. 'How could you do this, after all you promised?'

As he ran down the hallway, his grandmother came out of the front room and grabbed hold of him. He looked anxiously into her face. Something was wrong, very wrong; he could see it in her eyes. 'What's wrong, Gran? Why's Mum so angry?'

'Come to the kitchen John, your mum's busy on the phone. I'll make us a nice cup of tea and you can have a wee biscuit,' she said, guiding him to where Alex was already sitting at the table.

'Is she talking to Dad?' he asked, craning his neck to try to hear what she was saying.

'If that's the case, you'd better come and get the kids,' he heard her say, and then the receiver being slammed down. The next moment Josephine came rushing into the kitchen, barely able to contain her anger. 'Can you believe it! He's changed his mind again, he's going off with that woman,' she said, pain spreading across her face. John stared at his mother. There was something in her voice he hadn't heard before, something that sounded cold and hard. Before he could say anything, Gran grabbed his mother by the arm and propelled her out of the kitchen towards the bedroom. John rushed after them, but stopped in his tracks as the bedroom door was slammed shut in front of him. He felt an iron grip of fear in his chest. He knelt down and pressed his ear against the keyhole.

'He's changed his mind. He's going back with her, with that, that, woman. Did you know she was here in Scotland?' he heard his mother say with a sob.

'Yes, but I didn't think much of it,' Gran tried to pacify her.

'Why didn't you tell me?'

'She has her family here in Scotland, so I assumed she had come back to stay here permanently.'

'What am I going to tell the children? Especially John; he dotes on his father.'

'If he does that, he's no longer a son of mine,' Gran said firmly.

'Well, you'll be able to tell him that yourself, because he said he's coming round to collect the papers about the court case. He seemed more interested in them than in anything else.'

'That adulteress woman will never set foot in this house, that he must know,' Gran said.

'I don't think I can face him. What about the kids? Is he going to say anything to them, explain why he's deserting them, why he's leaving us here to fend for ourselves?' Jose collapsed onto the bed and buried her head in her hands.

John's mind was racing, but his thoughts were interrupted when the bedroom door swung open. He scrambled to his feet. 'How much have you heard?' his grandmother asked, fearing the answer.

'That Dad's not taking us back with him,' he said, his face contorting as he fought back the tears.

Just then his mother came out, her face awash with tears, make-up streaking down her cheeks. She bent down and gathered John and Alex up in her arms. 'Your dad has made some changes to the plans…' she began, looking at them and knowing that what she said now could change the course of their lives.

'… and he's not taking us with him,' John cut in before she could finish the sentence.

'No, he's not taking us back with him,' she sighed.

John broke free from her. 'I hate him! I hate him!' he screamed and ran to the front door, flung it open and rushed out.

His mother wanted to follow him, but Gran grabbed her arm. 'Let him go, he needs time. He's hurting, just like you.'

Gran had been standing looking out of the front window for a long time before she saw Lex's car draw up outside. She watched him get out, go around to the passenger side and open the door. 'I don't believe it! He's brought that woman with him! Well, she's not coming in here, that's for sure. I won't have her in this house,' she murmured to herself as she headed for the front door.

Jose came out of the kitchen, with John following behind her. 'Is that him? Has he arrived?' she asked anxiously.

Gran turned back to look at her, her face stern. 'You stay back, let me deal with this,' she said, and opened the door.

'You will keep that adulteress away from this house. Tell her to stay in the car!' his mother shouted at Lex, as he and the woman approached the house.

'She's coming in with me. I just want to collect the papers and I'll be gone,' he said.

John suddenly recognised the woman. He had met her with his father while his mother was in England. He remembered going out to play with her son at a local park in Durban. She was wearing the same kind of clothes she had worn then—a flowery blouse with flared slacks and platform shoes. She was a bit stockier than his mother, and had mousey hair.

His mother, a red flush of anger and humiliation spreading over her face, charged forward to attack the woman, but his father stuck his arm out across the doorway to stop her. As she tried to force her way past him, he pushed her back rather forcibly, and she hit her back on the side wall. Alex sat down on the floor and began to cry.

'How dare you bring that trollop here?' she shouted as John came rushing forward, screaming, 'You leave my mum alone! You're a liar and I hate you!' His mother held him back before he could get to his father.

Lex gave John a puzzled look. He had never seen him behave like this before, had not expected this reaction from him. But now there was hatred in his eyes.

Lex looked around as people from the neighbouring flats started coming out to see what all the noise was about. 'Liz, I think you'd better go and get back in the car,' he said. 'This is not turning out the way I thought it would.'

Gran stepped forward and looked at the neighbours watching the drama unfold in front of them. This provoked her anger all the more, as the family reputation was something she cared about above all, and here was her own son showing her up right in front of them. She knew that they would all soon be gossiping about it, but it was too late to worry about that now. She turned her scorn back on Lex.

'And how *did* you think this would turn out? Did you think we would all welcome her with open arms? That's your wife in there. The one you married in the sight of God and gave your vows to. Have you no shame to... to...' she struggled to find the words as she watched the woman walking back to the car. 'You know what? You stay there too. I'm not allowing you into this house either. I'll get the papers and then you can go.' She closed the door to prevent Lex from coming in. He stayed outside, looked back over his shoulder and gave a shrug, as if to say sorry, there's nothing I can do about this. His mother opened the door again. 'There you are, be on your way and don't set foot here again. You're not my son any longer. Off, off with you!' She waved her free hand dismissively as she glanced around at the neighbours who were still watching. Then she stepped back inside and slammed the door. She gave an audible gasp as she walked back into the living room where Jose was cradling Alex in her arms. John was holding her hand and they all stood looking out of the window with tears streaming down their faces. They saw Lex get back into the car, lean over and give the woman a kiss on her cheek.

'It's strange how often men go for women completely opposite to their wives. I don't know what he's thinking, you're so much prettier than she is,' Gran reflected.

Jose sighed. 'I should have seen this coming. He's done this kind of thing before.'

Gran looked surprised. 'Done it before?'

'I mean, just cut people off. You remember Ronnie McGregor?'

'Of course, yes. They grew up together, went to school together, they were inseparable. He and Mary were the reason you went out to South Africa.'

Ronnie had been best man at Lex and Jose's wedding. Everybody thought nothing could separate them, but things changed when Ronnie became a born again Christian. Lex thought it a load of rubbish and promptly cut him out of his life.

'Religion was never Lex's strong point,' Gran sighed when she heard the story.

'And now Lex has done the same with me. I remember Ronnie's parting words when Lex told him he never wanted to see him again: "Friends may come and go, but Jesus will never desert me or let me down. If you come to know Him He'll never let you down either." Those words have always stuck with me.'

The following week Jose and the boys headed back to Birkenhead to see her father in hospital. Although they had been expecting it, it was still a shock when Granddad Curtis died a few weeks later. With his mother mourning the loss of her father, John could only look on in anguish while his mother and grandmother were seemingly crying all the time. A dreadful grief welled up inside him at the realisation that he too had lost a parent and a grandparent.

Two months passed while John struggled to settle at school. He missed South Africa, his friends, the sunshine and most of all, his father. The days seemed to drag on with nothing to look forward to, but he was determined not to let anyone see him cry.

Getting home from school one evening he found not just his mother in tears, but Auntie Ruby too. 'What's happened?' he asked.

'Your gran died today, darling' Auntie Ruby said between sobs. John stood there, stunned. He knew his grandmother had lost her will to live after losing her husband, but this was too much! He looked at his mother and saw such sadness on her face that he rushed to her, grabbed her hands and said, 'I'm so sorry Mum, I'm so sorry. I don't know what to do.'

Later that month Jose received a letter from her mother-in-law saying that Lex had shipped all Jose's belongings to her in Glasgow. Jose took it as a signal to try and start a new life elsewhere, to make a clean break and move forward.

'I've got some good news for you, John darling. We're going back to Scotland.'

'Why?' he asked, shocked and surprised at the news.

'Because it's going to be better for all of us, darling. We'll be able to get our own place that won't be so crowded. Dad has sent all our belongings to Gran, so we have to go up there anyway,' she said, watching his reaction.

CHAPTER 4

MOTH AND RUST CORRUPT

1977

In the block of flats where his Scottish grandmother lived, most of the old coal bunkers with their large doors had been cleaned out and turned into storage sheds. With nowhere else to put it, Gran had stowed the trunk there. Jose gave a little shriek of horror when the shed was opened, for it was the same green trunk they had used when they set sail for South Africa. Here it was back again, having done the full circle. The end of an era.

Jose and Gran dragged the trunk out of the shed and hauled it to the flat, with John and Alex helping by pushing it from behind. Once they had got it into the flat, John paced around, anxious to see what was inside. It had two heavy brass hinges, each secured with a padlock. Her hands shaking with anticipation, Jose inserted the keys, unlocked the padlocks, slowly raised the lid and looked inside. Everything was neatly folded and packed.

'He didn't pack this,' she said, as she picked up one of her dresses. 'Only a woman would fold a dress like this, and we know who that was,' she added with a look of distaste. 'I want to throw it all away, burn it. I can't bear the thought of that woman's hands all over my clothes, my underwear, everything. It makes my skin crawl.' Jose fell to her knees and began to delve deeper into the trunk. 'Look at these,' she said, as she took out the photo frames one by one and spread them out on the floor. 'These are all our pictures, even our wedding photos.' She held one of the frames and her hands began to shake as she gazed at the photo. It showed her and Lex hugging each other. She was looking out from the picture with big seductive eyes under long lashes and there was an air of vitality and happiness in her smile. It made her think about him as she had known him; about the happy times they had together. How being with him had felt so right; the way he stood, his hair, his smile, his spirit, his smell, how his skin felt firm under her touch. She held the frame for a moment longer and then let it slip from her hand and drop to the carpet, her face bewildered, tears flooding her eyes.

'I can just see that woman looking at these photographs and saying I'm not having any of them here. How could he not want to keep some memories of our lives together?' she asked, looking up at Gran. 'Did none of it mean anything to him? Has he no feelings left in him?'

Gran looked sympathetically down at Jose. 'Most of the time you only ever see the good side of the person you love, but it's moments like this when you see the other side, the real side and we are both now seeing his real side. You're well rid of him, my dear. He has shamed you and in doing so he has shamed me.'

She looked across at John who had picked up one of the pictures of him and his father, the father he worshipped, dressed in his police uniform, teaching him to shoot. As he stared at the photo he began to cry, the tears splashing onto the glass of the frame and blurring his father's face. He tried to wipe the tears away but it only blurred his father's image more. His mother leaned across and looked down at the blurred image of Lex and wondered if this was another sign that she should blur him from her memory. She reached back into the trunk and pulled out her jewellery box. She reached in and took out a few of the pieces and examined them. 'I suppose she had a good look at these too. Oh God, how I hate that woman!' she cried out, and let what she was holding slip out of her hands and fall back into the box.

Digging deeper into the trunk, she felt something hard. She moved the clothes aside and a soft smile touched her lips when she took the object out. 'Here John,' she said, holding it up for him to take. 'Remember this?'

John's eyes widened with excitement. 'McBoozer!' he exclaimed and reached out to take it from her. He loved the musical decanter of an old Scotsman in a kilt which his Granddad Curtis had given him when they left for South Africa.

Alex jumped up and down crying out excitedly, 'Can I wind it up please?'

'No, you can do that another time, we have to get ready to go to Auntie Betty's for the night so that your gran can have some peace and quiet,' Jose said, reluctantly closing the trunk.

Lurking in the shadows of the back garden, two young men watched Jose and the boys leave before sneaking up and knocking on Gran's door. 'You two!' she said, surprised at seeing her two sons standing there. She stepped aside to let them in.

George, aged nineteen, was the tallest of the four Lawson brothers. He moved towards the front window, his heavy body looking cumbersome in the confined space of the living room. He had a face that looked as if he was ready to hurt someone, but his mass of curly hair helped to soften the harshness. His freckles had earned him the nickname Spot. George was a petty criminal, not able to stay in one place for any length of time, as he was constantly on the run from the police.

Dave was twenty one, shorter and leaner, just as villainous and also on the run. He had once escaped arrest by climbing naked through the back window of their home and leaping over the fence into the graveyard while the police were trying to break down their front door. He always managed to avoid arrest by keeping one step ahead of them.

'How's Jose taking it?' George asked his mother, without looking away from the window.

'Pretty hard. Your brother just sent all her possessions back in the trunk with no letter, nothing.'

'That's not right. I'd like to get my hands on him and let him know how he's disgraced this family,' George said with a quick glance at his mother before turning back to the window. She had seen that look before, and knew what it meant to those who were unlucky enough to be on the receiving end of it.

'I don't think that's likely. I somehow don't think we'll see him again,' she said with an air of finality. 'He's out of our lives, and I for one am glad.'

George looked at his mother, surprised by her words. It made him look at her in a new light, and it showed. 'He's still your son, Ma' he said.

'Not anymore, I've disowned him,' she said.

Dave stood up and nodded at his brother, signalling it was time to move on. 'We'd better be off, Ma. We cannae hang around too long in case, you know...' he trailed off.

'What is it they want you for this time?'

'You don't need to know, Ma,' he said dismissively.

'You're in enough trouble as it is, and so is George. Why can't you two try to be more like Alan? At least he's married and settled down. I don't want the pair of you getting into more trouble than you already are. I'll tell Jose you asked about her,' she said, equally dismissively, not really wanting to know the details of her son's criminal activities.

'Tell her I'll come by again when I can to see how she is. Tell her not to sit there and let life happen to her. Tell her to go out and find a new life. She's worth more than he'll ever be,' Dave said, turning to hurry out.

Life at Auntie Betty's was good. John had his cousin Thomas to play with and Alex was pleased to have the younger cousins, Kenny and Amanda, to keep him occupied. John was enrolled at Cadder Primary, which was just around the corner. On his first day he also experienced his first fight. It was customary for the new boys to be confronted by the 'cock of the school', and John's refusal to give in to him cemented his position as 'one o' the boys'.

After school he headed home, excited to tell his mother that he had made a load of new friends. But as he walked into the living room he saw his mother biting her nails and looking distressed. 'What's the matter, Ma?' he asked nervously.

Jose hesitated, wondering how to break the news to him. 'Something bad has happened, John,' Uncle Tommy cut in. 'You stay here with Thomas, we have to go up to Gran's.'

'Why, what's happened to her?' John asked anxiously.

'Gran's fine,' his mother said, but nobody told him more.

'We won't be long,' Uncle Tommy said as he put on his coat.

'I'm going with you,' John said determinedly.

His mother gave a shrug and looked at her brother in law. 'He may as well come, he'll only fret if we leave him here,' she said.

Gran was standing at the shed when they got there. The door had been ripped open and was barely hanging on by one remaining hinge. The green trunk that they had returned to the shed had been forced open and what was left of the contents was strewn around it. Jose fell to her knees and covered her mouth with both hands. 'Who did this? It's all gone, my clothes, my jewellery, the photos, everything! Why would somebody want to do this?' She struggled to her feet, her legs weak with shock, but Tommy managed to catch her. 'Help me get her inside,' he said to Betty. Betty took her other arm and they half carried, half walked her inside.

'Right, don't anybody touch anything. I'm going to phone the police. We may be lucky, there could be fingerprints,' Tommy said once they had got Jose into the living room and into one of the chairs.

'What have I done to deserve this? I've lost my husband, my father, my mother and now this. I don't know how much more I can take. I've done nothing wrong and yet I'm being punished!' Jose cried out in anguish.

Gran looked at her with sadness and lowered her voice to give it an air of reverence. 'The Bible tells us, "Do not lay up for yourselves treasures on earth where moth and rust destroy and where thieves break in and steal, but lay up for yourselves treasures in heaven where neither moth or rust can destroy and where thieves do not break in and steal, for where your treasures are, so will your heart be also."'

Jose looked up, the words seeming to sooth her. 'I know Mum, but it's not only the treasures, it's my clothes. I've been walking around in the same clothes since I came back, and now it looks like I'm still going to have to, and John and Alex too.'

'I've spoken to the police and they're sending someone round,' Tommy announced as he came back into the room.

Lex's younger brother Dave was hiding in the shadows on the other side of the street, watching the policeman get into his car and drive off. He waited until it had turned the corner before crossing the road. 'What was the police doing here, Ma?' he asked anxiously as soon as he got into the flat. 'Was he looking for me?'

'No, they've found some of Jose's things that were stolen.'

'Stolen?' Dave exclaimed. 'What the hell's been stolen? Nobody told me anything.'

'You remember your feckless brother sent a trunk over with all Jose's possessions? Well, someone broke into the shed, forced the lid and took everything,' his mother explained. 'And the policeman you saw was returning what had been found dumped in the midden just a few streets away.'

An angry look spread across Dave's face. 'Nobody steals from this family, nobody! I tell you, George and I will find out who did it,' he said, his voice thick with anger.

His mother looked at him despairingly. 'No, David, you and your brother stay away from it, please. Let the police do their job.'

'The police will nae find out who did it, they're useless. They couldnae find a needle in a haystack if the needle was sticking up their arses. We'll get the scumbag who did this.'

'How are you going to do that Uncle Dave?' John piped up, having heard the discussion.

'Dinnae worry son, me and Spot have our ways. We'll get your things back, you wait and see,'

'Who's Spot?' John asked curiously.

'Ah, that's your Uncle George's nickname on account of his freckles, just like yours, ma boy,' Dave said, ruffling John's hair.

They didn't have to wait long. Within a couple of days John and his mother were at his gran's going through the items his uncles had recovered. Jose was pleased to see most of her good clothes and underwear, her winter coat and jewellery, as well as John and Alex's clothes. 'How did you get it?' John wanted to know.

'I don't think it would help for you to know, and I certainly don't want to know,' his gran said.

'Let's just say with a little gentle persuasion,' George said with a smile.

'They were a couple of junkies and I tell you one thing, they'll have a lot of trouble using their arms to make a spliff again,' Dave said casually.

John looked at his two uncles with admiration.

'Yeah, and the guy that bought the jewellery won't be fencing anything for a long time. We told him if he does any more fencing we'll nail him to the nearest one,' George said, and it made John smile.

CHAPTER 5

DRUMCHAPEL

1978

Jose walked nervously along the hallway to Betty's front door when she heard the letter box flap open. She saw a brown, official looking envelope drop onto the carpet.

'Who's it for?' Betty called out from the kitchen.

'It's for me, from the council,' Jose called back.

'What does it say?' Betty came into the hallway.

Jose opened the letter and her eyes brightened as she started reading. 'We've been allocated a two-bedroomed flat in Drumchapel!' she exclaimed, a mixture of joy and unease spreading across her face. She knew that Drumchapel had recently been labelled the worst housing estate in Europe. Her favourite comedian, Billy Connolly, called it 'A desert with windows,' but at least they would have a place of their own.

Betty rushed forward and embraced her. 'When can you move in?' she asked excitedly.

'It says we can take possession immediately.'

'Fantastic! Tommy can drive you over tomorrow to have a look at it,' Betty suggested.

'That would be lovely. It might be Drumchapel, but at least it will be a place of our own, I can't believe it! A bedroom for John and Alex; they'll be so excited. I thought it would never happen,' Jose said, putting the letter to her lips and kissing it.

There was a buzz of excitement on Saturday morning as Tommy loaded them all in the car and set off for Drumchapel. As they drove out of Glasgow John watched the landscape open up into large areas of trees and greenery. *Maybe it's going to be a bit more like South Africa*, he thought as he gazed through the window. 'This looks like fun! It's going to be so nice to play out in the open again. Just like in South Africa,' he said.

Tommy said nothing, but it didn't worry John because he felt so good to be getting away from the overcrowded, built-up city. As they got closer to Drumchapel, he saw a massive structure on top of a hill. From the distance it looked like a prison or a fort.

'What's that up there?' John asked.

There were a few moments' silence, then Tommy said, 'That's Drumchapel; that's where we're heading.'

Doubt started tugging at John's emotions as they drove up the hill and into Drumchapel. Suddenly everything was closing in on him. They passed building after building, all looking exactly the same—square concrete boxes surrounded by concrete pavements and roads. The roads were uneven, with potholes that tested the car's suspension to the limits. They were littered with rubbish, and there was graffiti scribbled on almost every wall.

'This is it,' Tommy announced as he pulled to a stop at Moneymusk Place. John watched his mother get out and look up at the block of flats. He suddenly had an uncontrollable urge to ask his uncle Tommy to turn around and take them back to Glasgow. Any place has to be better than this; even Glasgow.

'Come on John, we're going to have a look at the flat,' his mother said, opening the rear door for him.

'It looks terrible, Mum!' John said, reluctantly getting out and lifting Alex out onto the pavement.

'Look John, we have the chance of a place of our own and you and Alex will have your own bedroom. Won't that be nice?'

John looked up at the pebble dashed concrete walls with square holes for windows. He followed his mother and Tommy, with Alex lagging behind. 'What number is it?' Tommy asked as they got to the hallway. There was graffiti everywhere, not only on the cracked and peeling walls, but on the doors, the floor and even on the ceiling. An acrid smell of urine and stale cigarette smoke stung their nostrils.

Jose took the letter from her handbag and checked the address. 'Number twenty eight, on the fourth floor' she said.

'Right, let's go,' Tommy said, heading for the stairway.

'Isn't there a lift?' Jose asked, surprised, but started walking to the stairway.

'No, no lifts here, I'm afraid,' Tommy said with a half smile. Following one another they trundled up the eight flights of concrete stairway. John noticed a name that seemed to feature prominently in the graffiti—Monkey Melrose.

At the front door Jose took out the key and apprehensively unlocked the door. Their steps echoed on the bare floors as they walked in, and when they got to the living room, Jose gave a gasp. It was completely bare, except for a metal bucket at the fireplace. There was a strange smell of damp coal in the air. Jose noticed the damp spots and mildew in the corners of the room. She quickly moved to look at the other rooms. The kitchen seemed to be in reasonable condition, with a few cupboards fixed to the walls, a metal sink and draining top, but no cooker. The floor was covered with well-worn linoleum. Both bedrooms, as bare as the living room, had the same smell of dampness. Jose walked back into the living room with John following behind her. She was fighting to hold back the tears.

'I can't live here. This place is disgusting; it's filthy and there's damp everywhere,' she said to Tommy.

'Look Jose, I know it looks rough, but I'll help you clean the place up. You'd be surprised what a lick of paint can do. Johnny boy here will help me, won't you, son?' John didn't answer, unable to take it all in.

'Look, you don't have to move in right away, and...'

'How can I move in right away? There's no furniture, no beds, no cooker. Where am I supposed to find all that?' she asked despairingly.

'We'll help you find all that. What we need to do first is get the place cleaned up. We'll re-paper the living room and the bedrooms, put some curtains up and then get a cooker and the other bits and pieces,' Tommy said, trying to sound as cheerful as he could. To show how willing he was, he walked over to the far wall and dug a finger into the wallpaper, which came away easily in his hand. He looked down at the damp paper and saw that there were at least eight layers. 'My God, they've just kept papering over the paper already there. It will all have to come off, but by the look of it that won't be too difficult; it's almost falling off,' he said, throwing the chunk of wallpaper on the floor.

'Look Jose, I promise you we'll make this place fit for a queen, you'll see,' he said, giving her an encouraging hug. 'Now let's get back to Cadder.'

Tommy was as good as his word, and set about redecorating the flat. With John helping him, they stripped off all the wallpaper, which revealed soaking damp walls. There was a coal fire in the living room, but no coal in the grate, nor was there any in the coal bunker in the hall opposite the front door. The only way to help dry out the walls was to open all the windows and let the air circulate.

As luck would have it, they heard the coalman calling out and Jose rushed down to see him. 'We've just moved into number twenty eight. Could I have a bag of coal, please?' she asked politely.

'Are you alright?' he asked, wondering why she was shivering so much.

'We've just moved in and the place is so damp we've had to open all the windows in the hope it will dry out,' she told him.

'Well, once you get the fire going, it'll soon warm up. How many bags do you want?'

'One bag please, that's all I can afford,' she said, with a look of embarrassment.

The coalman studied her for a brief moment. 'You're gonnae need more than one bag to dry the place out if it's been left empty for a long time. So I tell you what I'll do. You pay for one bag and I'll let you have another on credit, since you seem a nice person, not like some of the people around here,' he said, his eyes shining brightly in his blackened face.

'Thank you, that's very kind of you. I'll make sure you're paid when you come around next time.'

'Dinnae worry yourself, I'm sure you will. Right, top floor, is it?' he asked, lifting one of the bags onto his shoulder and started up the stairs. He poured the coal into the small bunker in the hallway and headed back down for the next bag.

'John darling, take this bucket and fill it with coal so we can get a nice fire going,' his mother said. 'That's going to be your job, to empty the ashes every morning before you go to school, and to top up the coal bucket when you come home.'

Incredibly, the coal fire quickly dried out the rooms, and within a few days Tommy was able to re-paper the walls of the living room and the two bedrooms. Once that was done, he used his connections to find three second hand single beds and some bedding, a used cooker with some cooking utensils, plates, cups and cutlery. He even managed to blag some curtains and odd pieces of carpeting to soften the effect of the bare floor.

With all that in place Jose was ready to move in and start a new life.

CHAPTER 6

WHEN HELL FROZE OVER

1979

The winter of 1979 had set in with a vengeance. There was snow and ice everywhere. Jose started finding it hard to make ends meet, with all the extra coal needed to try and keep the flat warm as well as wanting to save money for Christmas, which was just around the corner.

Tommy and Betty could see the strain the family was under and how it affected the boys. John hid his feelings, but Alex was wetting his bed and sleepwalking. They also found out that Jose was going without food at times, so they decided to invite her and the children to spend Christmas with them.

John and Alex were excited about the opportunity to be with their cousins. The beautiful house was warm and Uncle Tommy, being a baker, was always bringing home lots of lovely cakes and pies and Gran was just up the street too.

On Christmas day John and Alex woke up to be given their presents. John could not believe his mother had found enough money to buy him a silver Raleigh Chopper. Although second hand, it was still one of the best bikes on the market. Alex was equally excited about his Scalextric set, which John helped him put together and they spent much of the Christmas period racing cars. The Chopper was John's pride and joy and he rode around on it whenever he got the chance.

Like all good things, the Christmas period came to an end and it was time to go back to Drumchapel. They had to take the bus because Tommy had to go to work at the bakery.

Jose stood at the bus stop with their heavy suitcase, wriggling her toes to keep them from going numb with cold. John was holding onto his bike and Alex was clutching his Scalextric box. The bus arrived and the bus driver pointed at the Chopper. 'Eh, you cannae bring that thing on the bus.'

For a moment Jose stared at him in consternation, then pushed John and the bike forward onto the bus. 'We've been standing here waiting for you for ages, and if you think I'm going to let my children freeze out here for another minute, you have another thing coming. What do you expect him to do, cycle all the way to Drumchapel? It's Christmas, in case you don't know! So please, show some consideration.' Somehow the driver realised he was not going to win the argument, gave a shrug and allowed them to squeeze into the aisle.

Back in Drumchapel the streets and pavements were covered in snow and ice. An arctic wind was furiously pounding the tall buildings and splattering the family with ice particles as the wind whirled around them. Their faces were stinging as they started the climb up to Moneymusk Place, slipping and sliding on the ice.

As they reached the top of the hill, catching their breath, the freezing air tearing at their lungs, they saw their tenement block covered with icicles dripping from the roof and every window and doorway. Then they noticed that all the windows were boarded up except theirs.

Jose felt her strength drain away. 'What the devil is this? What the hell has been going on?' she said, hurrying towards the entrance, but the steps were completely iced over, making it impossible to climb them. All they could do was to chip at the ice to get a footing on each step and to pull each other up. Reluctantly John chained his beloved Chopper to the lamp post with his new combination lock. Being the fittest and strongest, he started chipping away at the ice with a piece of broken pipe he had found amongst the litter lying around. He scrambled up and then set about helping to pull his mother and Alex up.

Inside the building there were icicles hanging from the ceiling, giving it an eerie cave-like feel. All the neighbours' doors were boarded up. The stairwell and the steps were covered in ice as if water had rushed down them and frozen in an instant. 'There's no way we're going to get your bike up those stairs, John,' Jose sighed.

As they got to their flat, Jose shrieked when she saw ice protruding from underneath the front door. She nervously put the key into the lock, but it wouldn't turn, no matter how hard she tried. She took out her cigarette lighter and used it to heat the key. Once it was really hot, she wrapped her scarf around her hand to insert it, but it still wouldn't turn. It took several attempts at heating the key before it melted the ice enough to free the lock.

Jose pushed at the door, but it was frozen to the frame and it took all three of them to heave at the door with their shoulders before it started to give way. The ice cracked and gave them just enough room to squeeze in through the gap. The lounge lay in front of them like a skating rink, the floor completely covered in several inches of ice. It was as if they had walked into an igloo. Even the furniture was covered in ice. There was a gaping hole where part of the ceiling had caved in.

They carefully made their way to the other rooms which were in the same state. The beds were covered in ice and there were icicles dripping from the wardrobe. The curtains looked as if they had frozen while caught in a breeze. The kitchen too looked as though it had been frozen in time. There was an eerie silence as the three of them stood hypnotised by the scene around them.

'We've only been away a week, how could this have happened?' Jose wondered out loud. But before she could answer her own question there was a heavy banging on the door.

'Man, it looks like hell's frozen over,' the man gasped, and squeezed through the half open door. Jose spun around at the sound of his voice, but there was no welcoming smile on her face. She glared at him and asked, 'What the blazes happened here?'

'That's exactly what I've come to ask you,' the man retorted, as he edged his way further into the room.

'How the blazes would I know? We've only just arrived back. We've been away for a week,' Jose said, her face pale and anxious.

'That's why we hadn't boarded your door up like the others,' the man explained. 'It must be because you were away, missus; with no heating in here the pipes burst,' he added with a hint of accusation.

'You mean to say this is my fault because we went away for a week?' Jose was outraged.

'Well, if the flat had been heated... I mean, we've been experiencing unusually cold weather. It's been up to twelve below. So perhaps if there had been heating, then maybe...'

'Do you really think one miserable coal fire would have made any difference?' Jose snapped, before pointing up at the ceiling. 'Does that look like a burst pipe to you? That looks more like a burst water tank to me, and I bet you it was never lagged. So we have a bit of bad weather and this is the result. So before you get all official and try to blame me for the council's shortfalls,' she said, 'I'd like to know what you intend doing about re-housing us. You don't surely expect us to stay here? Or do you?'

The council man was taken aback by her outburst. 'No, of course not,' he assure her. 'Everyone from this block has been relocated to temporary accommodation in Summerhill, and we've made the same provision for you and your family.'

'And what about furniture, all of this is ruined!' she said, with a sweeping gesture of her hand. 'Even our clothes are ruined.'

'There is some basic furniture there, but dinnae worry, we'll supply you with anything you need once you're settled in,' the council man tried to appease her.

The flat on the Summerhill Estate about a mile down the hill was identical to the one they had vacated, with the exception that it was situated on the ground floor. This block too was covered with graffiti, and there was litter strewn everywhere. It mystified Jose that nobody seemed to care about the state of the area or seemingly took pride in where they lived.

The move meant John and Alex had to change schools again and John enrolled at Summerhill Secondary School, which also had its bullies wanting to prove they were tougher than anyone else. Many of them, to their regret, discovered that John was not only a lot tougher than they were, but he was also a Lawson.

Jose tried her utmost to remain strong for John and Alex, and she knew they had to get out of Drumchapel. She applied for accommodation with one of the housing associations in Birkenhead, and to her delight news came within a few weeks in the form of a large envelope in the letterbox. It was from the Methodist Housing Association informing her she had been allocated a two-bedroomed house in Birkenhead with immediate occupation, requiring a decision by return. She didn't need to think twice. As bad as Birkenhead was, it would be a damn sight better than Drumchapel. In fact, any place had to be better than Drumchapel.

CHAPTER 7

BREAKING AND ENTERING

1980

Number 29 Hilbre Street was just off Corporation Road in the dock area of Birkenhead. It was a small, two-up and two-down house, with the front door opening from the street straight into the living room. The back yard was concreted and surrounded by a high brick wall, and the house next door was derelict.

Gradually things settled into a routine, with Jose working in the local Bingo hall to supplement their meagre benefits, and soon she was able to buy curtains and other necessities to make a home she wanted to be proud of.

John, having his Chopper bike, was able to cycle over and meet up with his old friend Flemmo and he loved cycling through Birkenhead park every day. The family was happier in Hilbre Street, but they were wrong to think they were in a safer and more respectable neighbourhood than Drumchapel. With the high wall surrounding their backyard John didn't consider it necessary to chain his bike up at night, and it wasn't long before someone scaled the wall and stole his pride and joy. John was filled with anger and for the first time in many months he cried about the injustices of life.

He now had to walk the five miles to meet up with Flemmo, who like him had developed an interest in Bruce Lee and Kung Fu fighting. John borrowed as many books as he could from Flemmo and studied them avidly. Fascinated by the nunchakus that Bruce

Lee made famous in the movie, *Enter the Dragon*, he made his own by sawing two lengths off the broom handle. He then broke off the metal chain from the cistern in the derelict outhouse next door and fixed it to the sticks. Now he had his own nunchaku, and he practised every move until he got them right without hurting himself.

His mother, of course, was furious when she got home and found the broom with a much shorter handle. John determined he would steal a new broom handle from the local hardware store as soon as he got the chance.

Jose got to know Linda Smart, who lived three doors away. Linda was known as the matriarch of the area. If one needed anything—a telly, curtains, carpets, clothes, in fact almost anything—you went to Linda. Shoplifting was on the increase and most of the loot found its way to her.

Linda had a sister Rita, who was known as Nelly, a brother Michael, known as Midgee and Phil, who for some reason didn't have a nickname. Phil was always in and out of young offenders' prisons known as Borstals for thieving and other misdemeanours and he had just returned home from another short spell away. John was a little wary of Phil but also admired his rebellious attitude, especially when out of the blue one day Phil said to him, 'You see that factory over there?'

'Yes, what about it?'

'It's a car repair garage and it's loaded with tools and it's got a safe too. I'm thinking of doing it over. You want in on it?' Phil asked, holding his gaze steadily.

John thought hard for a moment. He knew what he could do with the money. He wanted a new Chopper, he wanted more books on Kung Fu and he really wanted some training gear too.

'Yeah, I'm in. Let's have a go,' he said cheerfully.

'Good, we'll do it this Sunday afternoon when the place is shut and there's no one around.'

On the Sunday afternoon John met up with Phil, who was carrying a good length of rope, a strip of metal and some holdall bags. With him was David Robinson, another local boy.

'What's he doing here?' John asked.

'We need three of us on this job, so no messing, let's just get on with it and earn ourselves some dosh,' Phil said, moving off across the road.

They climbed over the concrete fence of a tea factory, then scrambled up onto the garage fence on the other side. Phil tied the rope to a concrete post before he leapt across onto the roof of the garage. John and Dave followed and they all moved across to the skylight. Phil used the strip of metal to lever the skylight open, lowered the rope through the opening and they all climbed down. There was a mezzanine floor with offices some twenty feet above the ground floor, so they only had about eight feet to drop. Phil looked over the balcony and said, 'You two get down there and grab as many tools as you can. Look for the expensive ones and don't waste time with the crap. I'll see what I can find here.'

Dave and John had to adjust their eyes to the dark as they made their way down to the ground floor. There was an abundance of tools to choose from—power tools, grinders, spray guns and expensive sets of spanners. They grabbed as many of the power tools as they could and carried them back to the mezzanine. Having got used to the dark they went down again and gathered some of the grinders and spanner sets. Dave then climbed back up the rope onto the roof while John bundled as many tools as he could into the holdall and tied it to the rope so that Dave could haul it up. Just then they heard Phil say, 'I've found the safe! I want to see if we can haul it up.' But what he didn't know was that the safe had a pressure mat and as he stepped on it, it triggered the alarm. 'Crap! Let's get the hell out of here!' he exclaimed, beginning to panic, urging John to clamber up the rope. Once they were back on the roof they hauled the rope up and grabbed the holdalls.

Back in their own street they took the bounty to the derelict house and hid it in the back room upstairs. John was surprised to see empty beer bottles, pages from porn magazines and even human excrement on the floors. *What kind of people are using this place?* he wondered.

'We'll leave it here for a few days, just in case the bizzies come looking around, then we'll sell the stuff,' Phil said.

'What's the bizzies?' John asked.

'What planet av you been livin on? The police, the pigs, man,' Phil explained.

John felt a pang of guilt, wondering what his mother would say if she had to find out what he had done. He hated lying to her; she was working so hard at the Bingo hall, even on Sundays. She didn't like him mixing with Phil, because she knew about the things he'd been up to.

In the back of his mind John always remembered what Uncle George had told him when they were sitting at the canal in Cadder: 'Don't ever tell your mother what you're up to. Don't cause her any aggravation. She's been through enough as it is. Always tell her everything's okay; just stay under the radar.'

John had known for some time that some things were worth being afraid of, and some not. The things he had done before had never made him this fearful, and for several days he feared that there was going to be a knock on the door and a policeman would be standing there wanting to question him about the break-in.

Phil announced a few days later that it was time to move the stuff, and that he already had some buyers, and this went a long way to allay John's fears. The three of them went to the derelict house, careful not to step on any of the mess, gathered up the holdalls and set off to sell the goods. Phil was as good as his word and managed to sell the lot for one hundred and twenty pounds.

'Here's twenty quid for each of you,' Phil said.

'I thought it was going to be a three-way split,' John protested.

'No, you've got a lot to learn, kid. I'm the boss and it was my idea. I planned it all and you get what you're given,' Phil said in no uncertain terms.

John gave him a half smile of acquiescence. At least he'd got twenty quid, which was more than he'd ever earned from any other caper. Now he could buy his own Kung Fu books and take the bus to Flemmo instead of walking. Maybe life in Birkenhead was not going to be so bad after all, he began to think as he made his way back home with the twenty pounds in his pocket. His face broke into a broad smile when he realised he could even buy that second hand stereo record player that he'd had his eye on for a long time for his mother. It would make him feel good to do something for her. Yes, he felt he could be happy in Birkenhead, he told himself.

CHAPTER 8

THE NEIGHBOUR FROM HELL

1981

Winter was coming to an end. The trees were beginning to bud, the birds were returning, the daffodils were starting to flower, the dark clouds were lifting and the skies were becoming brighter. It made everybody feel happier and people seemed to have a spring in their step.

On a quiet Saturday evening Jose was working at the Bingo hall and John and Alex were at home playing the tennis game on John's Sinclair ZX 81 Spectrum computer. They were becoming very good at the game. Alex's game was improving and John had to fight for every point. The only noise in the house was the boys cheering when they won a point.

A sudden banging on the front door made Alex look at John nervously. 'Don't open it. It could be that nasty man Peter again,' he said with fear in his eyes.

'Please let us in. Please hurry!!' a woman's frantic voice called out from outside.

'That sounds like Mary Holloran,' John said, leaping up and rushing to open the door.

Mary and her four children rushed in exactly as they had done on Boxing Day when Peter, her husband, had virtually destroyed their house in one of his drunken rages.

'Close the door, close the door, Peter's out there! He's been on another bender!' she screamed, ushering the children into the room.

John managed to slam the front door shut just as Peter reached it and started hammering on it with his fists, shouting, 'Come out, you bitch, or I'll break this door down!' He started kicking the door, making it rattle in its frame.

'Get in the back room,' John told them, realising the front door could give in at any moment. As soon as they were all in the back room, John shut the door and moved the kitchen table up against it. It didn't take Peter long to kick down the front door. Once inside he charged at the dining room door with his shoulder, but with the table wedged against it, the door held.

'This door won't stop me!' he shouted. 'Get my wife and kids out here NOW and tell that Scottish tart I'll get her as well, so open the door NOW!' He picked up the nearest chair and smashed it against the door, tossing the part he was left holding across the room. He then began to pound the door with his fists, managing to punch a few holes in it. The children started screaming and shaking with fear. Between them they tried to drag the washing machine from the laundry room to support the table. Mary, already suffering a black eye, became quite hysterical when Peter thrust his hand through one of the holes and tried to grab onto anything he could.

'We've got to do something or he's going to break this door down!' Mary screamed in terror. John looked around anxiously for any kind of weapon. If only he had his nunchakus, he could really do something, but they were in his bedroom. He was running out of time. Then he spotted the screwdriver he had been using to fix a mirror for his mother. He picked it up and stabbed it into the back of Peter's groping hand. Peter screamed in pain and quickly withdrew his hand, but it only seemed to make him angrier, and he thrust his other hand in. Again John stabbed as hard as he could and saw the point of the screwdriver penetrate the flesh on the back of Peter's hand. This time the scream was much louder and blood splashed on the door as Peter pulled his hand back.

'You Scottish tart, I'm going to make you pay for this, you wait and see!' Peter screamed at the top of his voice, thinking it was Jose who had stabbed him.

Hearing his mother being called a tart sent John's temper flaring, and he felt all fear drop away. 'No one calls my mother a tart!' he raged, and started to drag the table away from the door, finding strength from the adrenaline building up inside him. He flung the door open, expecting Peter to be standing there, but he had gone. John rushed out into the street and saw him stumbling off, holding his injured hands.

' I'm going to kill you!' John yelled after him, his face distorted with rage.

Peter turned and saw John rushing at him, the screwdriver still in his hand. He managed to knock it out of John's hand and grinned at him. 'You stupid little dickhead, you think a scrawny teenager like you can hurt me? You go back and tell that stupid tart of a mother of yours I'm going to get her. No woman messes with me, especially a jock tart like her.'

John's heart pounded in his ears. His jaw tightened as he gritted his teeth, his cheeks flaring an angry red as he felt another bolt of adrenaline shoot through him. Instinctively he turned sideways and lashed out with a powerful side kick which caught Peter completely by surprise and sent him sprawling backwards, landing hard on the pavement. He lay there dazed, his alcohol drenched brain trying to work out what had happened. Being a strong man, he managed to get to his feet and swung a vicious punch at John which, had it connected, would almost certainly have taken his head off. But John was too quick for him. He dropped beneath the punch, spun around and delivered a perfect leg sweep which took Peter's feet right out from under him. Before Peter could work out his next move the decision was made for him—by the distant sounds of a police siren. He scrambled to his feet and ran off in the opposite direction of the approaching cops.

Waiting for the police to arrive, John bent down and picked up the screwdriver, which still had blood on it. There were splashes of blood on his shirt as well. 'Drop that weapon!' the police officer shouted as he got out of the car. John looked at him in surprise, still clutching the screwdriver.

'I said, drop the weapon!' the officer repeated.

'Look, you don't understand. You should be going after...' John tried to explain.

'I won't ask you again,' the police officer said, reaching for his truncheon. John did as he was told and let the screwdriver drop to the ground.

'Now what have you been up to, lad?' the officer asked in a not too friendly manner.

'Me? It's that b****rd Peter Holloran who's just run off you should be after,' John said angrily.

'There's no need for that language, lad. Just tell me what you were doing with that screwdriver,' the officer said, already convinced that John was the trouble maker.

'Defending myself from the drunken b****rd that ran off,' John retorted, unsure of the implications. 'You have no idea what we've been through. If you lot had turned up on Boxing Day when he smashed up their house, maybe none of this would have happened today!'

Just then Mary came out of the house, followed by the children. 'Aren't you going after him?' she asked the police officer.

'After who, Madam?' he asked brusquely.

'My husband, who caused of all this,' she said, pointing to the broken front door.

'That's what I tried to tell him, but he didn't take any notice. More interested in what I was doing with a screwdriver,' John said, resentment brimming in his voice.

Ignoring John, the police officer turned his attention to Mary. 'Perhaps you'll be good enough to tell me what happened?' he said.

'My husband came home in one of his drunken rages, punched me in the face and shoved little Peter against the wall. I knew I had to get us out of the house and away from him, so I rushed to my friend's house. But as you can see, he kicked in their front door and broke an inside door too. If it hadn't been for this young man I don't know what would have happened to us. So I suggest you leave him alone and go and look for my husband; lock him up and throw away the key,' Mary said with as much venom as she could muster.

'Difficult to catch him now; he could have gone anywhere,' the officer said with little enthusiasm.

'Why don't you try the Piggy in Victoria Street, he's probably there getting even more drunk,' John volunteered.

The policeman gave John an irritated look. 'What's the Piggy?' he asked.

'Everybody knows it's the Victoria Vaults, except you lot of course.'

'Watch your language, lad.' The officer turned his attention back to Mary. 'So the man's your husband?'

'Yes, unfortunately.'

'Then this looks like a domestic, so there's not a lot I can do about it. I'll take a few notes and...'

'Domestic? What do you mean? That maniac kicked our front door in for starters!' John's voice rose with anger and disbelief.

'If I hear another word out of you, I'll put you in the car and take you down to the station,' the police officer warned him. He took his notebook and pencil from his breast pocket and started making notes. 'Right, I'll report this matter, and I advise you to ring the housing association and have them secure the property,' he said, replacing the notebook and pencil.

'So that's it, you're going to let him get away with it?' John asked ominously.

The officer's face flushed as he stared at John. 'You've got a big mouth for a young lad and I advise you to keep it shut. As for you, Mrs Holloran, I suggest you take out an injunction against your husband.' He walked off to his car, got in and drove off.

My uncles were right, don't trust the police. If you want anything done, do it yourself. I so wish they were here now, John thought as he watched the car drive off.

Walking home from the Bingo Hall that night, Jose reflected on how she had managed to bring a sense of normality back into John and Alex's lives, even though she was not over the loss of her husband and her home. She was determined to make sure the children felt loved and cared for despite not having a father. She quickened her step, anxious to see her boys, but she came to an abrupt halt as she turned the corner into Hilbre Street. A flush of anxiety and anger coloured her cheeks at the sight of her front door. She rushed to the house, pushed at the damaged door which swung open freely, leaning over at an odd angle, the top hinge having been wrenched from the frame. John came charging out of the back room still holding on to the screwdriver, but Mary pushed past him. 'Thank goodness you weren't here, Jose; Peter tried to kill us! He went berserk, smashed the front door in and would've got to us in the back room if it hadn't been for John here,' she said, embracing Jose. Jose's arms hung limp at her side. The house that she had worked on so lovingly was a wreck. Mary felt her body trembling. 'We'll help get the place straightened,' she said encouragingly, but as she said it, she knew they were empty words. It was going to take a bit more than just straightening up.

'You should have seen what John did to Uncle Peter, Ma, it was brill!' Alex piped up, in awe of what his brother had done.

Jose looked at John. 'And what were you going to with that, try and kill him?' she demanded, pointing at the screwdriver he was still holding in his hand.

'Yes, if it I had to, after what he said about you!' John's eyes blazed defiantly.

'And what good do you think that would have done? Isn't there enough trouble without my son going around wanting to kill someone with a screwdriver?' she said reproachfully.

'That b****rd deserves to die for what he did, and...'

'Don't you dare swear like that, or I'll wash your mouth out!' Jose shouted, her voice quivering. John dropped the screwdriver to the floor, his hurt at the injustice and the harshness of his mother's words etched on his face. Jose looked at him in silence. Here she was lashing out at him as if it was all his fault. 'I'm sorry, John darling. It was just too much of a shock to come home to this,' she said, collapsing into the nearest chair.

'I'll make you a nice cup of tea,' Mary offered, going off to the kitchen.

Jose looked up and smiled a thank you. 'And here I thought we'd have a safer and happier life here, but it's no different from any of the other places. Look at this place, after all my hard work. It's just not fair,' she said, shaking her head.

'We'll be alright, Mum; we'll get the house cleaned up, you'll see,' John said. He knelt next to his mother and took both her hands.

Jose looked into her eldest son's eyes. 'You're a good boy John, and I'm sorry I shouted at you.'

'It's alright, Mum. It's Mary and the children we have to worry about.' John spoke with such quiet conviction that she suddenly felt proud of him.

'Yes, you're right, she must be feeling awful.'

Just then Mary came back into the living room with a cup of tea. It always amazed John how people seemed to think that a cup of tea could cure everything. 'Have you phoned the housing association?' Jose asked, her nerves steadying.

'No, I don't think they'll believe me.'

'Then I'll do it,' Jose offered, and got to her feet.

CHAPTER 9

THE NORTH END

1982-1986

Jose was on her way home, bristling with excitement about the news she had just received. Her boss, Mike Jeffries, the general manager of the Bingo company had told her he was moving and the house he was renting was becoming available and he would happily recommend her as a tenant.

Number 1 Thorneycroft Street was a much larger house, with large living room, a dining room and a separate kitchen. Upstairs it had three bedrooms and a bathroom.

Life had settled into a comfortable routine which was disrupted when they learned that John's uncle Dave had been involved in a motorcycle accident, that he had suffered serious brain damage and was in a coma. John wanted to rush to London to go and see him, but neither he nor his mother had money for the fare. He had finished sixth form at school, obtained a City and Guilds in Technical Engineering and it was time for him to start looking for a job.

John had made one good friend at school. Jamie Lowe joined the school in their fourth year after his father had committed suicide a few months earlier. He was introverted, kept to himself and appeared not to want to mix with the other lads; a situation John had learnt from experience always attracted the bullies. Before long they started calling Jamie 'ballhead' and other derogatory names, and Jamie seemed unwilling to challenge them, even though he was a talented amateur boxer. John decided to intervene on Jamie's behalf, and this cemented their friendship.

Job hunting was tough going and the odds seemed to be constantly stacked against John. It was a time of mass unemployment, and he hated having to go to the dole office and be looked down upon as a scrounger by people who thought they were smarter, more successful and stronger than him. The only good news at this time was that Uncle Dave had regained consciousness, although he was suffering from memory loss.

Eventually John found a job as bartender in the St James' night club, nicknamed The Jimmy's. It was a rough kind of club owned by the Demetrios family and was situated near the ferry terminal. There was always trouble there and they needed bouncers to keep order and get rid of the trouble makers.

John's baptism of fire came sooner than he expected. He had been assigned to what was known as the VIP bar where the well-heeled preferred to sit and drink. It was early evening and there was only one customer, who had slumped into a chair after having far too much to drink. Feeling a little concerned about him, John left the bar and went up to the man, shook him gently and said, 'Mate, you can't sleep here, would you like me to call you a...' but he didn't get a chance to finish the sentence. The man jumped up and tried to head butt him. John saw it coming and managed to raise his arm, which caught the man on the cheek and sent him flying onto his back. To John's amazement the man jumped up and came charging at him again. John swiftly side-stepped him, sending him crashing over a table. Again the man got up, blood running down the side of his face where the sharp edge of the table had cut him. With a crazed grin he came at John again and grabbed his arms, but being proficient in martial arts, this gave John the perfect opportunity to force the man's arms wide open, which exposed his whole body as a target. John kneed him hard in the groin, which caused the man to double over, and with his head lowered, he elbowed him on the side of the temple. This should have laid the man out for good, but he got back on his feet and said, 'Is that all you've got, mate?'

John stood poised, amazed at the man's ability to absorb such punishment and still wanting to fight. 'I'm going to kill you!' the man screamed as he charged, but John swiftly stepped back and delivered a perfectly timed roundhouse kick to the man's head, telescoping him to the floor with a thud. At that moment the bouncers came rushing in, leapt on the man and held him down until they could get a firm grip on him. The man was struggling violently and screaming like an animal, 'I'm going to get all of you, and kill the lot of ya!' It took three bouncers to control him and get him to his feet. John followed as they dragged him out of the bar.

When they got to the main door, one of the bouncers punched the man in the stomach.

'Get the hell out of here and never come back or you'll get more of this,' he said, cracking the man over the head, expecting him to go down, but he didn't. He just turned his head and said, 'I'll be back to do you all in.'

The remark threw the bouncer into a rage. He grabbed the man by the throat and started throttling him. Big Vic, the head doorman, quickly pulled him off and said, 'Just throw the idiot out.'

They watched the man walk off as if nothing had happened. 'You seem to have handled yourself well, kiddo. I saw that roundhouse kick as we came running in,' Vic said appreciatively. 'He was obviously high on speedballs.'

'Speedballs, what are they?' John asked.

'A mix of heroin and cocaine, my friend. They can either make you lethargic or violent, as you saw. You don't feel any pain; nothing and nobody can hurt you. You could have hit him with a brick and he wouldn't have felt it, but I tell you one thing—when he wakes up tomorrow, he's going to feel it and probably need an ambulance,' Vic said with a chuckle.

'You seem pretty well able to handle yourself. Have you done any training?' another bouncer Paul asked.

'Yes, I practise kung fu and karate. Taught myself, mostly,' John said with an air of pride.

'You should think about becoming a bouncer; how old are you?' Vic cut in.

'I'm nineteen, well almost twenty. Any jobs going here?' John asked.

'Not at the moment, but we'll let you know if one comes up. If you want to try for a job somewhere else, you can always get them to call me for a reference,' Vic smiled.

'I may take you up on that,' John said as he strolled back to the bar.

John learned that, due to his accident, his uncle Dave's criminal record had come up. He was a wanted man, and as soon as he was well enough, he was arrested and sent to prison. As a result Dave's brother George decided to go back to Scotland.

John had a compelling urge to find out more about Dave's circumstances and how long he was going to be in prison. With his mother's blessing he took the train to Glasgow. George met him at the station, took him to the house he was renting and put him up in the spare room. It appeared that George had given up on crime and started a picture framing business he called Cairnlandia. He was producing pictures using all kinds of light metal in a way that had not been done before. To John's joy George asked him to come and work for him and to help make and sell the pictures. But the people of Glasgow didn't seem to take to this modern art form, and the business failed before even getting off the ground. Dismayed at the failure and with no job prospects, John went back to Birkenhead with a gift of a metallic picture of a snow leopard, and George headed back to London.

CHAPTER 10

WIGAN
1986

'How do you fancy a trip to Wigan over the weekend?' John's old school friend Jamie suggested when they met up for a drink at the local pub.

'Sounds great. I've heard there are loads of nightclubs down there, and some tasty birds,' John enthused.

'Then Wigan here we come. The birds better watch out, but if we don't manage to pull, we'll spend the night in the park and head back home,' Jamie said, raising his glass.

In Wigan they headed for King Street, which was well known for its clubs and nightlife. They decided on a club called Scott's, where something was to happen that would change John's life forever.

Jamie and John sat down at a table and scanned the dimly lit club, trying to pick out the most likely girls to pull. John noticed two girls sitting on their own. One had flaming red hair, her face animated and eyes sparkling brightly as she sat talking to her friend. 'How about those two over there?' he suggested. 'I bag the one with the red hair,' and they moved across to ask them for a dance.

As John got close to the girl with the red hair, his eyes instinctively travelled over her body, starting at her legs, moving swiftly to her hips and waist before finally settling on her face. Lifting her eyes to meet his, she smiled, pleased with the appreciative look on his face. She was about five feet four, with a pale, lightly freckled face. Her large blue eyes shone with mischief. Her makeup was smooth, not overdone, her nails painted a gentle red. Her black leather mini skirt accentuated her shapely legs, and her low cut blouse displayed a fair amount of cleavage. She told him her name was Jackie and her friend was Louise. To John's delight they seemed to hit it off straight away.

Jamie was immediately taken by Louise. She was equally voluptuous, the same height as Jackie, but had short curly brown hair, brown eyes and large pouting lips.

As the evening came to an end, they were still with the girls, all of them wondering what was going to happen next. John and Jamie knew what they would like to happen, but they were too shy to suggest it. The situation was resolved when Jackie said, 'You two aren't thinking of driving all the way back to Birkenhead tonight, are you?'

John and Jamie exchanged glances. 'No, we were going to look for somewhere to stay, but I guess we've left it a bit late. You wouldn't know of a place where we can crash out for the night, would you?' Jamie asked awkwardly.

Jackie and Louise exchanged glances. 'The only thing I can suggest is that you come back with us,' Jackie said with an inviting smile.

John and Jackie ended up in bed together, both too drunk to attempt anything as vigorous as making love. Jamie and Louise made a bed on the living room floor, and judging by the grunts and groans emanating from there, they didn't do much sleeping.

The following morning, refreshed by a good night's sleep, John and Jackie made passionate love; an exhilarating experience for John, as Jackie was totally uninhibited and led the way. Although John had had several girlfriends, this was the first time he slept with a woman. He had often wondered what it would be like to be in bed with a naked woman and to make love, but it far outstripped anything he had ever imagined. None of the girls he knew were anything like Jackie. She was eight years older than him, experienced and insatiable, and she revelled in teaching him everything she knew.

The next morning, when John was preparing to leave, he discovered that Jackie had two sons from two different fathers—

Stephen, aged three and Craig, aged five. Over time he drew quite close to them, mainly because their fathers appeared to show no interest or care for them, something with which John was able to identify. At the same time he was beginning to feel unhappy at home. Things were becoming difficult with his mum and they were starting to tiptoe around each other like strangers. Even Alex was getting on his nerves, and the whole situation was becoming untenable. John wanted to become more independent and get a place of his own. He was working, so he could afford it, and there was something else tugging at his heart: He was falling in love with Jackie.

There was an uneasy silence when he told his mother that he was moving in with Jackie. After a while she said, 'Do you really know what you're doing?'

'Yes Mum, I do. I need to get away. I'm twenty now and we're beginning to get on each other's nerves. It upsets me that we argue and I'm sure it upsets you too,' he said, kneeling next to her and taking hold of her hands.

She pulled her hands away and covered her face. Choking back her hurt, she said, 'I know it's not been easy for us, but I want you to think hard about this. How well do you know the girl? You tell me she has two young children. Do you really want to take on that responsibility at your age?'

'They're good kids and they don't have a father either,' John said, the smile on his face freezing at the realisation of what he had just said. 'Sorry Mum, I didn't mean it that way.' He took hold of her hands again.

'I know you didn't son, but I want you to think carefully about it. I'm not ready to be a grandmother and you're far too young to be a father,' she said wearily.

'Don't worry Ma, I'm not planning to start a family yet,' he assured her.

'Are you planning to get married?'

'I don't know, we haven't talked about it.'

'Do you love her?'

'I think so,' John said hesitantly.

Her eyes came up and fixed on his face. 'I want you to promise me one thing. If you do get married, you stay married and you never ever behave like your father. At least promise me that.'

'I'll never do that and I'll never desert you. I'll always be there for you,' he said, almost choking on the words. 'I won't be that far away and I'll come and see you and Alex often.'

A blanket of sadness fell over her as she watched him walk out of the room, and she wondered whether this was another turning point in their lives.

Jamie had broken up with Louise and as a result he and John were drifting apart. John moved in with Jackie, who was renting a house on the Worsely Hall Estate, a rough area riddled with petty crime, drugs, gang fights and a general disregard for the law.

With the responsibility of Jackie and her two children, John decided to get a job as a bouncer, remembering what Vic had told him at The Jimmy's. He walked along King Street enquiring at various clubs, but with little success. He went to Scott's, where he had met Jackie, and they didn't have any vacancies, but they told him there was a club called Gigolos in the basement at the back of their building that was looking for a bouncer. John made his way there. It seemed even seedier than the other clubs, but he needed this job.

The manager introduced himself as Anthony. He was very slim and his hair was greased straight back. By his manner and the pink silk handkerchief protruding from his breast pocket, it was obvious that he was gay, which seemed rather incongruous in such a tough nightclub.

'So where have you worked before?' Anthony asked, looking him over in a way that made John feel uncomfortable.

'I worked as a barman at a club in Birkenhead and had to deal with some awkward customers. One of the bouncers there said I should become one myself, so here I am. I know I can do the job. I do a lot of kung fu and karate. I tell you what, how about you give me a month's trial and if I don't measure up, then fair enough. How's that?'

'Okay, John Lawson, when can you start?'

'As soon as you like.'

'In that case you can start tomorrow night. The pay is fifty pounds a night, in cash, and you're responsible for your own tax and other things.'

'Sounds fine to me,' John readily agreed.

'Right then, you better come and meet the boys you'll be working with,' Anthony said, walking off with a fluffy wave of his hands.

'This is John Lawson, our new man, and this is Dave, Billy, Graham and Steve,' Anthony said, gesturing to each one in turn.

'Hi, good to meet you,' John said, shaking each one's hand with a smile.

'John will be starting tomorrow, so one of you can have the night off,' Anthony said and sauntered off.

'Bleedin' poof,' Dave scowled. John noticed that Dave stood out from the others. Though he was smartly dressed, he looked every bit a thug; very muscular, head shaven and tattoos around his neck.

On his first night, John was shocked by the bouncers' behaviour. Dave in particular acted exactly like the thug he was. A man and woman were sitting opposite each other having a loud argument and suddenly the woman slapped the man across the face. Dave stormed over and punched the woman in the face, knocking her to the floor. When the man protested, Dave swung a left hook and sent him sprawling too. A young couple, a few seats away, started to protest and they got the same treatment. Within a minute four people were lying unconscious on the floor. Billy and Graham, the other two bouncers on duty, stepped in to help Dave haul them to their feet and throw them out.

'Blooming heck, Dave's a bit quick with his fists, isn't he?' John remarked.

'Yeah, we call him the removal man,' Billy said ruefully.

John resolved to try and show the men that there was a better way of dealing with trouble makers. He would warn the culprits that if they didn't calm down they could get seriously hurt. It usually did the trick, but when Dave was around, his love of violence won the day. John felt compelled to talk to Anthony about it. He felt very strongly that men who beat up women are not men, they're bullies. He also feared that they could end up with a dead body on their hands because of Dave's behaviour.

When John reported for work the following night, Dave came charging out of the office, his face purple with rage. He deliberately bumped into John and stormed off. Realising something was wrong, John went straight to Anthony's office. His instincts were right—Anthony was lying flat on his back, his face covered in blood.

'What the hell happened?' John asked as he helped Anthony to his feet.

'I told him I couldn't take any more of his violent behaviour and that I'd fire him if it didn't stop. He told me I could shove the job up my poofy arse and then smashed me in the face. I think he's broken my nose,' Anthony said, putting his pink hanky to his bloody nose and collapsing into his chair.

'I think you'd better get to a hospital,' John said in an effort to be useful. 'I'll phone for an ambulance.'

'Okay, but just say I tripped and fell on my face. I don't want the police sniffing around here. And by the way, I'm going to need you more now. Consider yourself a permanent member of the team.'

John allowed himself to smile, pleased with what Anthony had just told him and pleased that Dave would no longer be around.

John and Jackie had been together for three months when Jackie was offered a much larger house on Severn Drive, around the corner from her mother's house on the Norley Hall Estate.

John hired a Ford Transit van for the day and started moving the furniture across. By the end of the day there were still a few items to be collected from the old house, which was only about a mile away. John decided to borrow a trolley Jack and wheel the last few items across himself. The children were at their grandmother's, so Jackie came along to help in any way she could.

When they got to the new house, John almost let go of the trolley handles and Jackie let out a gasp when she saw their front door standing wide open. 'You did lock the door, didn't you?' John asked as he gently lowered the trolley.

'Of course I did,' Jackie scowled, and they both rushed inside.

Virtually everything John had delivered to the house was gone—the television, video recorder, the Hoover, the stereo and his precious picture of the snow leopard were nowhere to be seen. John realised that someone must have been watching them move in and just waited for the chance to break in. 'You can rob a bank, steal from a factory, but you don't steal from your family or your neighbours!' he raged. He knew there was very little chance of getting anything back, but he was determined to find out who had done it.

What gnawed at him most was the loss of the picture that his uncle George had given him. It wasn't worth much, but it was the only one of its kind.

Setting off for work one evening, John walked past a house with the lights on and the curtains wide open. He stopped dead in his tracks and blinked once or twice before realising that he was looking at his picture of the snow leopard hanging on the lounge wall. Without a second thought he stormed to the door and with one furious kick the door burst open. He charged in just as a man nervously poked his head out of the lounge door.

'Where did you get that picture?' John shouted at him as he barged into the lounge where a woman and two children were watching television. 'That's my picture and I want it back!' he continued without waiting for an answer.

'I bought it. How do I know it's yours?' the man said, trying to control his fear.

John rushed over, yanked the picture off the wall and turned it over. 'You see that?' he said, jabbing angrily at the sticker with his thumb. 'That's my uncle's company and he gave me this picture. It's the only one of its kind. Do you want me to call the police?'

'No, please, just take it and leave us alone,' the man said nervously.

'Where did you get it?' John demanded.

'I bought it off a guy called Banny Wharley down at the local pub,' the man said.

'And where does this scumbag live?'

'On Serven Drive on the Norley Estate, number 303, I think.'

'What!' John exclaimed. 303 was the house right next door to them. 'Look, I'm sorry I burst in on you like this, but I hope you understand that this guy, my neighbour, stole it from me. But he'll pay, oh yes, he's going to pay for this,' he added.

'I understand, but please, can you go now,' the man pleaded, becoming more nervous at the sight of the anger on John's face.

'Good evening Madam, sorry to have disturbed you,' John said, forcing a smile as he turned and walked out, clutching his picture.

John was determined to teach Banny Wharley a lesson. He asked around about him and found out that he was a real heavy, into drugs and anything else that could make him money. He had his own gang, which meant he was not a man to confront face on. John thought about what Uncle George had told him. 'Lay low, stay in the shadows, be patient, wait for the right moment, which will come, then strike and when you do, make sure you do it well and it can't be traced back to you.'

John waited until he could get Banny Wharley somewhere on his own. Having him next door made it easy to keep an eye on his movements. John soon became aware that Banny had the habit of going into his back garden every night to roll a joint and smoke it.

One night, as Banny came out into the garden, John slipped on his black coat, took the balaclava out of its pocket and pulled it over his head. He grabbed the piece of two by four he had prepared and quietly slipped out of the back gate of his garden into the alleyway.

He took the few steps to the next gate, kicked it open and before Banny could do anything, John whacked him in the face as hard as he could. Banny went down and stayed down. Although his martial arts training had taught him never to kick a man when he's down, John gave him a few good kicks in the ribs and made his way back home, pleased with his revenge.

'What the hell have you been up to?' Jackie asked when she saw John pulling off the balaclava as he walked into the house.

He inwardly cursed himself for not taking it off before coming in, but he decided to tell Jackie the truth. 'I found out who stole our stuff. It's that thieving git next door and I've just given him a good hiding.'

Jackie was panic-stricken. 'Do you know who he is? He runs most of this estate. Do you imagine for one moment he's going to let you get away with it? How could you be so stupid? I've got two kids to worry about, in case you've forgotten!'

'Don't worry, he doesn't know it was me, that's why I wore the balaclava. But I have a rule—anyone who messes with me or mine does so at his own risk,' John said assertively.

'So what was the point of beating him up if you didn't want him to know it was you?' Jackie looked at him quizzically.

'I just felt he needed a good hiding for what he'd done to us. I know there's no chance of us getting our stuff back, but people who steal off their neighbours are scum, and he's got what he deserved.'

'That won't stop him stealing; everyone knows he's a thief and a junkie,' Jackie said with a hint of agitation.

The next day, as John and Jackie left their house, they saw Banny coming out of his front door. His face was bruised, he had a black eye, cut lip and he appeared to be walking with difficulty.

'What happened to you?' John could not resist asking.

'A group of thugs jumped me. Cowards, there were five of them and they had baseball bats, but I managed to fight them off,' Banny said bullishly.

'When did this happen?' John asked, struggling to look concerned.

'Last night.'

'You should have called me. I would have come and helped,' John told him.

'No, I can take care of myself. As I said, I beat them off and I don't think they'll dare to come around here again. Nobody messes with me and gets away with it,' Banny expanded boastfully.

As he and Jackie walked off, John's face broadened into a grin. 'Five men; what a dickhead.'

Jackie invited her friend Linda and her boyfriend Jimmy to dinner on one of John's evenings off. Unbeknown to John, Jimmy was a notorious burglar, who took John aside while the girls busied themselves with the washing up and said, 'You game for earning a bit of extra money?'

'Sure, I'm always game for a bit of extra money. What have you got in mind?' John asked enthusiastically.

'There's this working man's club. It's loaded with fruit and cigarette machines. So we break in, crack open the fruit machines, take the cash, smash open the cigarette machines, take the money and the fags and off we go. It's ripe for the taking,' Jimmy explained.

'Sounds interesting; when are you planning on doing it?'

'Saturday night's the best time. It's bingo night, which means the club is busy and the machines are fuller. I've checked the place out and I know where the alarm box is. We can get in through a kitchen window. You up for it?'

'I'm up for it.' John was getting excited.

'Good, bring a nice heavy hammer and a few pairs of strong socks; they're great to stash the pound coins in,' Jimmy said.

On the Saturday night Jimmy climbed onto the flat roof of the club and went straight for the alarm box, knocking it off the wall with a few heavy blows with a crowbar. But what he didn't know, was that the alarm alerted the police as well as the caretaker.

It was easy levering the kitchen window open with the crowbar. At the one end of the main hall of the club was a long bar, stretching the full width of the hall. All the chairs were still laid out facing the stage where the evening's bingo session was held. Jimmy and John weaved their way through the chairs to the fruit machines and immediately set about breaking into them, taking out the coins and stuffing them into the socks. Having emptied the fruit machines, they started on the cigarettes machines, removing the packs of cigarettes and throwing them into a bag Jimmy had brought. It all seemed easier than expected, until they heard a commotion in the front of the building.

'What's that?' John asked apprehensively.

'Probably nothing, but better go and have a look,' Jimmy said.

John moved cautiously to the entrance hall, crept to the front door and peeked through a crack in the curtains. There was a police car with a constable standing looking at the door. Another police car drew up, and the driver got out.

'The caretaker will be here any minute, he's got the keys, so we may as well wait. It could be just a faulty alarm,' he heard one of the policemen say.

John rushed back to Jimmy. 'It's the bizzies; they're right outside, but we've got a few minutes. They're waiting for the caretaker.'

'They'll come in through the front, so let's stack some chairs up against the swing doors to jam them so we can leg it out through the back. By the time they get here, we'll be gone,' Jimmy whispered.

They had just managed to wedge enough chairs against the doors when they heard someone say, 'Blooming alarms, they can be a damn nuisance sometimes. Can't see any sign of a break-in.' They heard the keys turning in the door as they gathered up their loot and quickly weaved their way through the chairs to the back exit. They waited until they heard the police and caretaker struggling with the chairs before they pushed down on the safety bar of the large fire door and rammed it open. There was a thud and a groan as a police officer, who had reached the exit, slumped to the ground, having been hit by the force of the opening door. They jumped over the dazed policeman and ran as fast as they could, managing to scale a wall at the bottom of the car park.

'That's what I call a good night's work,' Jimmy said once they had reached safety.

'Can I call you Dad?' Craig asked, looking up at John.

The word Dad stunned John and he didn't know how to answer. He liked Craig and felt for him. His brother Steven still had contact with his father and sometimes spent weekends with him, but Craig's father had left Jackie the moment he discovered she was pregnant, never to be heard of again.

'Can I?' Craig asked again, still looking up at John with warmth and expectation.

John knew better than anyone what it was like to hate one's father for not being there, but to still love him too. He'd cried many tears about it, and here was this boy, asking him to be his dad. 'Of course you can call me Dad,' he said, sweeping Craig up into his arms.

'You're crying, Dad,' Craig said, wiping away a tear with his little finger.

'No, I just got something in my eye,' John said, brushing Craig's hand away in an attempt to hide his emotions.

Later that day, when John sat at the dinner table before going off to work, his mind kept drifting, and he hardly touched the food on his plate.

'What's the matter?' Jackie asked, looking at him across the table.

'You alright, Dad?' Craig piped in. Jackie looked at Craig in surprise, but obviously pleased at the mention of the word.

'Did you tell him he could call you that?' she asked John.

'Yes, and I guess being called Dad has made me more determined to find my father. I have to know what went wrong, why he abandoned us,' John said with a lost look on his face.

'Why don't you start by trying to track him down through the police station where you said he worked?' Jackie suggested.

CHAPTER 11

HELLO DAD

1986

The walk through Johannesburg airport brought back a vivid memory of himself as a ten year old clutching his satchel and being led by an air stewardess in the opposite direction to which he was now walking. It was the time of the Rugby World Cup and with all the flights from Johannesburg to Durban fully booked, the only way of getting to Durban was by overnight train.

Finally, after a month of searching, his father had been surprisingly open to John visiting him, even offering to pay the air fare. John was nervous and excited at the prospect of seeing him again after ten years.

It was 7:30 in the morning when the train finally pulled into Durban Station. Eager and excited to see his father, John hurried to the exit. As was the case with all the stations in South Africa at the time, there were separate entrances and exits for whites and non-whites. In his eagerness John took the wrong exit and looked around anxiously, but could not see his father anywhere. He became increasingly aware of the odd stares he was getting from the people around him, and eventually it dawned on him that he was in the non-white area. He picked up his case and hurried back the same way he had come, frantically looking for the Whites Only exit. As he spotted the sign he saw his father hurrying towards him, not looking pleased.

'Where the devil have you been? We've had people searching the train for you.' He looked at his father's angry face as Liz and Tom quickly caught up with him. It was not the welcome he had hoped for. His father was dressed as John remembered him—in a denim shirt, jeans and black boots.

'Sorry, I came out the wrong exit,' John said sheepishly.

'Yeah, well that's just what the Kaffers want, to see whites mixing with them. We've got enough trouble as it is, what with Free Mandela and all that malarkey. So watch where you go and who you talk to,' his father said, and then surprisingly stepped forward to embrace him. 'My, you've grown up,' he said, holding John at arm's length 'You look strong and fit. Nice broad shoulders, just like a rugby player.'

'I used to play rugby for the school,' John said, feeling a little embarrassed as he sensed Liz and Tom watching him.

Liz stepped forward to kiss him on the cheek, her lips barely brushing his skin. 'Nice to see you John,' she said, her voice void of emotion. She still looked as he remembered her—a little frumpy, with oversized glasses and wearing a matching skirt and blouse.

Tom shook John's hand. 'Good to see you, John. I've been looking forward to it,' he said, and John felt the first bit of warmth in his voice.

'Good to see you too Tom,' he said, shaking his hand firmly. Tom was about seventeen now, quite tall and slim, with his brown hair cut fashionably with a long fringe on one side.

'Right, let's get you out of here' his father said, leading the way. John picked up his case and began to follow him. 'Is that all you brought with you, one little suitcase?'

'The other one was stolen at Johannesburg Station when I was checking the timetable board. It had all my clothes in it,' John explained sheepishly.

'Yes well, that's what the Kaffers do, they'll steal anything if it's not nailed down or chained to a wall,' his father said loudly, not caring about who could hear him.

It was a twenty four kilometre trip to Umhlanga Rocks and there was a nervous tension and very little said on the car journey home. John sat quietly in the back with Tom, taking in the scenery. Lex explained that he had joined the Umhlanga Rocks protection service a few years earlier, which effectively acted as the local police force, and that he had been allocated a large bungalow on Fairview Drive, which was situated in one of the more affluent areas of Umhlanga Rocks, with beautiful tree-lined avenues.

The bungalow had a wide driveway that led to a double garage. On the side of the driveway a concrete path led to the front door and to the left of the bungalow stood a large brick outhouse where the servants would have lived at one time.

'I'll make us a nice cup of tea,' Liz announced, making straight for the kitchen as soon they had stepped into the house. Lex watched her go and turned to John 'I think you should know, Liz and I got married; she's Mrs. Lawson now.'

'Oh. When did you get married?' John asked, almost choking on the words. To him there was still only one Mrs. Lawson and that was his mother.

'And Tom has also changed his name to Lawson. I hope you two are going to get on well together,' Lex added, ignoring the hurt he could see on John's face.

'Yeah, I'll show you around and we'll have some fun. Looking forward to it,' Tom said with a broad smile.

'Good, but first things first. I've managed to fix you up with a job that...'

'A job?' John was aghast.

Liz had come back with a tray of mugs and a plate of biscuits. 'Yes, you'll have to pay something towards your board and lodging,' she said.

'It's a video rental shop and I've arranged for the boss to see you tomorrow morning. If he likes you, as I'm sure he will, you can start straight away and everybody will be happy,' Lex said, grabbing one of the mugs and holding it up in a toasting gesture. 'Good to have you here, son.' It was the first time since his arrival that his father had called him son, and John was not sure what to make of it.

'Glad to be here, Dad,' John reciprocated.

'Right, I'll show you to your room,' Lex said. John followed him along the passageway that led to the bedrooms and he was amazed at the spaciousness of the house, and how luxuriously furnished it was.

'This is your room, Son,' his father said, indicating to the middle of three bedrooms. 'And the bathroom is back here.' Everything looked clean and sparkling, the towels neatly folded in a perfect line on the shiny chrome towel rails. Looking out of the window John could see a massive landscaped garden where a large white Alsatian was running around.

'Is that your dog?'

'That's Rolf; he's there to keep intruders out. He can stop a Kaffer dead in his tracks, but he's quite friendly once he gets to know you. You and Tom can take him for walks down to the beach,' Lex said. 'Just make sure you keep the bathroom clean, otherwise you'll have Liz on your back; she hates mess and untidiness.'

So she hates mess and untidiness. What does she think she caused when she broke up my parents' marriage? John thought as he followed his father back into the living room.

'I've made you a bite to eat. You look exhausted, so I suggest you get some rest. We're going take you out to dinner tonight at the Sands Hotel,' Liz said with aplomb, as she breezed into the room to join them.

'No, he's fine. I want him to come to my room first, then he can have a rest,' Tom cut in with what looked like a mischievous smile.

'Okay, if that's what you want to do,' Lex said dismissively. 'I've got to pop to the station to check on a couple of things, so I'll see you all a bit later,' he added, giving Liz a kiss on the cheek before making his way out.

John watched through the window as his father drove off in the police car.

'Come on,' Tom said, dragging him away from the window.

'Where's your room then?' John asked.

'I've got the outhouse. I've had it converted; it gets me away from Mum and Dad.' The fact that Tom was calling his father 'Dad' jarred John and he had to check himself to hide his resentment, as Tom was being very friendly towards him.

'Well, this is it,' Tom said with a sweep of his hands. 'I can shut myself away here and do what I like.'

'Looks great,' John said, slumping down on the bed and looking around. It was one large room with a bathroom and a small kitchen off to one end. 'What was this place used for before you converted it?'

'It was for the servants, in the days when people could afford to have servants, although I guess they didn't pay them much, if they paid them at all. We do have a maid though, called Edith. I call her One-eyed-Edith' because she's only got one eye,' Tom said. 'It must be her day off, 'cos I haven't seen her around. We've got a black gardener too.'

John looked at Tom, a frown beginning to crease his forehead. 'I don't get it, you're not supposed to mix with blacks, but it's okay for them to work for you?'

'Yeah, well it's cheap labour and perfectly okay, as long as they know their place and don't cause trouble, Dad always says,' Tom explained nonchalantly. 'Anyway, I'm sorry about what happened with him and your mum. I don't really understand what went on there,' he continued.

'Me too, but I remember coming over to play with you one time, which was the first time I met your mum.'

'Yeah, I remember that, I think we had fun together, and look at us now, step-brothers. Who would have believed that, hey?' Tom said with an affectionate smile.

'Yes, can you believe it?,' John said, feeling for a moment that he was betraying his mother.

'Hey, do you smoke dagga?' Tom changed the subject again.

'What's that?'

'Weed man, pot.'

'You mean drugs?'

'You bet, best in the world. Durban poison,' Tom said, coming out of the kitchen with something wrapped up tightly in newspaper.

'What's Durban poison?'

'What's the matter with you, don't you have drugs back home?

'No, never touched the stuff.'

'You don't know what you're missing. Here, have a whiff of this,' Tom unwrapped the newspaper and offered it up to John's nose.

'Phew, it stinks!' John exclaimed, jerking his head away.

'Yeah man, but when you smoke it, it's pure lekker.'

'What's lekker?'

'Lekker, cool man, real cool.'

'What does my... I mean our dad think about you smoking this stuff?' John said, watching with interest as Tom started rubbing the dagga in the palm of his hand to separate the stalks and seeds from the leaves before rolling a joint.

'That's the beauty of this place; he never comes in here, so he has no idea. I've even got my own stuff growing at the back. Here, come and have a look,' Tom said, moving over to the back window. 'If you look down you can just see them. It started by accident. I just threw some seeds out the window and they started growing and now I've got my own stash. They're not ready yet, they have to grow taller and the leaves have to turn a certain colour before they're ready.'

'But surely your dad must know about it?'

'He has no idea, boet. Like most of the police they never see what's right under their noses,' Tom said with a big smile as he went back to preparing his smoke.

'But what if they walked in now?' John asked.

'Then I guess I'll be in trouble.'

'I guess we both would, and hey, that's the second time you called me boot' John said curiously.

'Ha ha, not boot, its boet, b-o-e-t, it's Afrikaans for brother,' Tom grinned.

After a good night's sleep, John woke up bright and cheerful, got out of his comfortable bed, crossed over to the window and looked out at the clear blue sky. He felt good and he wondered what the day would bring.

'I see you're up at last,' Lex said, popping his head around the door. He was dressed in his police uniform, a gun strapped to his hip. 'Liz has gone off to work and the bathroom's free, so get yourself ready. Edith will make you some breakfast and then I'll run you down to the video shop.'

'Okay, I'll be as quick as I can,' John said, setting off for the bathroom.

The drive to Glenashley, where Video Venture was located, made the memories come flooding back of when he was a kid and used to drive around in the police car with his father. Tom had decided to come along for the ride, and both he and John were having fun asking what all the controls were for. This one switches on the flashing lights, this one the siren, that one switches on the speaker if you want address a crowd or warn someone and that is the radio switch to speak to HQ, Lex explained.

'You said Liz had gone to work, what does she do?' John wanted to know.

'She works at the Sands Hotel on the beachfront where we had dinner last night. She's one of the managers in charge of the laundry and housekeeping,' Lex said.

So that's why she was greeted so regally last night when we arrived for dinner, John thought.

'Good morning Officer Lawson,' the owner greeted Lex as they entered the video shop. Clive was in his mid-fifties, rather portly and balding on top. He was dressed in a safari suit that gave him the appearance of a colonial missionary.

'Good morning Clive, this is my son John that I told you about. He's over from England for a short while and looking for a job to earn his keep,' Lex said by way of introduction.

'Know anything about the video rental business?' Clive asked offering his hand at the same time.

'Over in England they get all the videos released long before we get them here, so John can tell you which ones have been really successful and which haven't, can't you John?' Lex said, turning to John.

'Yes, I suppose so,' John conceded.

'That would be very useful. We get offered packages from the distributors and we're never sure which to choose,' Clive said. 'Can you start straight away?'

That was something John had not expected. 'I only arrived yesterday and Tom here has promised to show me around today.'

'Okay, tomorrow will be fine. Can you be here at nine o'clock?'

'Sure, I'll be here,' John assured him.

'He's a bright boy and I know he won't let you down. Good to see you Clive,' Lex said, giving him a strong handshake.

John spent the rest of the day walking around the town with Tom, ending up playing on the golden sandy beaches of Umhlanga Rocks. They were late getting home and Liz had already set the table, with the evening meal ready to be served.

'Hurry and get cleaned up otherwise the dinner will be spoiled,' she said, a hint of annoyance in her voice.

John had to admit Liz was a good cook and the meal was enjoyable. Afterwards, when everybody was relaxed and Liz started to clear away the dishes, John felt it was the right moment and approach his father. 'Dad, I've got some things I want to ask you.'

Lex was a little surprised at the firm tone of his voice. 'I think we should go into the other room and talk quietly,' he suggested.

'No, sit and talk here,' Liz said as she came back into the room. 'We don't have any secrets around here, do we darling?'

Her sudden interference and the thought that she just wanted to hear what he was going to say, irked John and he said, 'No, I'd like to talk to you alone.'

'Okay, let's go and talk in the living room,' Lex agreed, and Liz turned and walked off in a huff.

'So, what's on your mind?' Lex asked, slightly irritably as he sat down in one of the leather armchairs.

'I want to know why you didn't stay in touch. Why you didn't write or phone. Why you never even sent me or Alex a birthday card, let alone any presents. Not that we were ever without presents, Mum made sure of that. But it would have been nice to have got something from you.'

'Liz thought it was for the best.'

'Whose best?' John retorted angrily.

'Everyone's. It was difficult resettling back here, sorting out everything with Liz and Tom. Before you realise it a month flies by and then a year and then another year and then you start to think you should have written. I should have phoned. But then you start to worry because you haven't been in touch and that it's too late and if you do, what sort of reception are you going to get? So you don't do anything.'

'It's never too late, Dad. Tell me honestly, would you ever have contacted any of us if I hadn't contacted you?'

'To be honest, no, I probably wouldn't have, but I'm glad you did,' Lex said, offering a smile.

'So as far as you were concerned, we were part of the past and that was it?'

'We can't live in the past John, we all have to move forward...'

'Like you, you mean? Dump one woman so you can move forward to the next, is that it?

'It wasn't like that.'

'Then how was it? Did you ever love Mum?'

'Yes, I did, but it's as easy to fall out of love as it is to fall in love. Your mum and I were young when we got married. We were both about your age and it all seemed so romantic and we decided to start a new life here in South Africa, and...'

'What I remember of those days is that we were happy and you used to teach me all sorts of things. I've still got the photo of you teaching me to shoot. I don't think you realised how much I worshipped you. You couldn't do anything wrong in my eyes and you seemed so happy with Mum.'

'I was, we were, but things change...'

'They changed when you met Liz; I still remember you taking me to meet her and then sending me off to play with Tom. Tom remembers it too. So it was already going on, you and Liz, when Mum went to England?'

'Yes, it was just one of those things that happen. I can't explain it. Maybe one day it'll happen to you and then perhaps you'll understand,' Lex said.

'I've already met someone and we're together, but the difference is, I'm not deserting a wife and kids to be with her,' John said with an air of derision, his eyes hard as he stared at his father. The accusation made Lex wince and shift uncomfortably in his chair.

'That's a bit harsh, John. I thought now that you've grown up you would understand.'

'I understand, but it doesn't mean I accept it, or that it takes the hurt away. You have no idea how devastated Mum was; the shame she felt at being tossed aside and left to fend for herself with two small children, and all we ever got from you was the trunk with our belongings in it. Have you any idea what that felt like?' The tension was building up in his voice. 'It was like the end of everything. Until I phoned you, because I needed some answers.'

'And how do you feel now? Have you got the answers you were looking for?' his father asked, hoping it would be the end of the conversation.

'You know Alex hates you. He didn't even want to speak to you on the phone, let alone come out with me. I bet you don't even remember when Alex was ten years old, he wrote to you, and what was your response? You criticised his handwriting, you even called him Alexander, not Alex or Son, and that was the only time he ever heard from you. He's never got over that. And because of that, Mum's had a lot of trouble with him. He was so traumatised, he couldn't sleep and constantly wet the bed, because he couldn't understand why he didn't have a father anymore.'

'And what about you, do you hate me?'

'I love you and I hate you. I love you when I remember the good times we had together and the beautiful country you'd brought us to,' he said. He paused and his face hardened at the thought of the painful memories, and his eyes filled with tears. 'But I hate you when I think about the filthy concrete jungle you dumped us in without giving a damn that we had nothing and nowhere to live. If it hadn't been for Mum and your family, we would have been out on the streets with only the clothes we stood up in. My mother didn't deserve that, she loved you and somehow, in a strange way I believe she still does. And what amazes me is that you haven't even asked how she is. You have no interest in how she has managed to cope over the years, bringing up the two of us all on her own, with no support from you whatsoever.'

'Look John, all I can say is I'm sorry and yes, you're right, I should have handled things better and I truly wish I had, but it's in the past and we can't go back. I'm glad we've had this conversation and I'm glad you're here and I'd like us to get on while you're here,' Lex said, getting up from the chair. 'I think we could do with a beer, don't you? I sure as hell could.'

'Okay, but I need to pop to the toilet,' John said, hurrying off, desperately wanting to wash away the tears.

That night John lay in bed, unable to sleep, feeling that the conversation with his father had not resolved anything. He started to feel guilty about his mother, wondering what she felt about him being here, and he was starting to miss Jackie too. He decided he would leave as soon as he could get enough money together for the return ticket. Ironically, it was the video shop that would provide that, but even if it did—which he felt confident it would—it was still going to take at least three months.

When John got home from work the next day, Liz was in the kitchen preparing dinner. 'Jackie called and wants you to call her back urgently,' she said, slightly disdainfully.

'Can I use the house phone?'

'Sure, go ahead, but don't be too long,' Liz cautioned.

Lex arrived home just as John was talking to Jackie, and he

stopped in the hallway to listen. John's face broke into a smile when he heard her voice. 'Hi, it's me,' he said.

'Hi me,' Jackie said.

'How are you?' John asked nervously, wondering what was so urgent.

'I'm pregnant,' Jackie said.

'You're pregnant!' Lex heard John exclaim, causing a wry smile to spread across his face as he watched John begin to shuffle uneasily. 'How far?' he asked.

'I've missed my second period, so it must be nearly two months,' Jackie told him.

'Two months,' John repeated. 'Then I'm going to have to get back as soon as I can. The problem is I'm having to work to get the money together for the return ticket...'

'You mean to say your loving dad that you were so anxious to see only paid for a single ticket? If I'd known that I would never have let you go. You idiot, who the hell flies anywhere in the world without a return ticket?' Jackie ranted.

'Yeah, I know, stupid of me. Anyway, I'll get the money and be back as soon as I can darling, I promise. How are you, are you being sick and all that?'

'A little, but it's not too bad. I hope you're going to be a better father than the others,' she chided good-naturedly.

'Don't worry, he'll have all the love I can give him.'

'How do you know it's going to be a boy?'

'Girl or boy, you forget I know what it's like not to have a father,' Lex heard him say.

'So Jackie's pregnant,' Lex said, more a statement than a question, after John had ended the call.

'Yes, and that's changed everything. I'm going to have to get back as soon as I can.'

'How do you know she's pregnant? She could just be saying that to get you back. I heard you say she was two months. In that case, if it's true, she could have told you before you left,' Lex said.

John looked at his father and sensed a coldness he had felt

many times before; a coldness that seemed to say 'If there's a problem in your life, then walk away from it.'

'No, I have no intention of doing what you did. This is my child and it's going to get all the love I never had from you.'

'You can stay here and live with us if you want,' Lex offered.

The offer surprised John, for it was the first time his father had shown any sign of wanting him there. 'You mean you would like me to stay here and live with you?'

'Yes, I would. Does that surprise you?'

'Yes it does, but it comes too late and in any case, I couldn't desert Mum like you did. It would break her heart.'

'Yes, I guess you're right, but I'm still glad you came.'

'Yes, sorry I snapped. I'm glad I came too, but I do need to get back. So all I've got to do now is save up enough money for the ticket,' John said, but thought to himself, *Any decent father would say, of course you've got to get back and don't worry, I'll give you the money for the airfare.*

'Well, business at the video shop seems to have improved since you started there, and there's a lot more money coming in,' Lex said. *For them yes, but not for me*, John thought grudgingly, and it gave him an idea.

Over dinner John asked whether his father was still in touch with Auntie Marion and Uncle Les. Lex told him they hadn't been in touch for a very long time, but that he did still have their address and phone number.

John spent a lovely weekend with Auntie Marion and Uncle Les, but something they told him shocked him and brought back some harrowing memories. He knew he would have to confront his father with it, but how or when he didn't know. When he got back after the weekend, Liz told him Jackie had called again and wanted him to call her urgently. She reluctantly allowed him to use the phone, and Jackie told him she had lost the baby. She sounded distraught and begged John to come back. He wanted to tell her he would be back very soon, but he knew he would be overheard, so he lowered his voice and whispered, 'I'm sorry, I'll be home as soon as I can.'

In the bus on his way to work, John sat contemplating when to tell his father that the time had come for him to leave. On arrival he was surprised to see a police car as well as his father's car parked outside the video shop. He took a deep breath, braced himself and entered the shop, where he saw his father standing with the owner.

'Hi Dad, what you doing here?' John asked, feigning surprise.

'What the hell have you been up to?' Lex shouted at him.

'What do you mean?' John asked, trying to maintain a look of innocence.

'Don't come the innocent with me! You're a thief! They say hundreds, maybe thousands of rands have gone missing since you started working here. Where are the records of the money the customers have been paying?'

John didn't meet his gaze, simply stared straight ahead.

'They want you out of this shop and I want you out of this country! I've managed to persuade them not to press charges, but if you were anybody else you'd be arrested. Get out and wait for me in the car!' Lex could hardly contain his rage.

There was an uneasy silence as they drove back, until Lex turned to John and said, 'You've brought shame on the family. And that after all I've done for you.'

'Done for me?' John snapped, and glared at his father. 'You've done nothing for me or for my mother or for Alex! You're so mean you wouldn't even pay for my return ticket! How else did you think I was going to get enough money together?'

'When we get back, I want you to pack up and get the hell out of my house and out of my life,' Lex said with an air of finality.

'We've been out of your life for ten years! I wanted to come and see you to try and get some answers. But you didn't care then and you don't care now. How else could you have locked me up in an apartment and left me there for days? I was only a kid, but of course now I know who you were running to.'

Lex braked hard, stopped the car and turned to John. 'And you've carried that with you all these years?'

'No, as a matter of fact, for some reason I'd blanked it from my memory. It was Auntie Marion who reminded me of how they had to break the door down to rescue me. What kind of father does that to a ten year old? I was there for days without food! Ten years old!'

Lex turned his head away and stared out of the window as if looking for an answer, guilt pressing down on him. From the way his jaw had tightened John realised he had touched a nerve. 'Well, aren't you going to say something?' he asked.

Lex slowly turned his head to look at John. 'I'm sorry,' he began, his voice tentative, his expression uneasy. 'I didn't mean to leave you that long. It was just that...'

'Liz was more important,' John cut in, not interested in what his father might say. Nothing he said could ever excuse what he had done.

The tension was broken when a voice on the police radio requested Lex to go to the assistance of another police officer dealing with a road traffic incident. 'I have to go. You'll have to walk the rest of the way. And I expect you to be gone when I get home,' Lex said.

As he watched his father speed off, tyres screeching, John was reminded of the previous time he had watched his father drive away, wondering if he would ever see his him again. This time he knew he would not.

'Have you spoken to your dad since you had the row, to say goodbye?' Auntie Marion asked as they were driving to the airport.

'No, there's no point. I've said all I wanted to say to him.'

'It's sad that it should end like this, after coming all this way to see him,' Auntie Marion sighed.

'It was silly of me to think we could ever be close again,' John said with a sense of remorse. 'He's made his life and I've got to get back and carry on with mine.'

Suddenly the music on the car radio stopped and the local radio station announcer broke into the programme. 'News has just come in of an incident on the freeway leading from Umhlanga Rocks,' she began. 'Protection Service Officer Lex Lawson had stopped a driver for a traffic violation on the M4 when a speeding car crashed into the stationary vehicle. Officer Lawson was catapulted over the car and severely injured. It is believed the first driver drew a gun in an attempt to flee the scene, and was shot and killed by Officer Lawson as he lay injured. The freeway has been closed while police continue their investigation. A further bulletin will follow.'

'Oh no,' Uncle Les said, slowing down. 'Do you want to go back?'

'No, it won't change anything. Let's get to the airport,' John said resolutely, but once again struggling with mixed emotions.

CHAPTER 12

BORN AND BETRAYED

1987

John and Jackie were reunited and family life resumed with John doing his best to block out the emotions of the previous months. He was delighted some time later when Jackie announced she was pregnant and they hastily arranged a wedding at the local town hall. Jackie gave birth to Daniel in August 1987 at Billinge Hospital in Wigan. John was present at the birth. The umbilical cord was cut and John's chest swelled with love and pride when he heard his son's first cries.

'I'll never leave you son, I'll never leave you,' he said as the nurse placed the baby in his arms. He looked across at Jackie. 'Thank you, my darling, for giving me such a beautiful and healthy boy. He's got your red hair alright.'

John was working as hard as ever and Jackie looked after Daniel. But Jackie had a restless spirit and began to miss going out to the clubs. She resented being left at home to take care of the baby while John was out at night, working as a bouncer, so she started taking the baby along when she visited her friends. This pleased John, and he encouraged her to go out more. It didn't bother him when she told him that she had been asked to babysit for a friend who had been invited to a party. And because they would be coming home late, Jackie said, would it be alright if she stayed over. John readily agreed and rearranged his shift at the club so he could stay home with the baby. He walked with Jackie to the bus stop, kissed her goodbye and strolled home with Daniel in his arms.

The babysitting became a regular occurrence, particularly over weekends. It seemed to do Jackie a lot of good, and she was more cheerful around the house. It also gave John the opportunity to take Daniel to see his mother, who by now idolised her grandson and loved every moment she spent with him.

It seemed an idyllic situation until one Sunday when Jackie was later than usual coming home and John began to worry. Stephen and Craig had gone off to play football with their friends and John needed to get some food for Daniel. While pushing Daniel along to the shops in his new pram, John bumped into Jackie's friend Diane, and politely asked how she was doing.

'Fine thanks. I see she left you to look after the baby again,' Diane replied.

'Well, you know how it is with Jackie, off babysitting for Debra and...'

'Debra?' Diane exclaimed with raised eyebrows.

'Yes, she's been babysitting for her. Why, what's the problem, why are you so surprised?'

Diane looked away, her eyes troubled as she struggled to decide what to say. Then a wry smile twisted her face and she said, 'You're a decent guy John, and here you are running around with a baby while your wife is...' her voice trailed off as she continued to struggle with her conscience.

'While my wife is what?' John asked, suspecting he wouldn't like the answer.

'She doesn't deserve you, John,' she began, with a look of sympathy on her face. 'She hasn't been babysitting. She meets up with this guy Michael and she's been staying at his place...' she hesitated when she saw John's body stiffen.

He was stunned, his heart hammering his chest, his eyes taking on a murderous look as he said. 'I have to go. Can you please do me a favour and look after Daniel?'

Diane looked at him hesitantly. 'I don't know John, I don't think I can...'

'Look, I'm going to have to sort this out and I don't want Daniel to...'

'Okay, but don't be too long. I'm sorry, I should have kept my mouth shut,' Diane said, her eyes full of pain, her mouth starting to tremble.

'No, you did the right thing and I'm glad you did. Someone only makes a fool of me once. I promise I'll be back to pick up my boy; he's everything to me,' John said, spinning around and running as fast he could down the road.

Oh God, what have I done? Diane sighed as she took hold of the pram and headed off to the nearest phone booth.

Jackie unlocked the door, breezily walked in and cheerfully called out, 'John darling, I'm home!' Then she heard the phone ringing. She waited to see if John would answer, but he didn't. She waited a little longer, thinking he might be in the garden, but still the phone kept ringing. She rushed over and snatched up the receiver. 'Hello.' Slowly her face changed and her legs went weak. 'You stupid cow!' was all she said before slamming down the receiver. She rushed to the front door, flicked the latch up, then ran upstairs and threw herself down on the bed. She buried her head in her hands and started sobbing. She raised her head and looked into the dressing table mirror as if looking for an answer, but all she could see was her tear-stained face, fear written all over it.

The answer she wasn't looking for came from John's voice shouting above his hammering on the front door. 'He's going to kill me,' she said to her reflection as if she knew that was the only answer there could be. She got up slowly, moved to the window and looked down at John hammering away at the door.

'Stop it!' she shouted.

John looked up, his face bristling with anger. 'Come and open this door NOW!' he shouted at the top of his voice.

'No, you need to calm down first and then we can talk. I don't know what you've heard, but it isn't true; the truth is...'

'I know what the truth is, I know what you've been up to. You've been sleeping with a guy called Michael! If you don't come and open this door I'll kick it in!'

Jackie knew that nothing she said would stop John from doing what he was threatening to do. She dragged a small chest of drawers over to the bedroom door and wedged it under the handle, then threw herself back on the bed and buried her head in the quilt in an attempt to block out all sound. It didn't take John long to break the door down. He ran up the stairs two at a time and charged at the bedroom door. A couple of heavy charges shifted the chest of drawers and the door opened. Jackie screamed as John threw himself on top of her and grabbed her by the collar. There was naked hatred in his eyes as he raised his fist, ready to smash it into her face. But something like a powerful force clutched at his wrist and restrained him, while a voice in his head repeated, *'Men who beat up women are scum.'* Suddenly he felt a calmness wash over him. He unclenched his fist and lowered his arm. Slowly he got off the bed and stood staring down at the petrified Jackie.

'You realise what you've done? I could have killed you! You've ruined what I thought was a happy marriage. I loved you, I loved your kids and above all I love the boy we made together. I always thought it was the other fathers who deserted Stephen and Craig, but now I know better.' He saw Jackie wince. 'I'll be back to collect my things. Michael, whoever the hell he is, can have you; our marriage is over.' He turned and walked out, leaving her straightening her blouse, shuddering at the thought of how close he had come to doing her serious harm.

John called his uncle George and told him what had happened. 'It's better to have got the hell out of it than to have been stuck with her forever,' George said. 'Why don't you get your arse down here? Dave and I will sort you out with...'

'Uncle Dave? Is he out then?' John said excitedly.

'Oh yes, he's out, and we've got some good things going. So get yourself here and we'll look after you.'

CHAPTER 13

SOHO, SEX AND SCAMS

1988

The eighties were turning out to be a golden era at the Marquee Club on Wardour Street in London's fashionable Soho. It had witnessed the early performances of stars such as David Bowie, the Rolling Stones, Led Zeppelin and countless others and had earned itself the reputation as the most important venue of its kind in Europe.

Gay bars were starting to multiply in and around Old Compton Street, but it was the oldest profession in the world that benefitted most from the new 'enlightenment'. There was no longer a stigma attached to prostitution, and the gangsters quickly set up shop, knowing there was big money to be made from the sex industry. It was turning over millions of pounds a year, most of which could remain unaccounted for and used to finance drug dealing and other such activities.

John was picked up from Euston Station by Uncle George in his shiny Range Rover. As they drove along Euston Road, John watched his uncle bring his knees up to hold the steering wheel, reach into his pocket and roll himself a spliff.

'Hold the wheel,' George shouted at John as the car started to veer.

'Nice motor,' John said nervously as he reached over and gripped the steering wheel.

'Sure is, cost a few bob, these. Anyway, great to see you Son, you'll be pleased you got away from that crap up there. This is where it all happens, where the money is, and we've got some good jobs lined up for you,' George said.

'Where's Uncle Dave?' John asked, watching George pull out the car lighter and put it to the end of his spliff.

'Oh, he's sorting out some problem or other with one of our clubs. You'll meet him later, and Uncle Tony too.'

'Uncle Tony? Who's he?'

'Well, while your Uncle Dave was banged up, he met this Maltese guy Tony who was doing time for tax evasion. He's apparently connected to the Maltese Mafia, but Tony isn't a violent guy. He's quite weak, actually, so some of the hard nutters in prison used to pick on him. One night one of the inmates tried to slash him with a knife. Well, you know what your Uncle Dave can be like. He drew a knife himself, and slashed the guy's face before he knew what was happening. Tony never forgot it, and told him when he got out there would be a job waiting for him. So when Dave found out the job was all about sex clubs, hostess bars and peep shows, he told Tony he didn't want a job, he wanted a partnership. And Tony agreed, can you believe it!'

'So what kind of job are you thinking of for me?' John asked slightly apprehensively.

'You'll be working the kiosk at the live shows.'

'Live shows?'

'Dinnae worry, I'll show you when we get there.'

They made their way through the busy streets of the West End along Shaftesbury Avenue, turning into Newport Street and parking the car in the car park behind the fire station. As they walked out onto Gerrard Street, John was amazed to see the glittering display of colours and the mass of tourists milling around. He gazed at the colourful Chinese arch with its tall red pillars, decorated with intricate designs and Chinese calligraphy, the roof covered with coloured tiles.

'This is called China Town, there's some great restaurants here. You ever had Chinese food?' George asked as they walked along.

'Yeah, we used to get a takeaway now and then.'

'Nah, I mean real Chinese food. I'll take you one night. You're in for a treat,' George said as they crossed back over Shaftesbury Avenue and walked up Greek Street. Entering Old Compton Street, Ed's Diner lay ahead of them. As they turned right, the road split, with Old Compton Street going off to the left and Moor Street to the right, creating an island of buildings in the centre.

'Welcome to Soho my boy, the home of sex, drugs and rock 'n roll. You see those buildings behind Ed's Diner? Well, Uncle Tony and your Uncle Dave own them. Oh, make sure you always call him Uncle Tony. The only one who gets to call him Tony is your Uncle Dave, okay?'

'You mean they own all of those?' John asked, stopping in his tracks.

'Aye, all of them. Come on, Dave will be waiting for us.' John followed his uncle until they came to a doorway with a large neon sign above it, saying PEEP SHOW.

Inside there was a small kiosk where a man sat and handed out change in pound coins to customers. The customer would then move across to what appeared to be a series of booths, open the door, slip inside and close it behind him.

'I'll explain all that to you in good time,' George said, as he worked the combination lock to a door. 'This is where it all happens,' he said and ushered John up a staircase. 'Go on up, right to the top,' he said, securing the door before following John.

'This is my flat,' George said when they reached the top floor. It was spacious and well furnished, with a good view over the area. 'We've got a nice little flat for you on the next floor down.' He handed John a key. 'Come on, let's drop your stuff and go and meet Uncle Dave.'

There was a row of well equipped single bed-sits that had originally been used by prostitutes, but were now occupied by the people working for the organisation. In the passageway there was a shower unit and a washing machine. On the next floor down was Dave's office, large and impressive, with an adjoining luxury bathroom and sauna. George led John down a small flight of stairs into a fully equipped gymnasium. 'You'll be able to keep fit in here,' he said with a sweeping gesture of his hands.

'I'm going to love this; just what I've always dreamed of,' John said, taking in the surroundings. There were all kinds of weight training equipment, punch bags, boxing gear, and hanging from the walls were swords, spears, body armour, protective headgear and nunchakus.

Just then Dave walked in, his huge afro haircut making John do a double take. 'Hey John, you made it alright?'

'Uncle Dave!' John exclaimed, excited at seeing him.

'Glad you got rid of that stupid lassie. You're with us now. Keep your nose clean and you'll do alright. I'll catch up with you later, I'm off to buy a roller,' Dave said chirpily.

'What's a roller?' John asked.

'It's a car, my boy. The best there is; Rolls Royce Silver Spirit.'

'Right, let's go for a drink and I'll explain everything to you,' George said as soon as Dave had left.

They went to the Admiral Duncan, a pub frequented by the gay community. It unnerved John to see a pub full of men with no females around. Some of them stood together in a very intimate way. George bought a couple of pints and found them a table. 'They're all poofs, dinnae worry about them,' he said, noticing John's discomfort. 'Anyway, we run the peep shows around here, and...'

'Peep shows?'

'You saw one when we arrived. There's a series of booths where men go to ogle at girls in skimpy leotards doing provocative poses. They work with pound coin machines. Most of the men finish up spending ten or twenty pounds at a time, so it's a real money spinner. But the big money is in the hostess bars. I'll show you those later, when we've had something to eat. Let's go across to the Compton, the food is good there,' George said.

The Compton was a larger pub, also frequented by the gay community, and here the customers were more overt in their behaviour. There were couples embracing and kissing, while some men sat on their partners' laps stroking their thighs. 'Oh no, come on Uncle, let's go somewhere else, this is kind of weird,' John said, turning to leave.

George grabbed his arm and pulled him back. 'Relax, you're in London now, where anything goes. You just have to get used to it. We're going to have a beer and something to eat. So go and order us two beers and two bangers and mash,' George said, slipping him some money.

'What you looking at?' John heard his uncle shout at someone as he crossed to a table. He found himself having to control his temper when the barman tickled the palm of his hand when he handed him his change.

It was beginning to get dark when they left the pub, and Soho at night became a very different place. The neon signs of the strip clubs and peep shows stood out in the darkening night, and there were hustlers, toms, pimps, transvestites, drag queens and prostitutes everywhere. So much flesh on offer, both in the pictures displayed in the windows of the porn shops and in real life on the pavements.

'This is Wardour Street, once the heart of the British film industry. All the major film companies had offices here at one time, but there are only a few left now. Anyway, there's another good pub down here, the Intrepid Fox. Up there is Oxford Street; you've heard of Oxford Street?' George continued his running commentary until they got to the corner of Old Compton Street.

'Yes, of course.'

'Well, that's where all the famous stores are—Selfridges, John Lewis, Debenhams and the rest. And the other way,' he said turning round, 'is Lower Wardour Street, which leads into Gerrard Street, which is the other end of China Town you saw earlier. So if you ever get lost, remember these landmarks and you'll find your way back.'

On the corner of Wardour and Brewer Streets George said, 'Along there is Madame JoJo's where all the trannies hang out and that's the famous Raymond's Revue bar. You'll find a lot of sex shops down that alley. We own this building here,' he said, pointing to the tall building on the corner where they were standing. 'It used to be called the Round House, apparently the Rolling Stones once played here, but we now call it the Erotica. The other building in Moor Street where you're going to be living and working, we call the Phoenix. You got it, this one is the Erotica and the other one the Phoenix, okay? They used the Erotica in the Bob Hoskins film, *Mona Lisa*, and your Uncle Dave got a nice bung for it.'

'So what is it used for now?' John wanted to know.

'Didn't you see the sign up there?' George said, indicating a neon sign with the words LIVE SHOW blazing out.

'Are they sex shows?'

'They used to be, but the Council clamped down on all that and now they're just fake sex shows. There's no real sex, just fake blow jobs. Anyway, this is where you're going to be working. Come on, I'll show you inside,' George said, leading him through the side door.

Inside was a kiosk, very much like the one he saw when he first arrived. 'Now your job will be to sit in the kiosk and take the money. The charge is two pounds and you issue them with a ticket and tell them that gives them entry into the club. This is Adam, by the way, who you'll be working with,' George pointed to the man sitting in the kiosk.

'Hi Adam,' John said, offering his hand, which Adam took with a firm grip and gave it a strong shake. Adam had a kind of Gothic appearance with his long black hair swept back and tied into a pony tail. He was wearing a long black leather coat and black boots. Some heavy guys standing around acknowledged George with a certain deference as he walked in.

The basement club was dark and dingy, with spotlights shining on low tables arranged in a semicircle around a bed. On each of the tables was a menu in a black plastic holder, listing the various drinks available, but almost illegible in the dim light. At one end was a bar with optics for the variety of spirits and other exotic looking bottles. Several girls, dressed in sexy underwear—stockings, suspenders and basques—sat around quietly waiting for their customers.

'Let me explain how this works,' George said, taking John aside. 'The customer—the punter—buys his entry ticket and comes down into the club. He sees the bed, so he thinks he's going to see a live sex show. He sits down at one of the tables and a hostess approaches him and asks if he would like a drink. They usually say no, because they've only come to see the sex show, but the hostess tells them they have to buy a drink or leave, because that's the rule of the club, which is clearly printed on a small sign at the entrance and also on the back of the ticket. The punter, not having read anything, doesn't want to leave for the sake of buying a drink, so he usually orders a pint of lager, which, if he had bothered to read the menu, costs twelve pounds. All drinks are non-alcoholic, of course, because we don't have an alcohol licence.'

'What about the optics showing the gin and the vodka, and those?'

'The bottles are genuine, but the contents are fake. The gin and vodka bottles are filled with water. The drinks are not actually served from the bar, they're prepared in the back room. Once he has his drink, the punter usually wants to know when the show is going to start. The hostess tells him they're just waiting for more customers. In the meantime she asks him if he'd like her to sit with him. Most of them think she's just being friendly and they say yes, why not? She then asks the punter to buy her a drink, and she of course orders the most expensive cocktail on the menu. Let's go and pretend we're punters so you can see what actually happens,' George suggested, looking around as the tables started to fill up.

As soon as they had sat down a man appeared and started walking around the tables.

'That's Martin, he's one of the Maltese gang; we call him the showman. He's someone you'll have to get to know once you start working here.'

They watched as one of the scantily clad girls got onto the bed and spread herself out in a provocative manner, while the other hostesses quickly presented their punters with their bills.

'How the blazes do you work this out? I only had a pint of lager!' John heard one of the punters complain.

'Did you not read the menu, sir?' the hostess asked politely, but John could see a few of the heavies ready to move in.

'Look sir, you've had your fun, and you're about to see the live show, but you have to pay like everyone else,' one of the men said with enough force for the punter to start worrying.

He hesitated for a moment, then said, 'I'll call the police and I bet they won't be pleased when they find out what kind of clip joint this is.'

'Okay, if that's what you want sir, but what do you think your wife will say when she finds out you've been watching live shows and flirting with sexy young women?'

'I hope you're studying all this,' George whispered to John.

'Just remember where you are,' the heavy reminded the punter. 'You're in the middle of Soho and we don't take kindly to people who don't pay their bills. So if I was you, I'd pay up and save yourself a lot of trouble.' There was no attempt to hide the threat of what could happen if he still refused to pay.

George continued his training. 'Watch what happens now. Once the first one pays, it has a domino effect and rest of them usually cough up without much trouble.' John watched in amazement as the hostesses moved around, collecting hundreds of pounds.

'Is it always this easy?'

'Not always, but that's where the fear factor comes in useful.'

Once all the bills had been paid, Martin, in a theatrical manner, began to build up to what all the punters had been waiting for. 'Right, we're going to do the live show now. This beautiful girl wants me and I'm going to give it to her, right gents?' he called out, clapping his hands above his head while pacing around the floor.

'Yeah, go on, let's see you give it to her!' one of the punters called out.

'Don't you worry Sir, I will,' Martin called back. 'One of the hostesses will come around with a box and the more money you put in, the more I'll perform, but no coins, just nicely folded notes, if you please,' he added, as he watched the girl move around the tables collecting the money.

When he felt they had collected all the money they were going to get, he got onto the bed. He stood up with his back to the tables and the girl got down on her knees in front of him. She raised her hands, unzipped his trousers and began to move her head backwards and forwards, simulating the sex act. She was, of course, just moving her head against his bellybutton while both of them made the appropriate noises. After a while Martin cried out in ecstasy, as if reaching an orgasm. Then he zipped himself up and turned to the punters. 'That's it gentlemen, show's over!'

George leaned over to John. 'This is usually the point where they get angry. You'll see how the heavies move in just in case any of them want to make trouble. You'll always get one or two awkward ones, but they always pay up in the end. Sometimes we have to rough a few up, but usually the threat is enough.' He stood up. 'You start in the kiosk upstairs tomorrow; it's a five hour shift and you get paid fifty quid per shift. You can always do two shifts a day in you feel up to it. We'll see how you go and then maybe move you up to bar manager. There you get ten per cent of the take. We make between two to five grand a shift.'

'Sounds great, Uncle George,' John said eagerly.

'Right, I'll take you back to your room so you can sort yourself out and get a good night's rest.'

John lay on his bed thinking about what had happened since his return from South Africa. It had been hard, harder than he had expected, Jackie's betrayal hitting him the hardest. But now he began to realise how naive he had been, and promised himself he would never fall into the same trap. His worst anguish was having to leave Daniel behind. He would visit him regularly to see to his well-being, to show him he still had a father who loved him and that one day they would be together again.

CHAPTER 14

THE MALTESE MAFIA

John lay on the bed, deep in thought. He had left Daniel with Jackie; was he deserting him as his father had done to him? He had sworn he would never do that to his own son, but that is exactly what he had done and it was troubling him. He stared up at the ceiling, tears running down the side of his face, determined to go back as soon as he could to try and sort something out with Jackie.

His thoughts were interrupted by a heavy banging on the door and his uncle George shouting, 'Come on, get yourself out of bed, you can't lie there all day, there's work to be done!' He wiped his eyes and heard his uncle banging on the next door and calling out, 'Come on Martin, time to get up!' He got out of bed, went to the window and looked out over Moor Street, not quite believing he was in the heart of London. To his left was Cambridge Circus with its mass of traffic. It was an exhilarating feeling. To the right the Palace Theatre's signs were advertising Les Miserables. Just then his uncle walked in and saw him standing at the window.

'Quite a sight, Soho, isn't it? I remember when I first arrived; I found it difficult to take it all in, but you'll get used to it. Get yourself washed, we're going to Café Bruno. They do a great breakfast.'

As they walked into the café, George handed him a twenty from a thick wad of notes. 'Here, order us some grub,' he said. While John was at the counter ordering two English breakfasts, Martin and Andy came in and joined George at the table. 'Make that two more!' he called out.

'So who's the new kid?' Martin asked, looking across at John at the counter.

'That's my nephew, John. You'll both be working with him and I want you to look after him, teach him the ropes. He's got a lot to learn but he's smart and he's pretty handy with his fists; been doing a bit of Kung Fu and Karate.'

John returned with the coffees. George waited for him sit down before he said, 'This here is Martin; he's got the flat next to you. We call him the showman. You remember you saw him doing his bit yesterday?'

'Yes, I remember. Hi Martin,' John said, offering his hand, which Martin shook welcomingly. Martin was Maltese, with a mop of a curly hair, a Roman nose and tanned skin.

'And this is Andy, Uncle Tony's nephew and the son of one of Soho's most celebrated ladies of the night. He's also the general manager, and takes care of the day to day running of the operation. Andy has one of the bigger flats on the floor below me.' Andy seemed unusually proud that his mother was a prostitute, nodding his head in acknowledgement. He was quite handsome, much like a young Mel Gibson. 'So, after breakfast I'm going to introduce you to some of Tony's guys. It's important you know who and they are and what they do,' George continued as he tucked into his breakfast.

'This is Bullets, this is Fingers and this is Diamonds,' George introduced the three men when they arrived at the hostess club. All three looked as if they had just stepped out of a gangster movie, and John had to stifle a laugh. They were all in their forties, stocky, and wearing pinstripe suits, spats on their shoes and sporting trilby hats; every bit the stereotypical Mafia mobsters.

'This is John. He's family and he's come to join us. To begin with he'll be in the kiosk of the hostess bar and we'll see how he gets on,' George told them.

'Good to know you, John,' Bullets said with a heavy Maltese accent. 'I sure we be bumping into each other all over da place.

Keep your nose clean and I sure you do alright,' he added, shaking John's hand.

'Yeah, good to know you, John,' the other two joined, each shaking his hand before turning and walking off.

John waited until they had left before he turned to his uncle. 'Are they for real?'

'You'd better believe it. They're connected to the Maltese Mafia and I'm telling you, you don't want to mess with them. They virtually run Soho. Tony's the boss man and they're his lieutenants. They guard their territory from other mobs moving in. There's a rumour that Bullet's dad chopped the head off a gang leader in the sixties in the café where we had breakfast. True or not, I don't know, but they're sure as hell capable of it. They even drove the Kray Twins out when they tried to move in. So be careful what you say to them. Dave is their boss, because of his partnership agreement with Tony, but it would only take one stupid move to unbalance things.'

'How did they get those names—Bullets, Fingers, Diamonds?'

George smiled. 'Well, Bullets has been shot several times. He wears the bullets they took out on a chain around his neck. Fingers, well, he's a brilliant card shark. You should see him shuffle a pack of cards; it'll blow your mind. And Diamonds just likes diamonds. You saw that huge diamond in his ear? Just remember, those guys have an assortment of weapons and they aren't afraid to use them.'

'So I'm starting in the kiosk?' John asked, anxious to get to work.

'Yes, but first you're going to run an important errand for us. I'm going to give you a bag that you need to guard with your life; I mean your life. You'll be carrying twelve grand in cash. You get a taxi and tell him to take you to Café Basilico in Covent Garden. Order yourself a coffee and wait. The owner will come over and tell you there's someone on the phone for you. That someone will tell you what to do next, okay?'

'Okay.'

On the corner of Greek and Old Compton Streets John hailed the first taxi he saw with the For Hire sign lit up. 'Where to, John?' the taxi driver asked casually.

Wow, everybody knows Uncle George and Uncle Dave. They even know my name, John thought, but said, 'Do you know the Café Basilico in Covent Garden?'

'You bet,' the driver said. He turned left into Shaftesbury Avenue, crossed over Cambridge Circus, turned right into Earlham Street and stopped at the corner of Neal Street. 'There you are, John, Cafe Basilico,' he said, pointing to a rather run down cafe on the other side of the street.

'How much is that?' John asked.

'Five pounds sixty on the clock.' John handed him one of the ten pounds notes George had given him and waited for the change. The taxi driver handed him the change, irritation beginning to show on his face that he hadn't been offered a tip.

'Do all the taxi drivers know my uncles?' John asked, pocketing the change.

'Who the hell are your uncles?'

'The Lawsons,' John said proudly.

'Never bleedin' heard of 'em, but I tell you one thing, I won't forget you John. Last of the big spenders!'

The Gaggia coffee machine was hissing and steam drifted across the café as John sat looking around nervously. He had finished his coffee and was trying to decide whether to order another when the pay phone on the wall started ringing. Just then a man came from behind the counter, snatched up the receiver, listened for a brief moment, and called out to John, 'Your name John?'

'Yes,' John answered.

'This call's for you.'

'Hello,' John said hesitantly. A gruff cockney voice told him to take a taxi to the County Arms Pub in Wandsworth, and the phone went dead before he had a chance to repeat the instructions. John hailed a cab and asked the driver if he knew Wandsworth prison.

'You planning an escape, John?' the cabby replied with a cheeky grin.

John laughed as he realised that London cabbies called all their fares John and blushed at his earlier ignorance.

As the taxi turned down Heathfield, John saw a sign that read: HMP WANDSWORTH on a huge building looming menacingly over the area. *That's one place I never want to go to,* he thought. The taxi turned into Trinity Road and pulled up outside the County Arms.

As John entered, he noticed two tough looking elderly gentlemen sitting at the back near the bar. One of them raised a finger beckoning him over and John approached them, clutching the bag with the money. Without saying a word, the second man pointed to the floor. At first John wasn't sure what to do, but he placed the bag on the floor and waited for them to say something. They said nothing, just stared up at him, so John waited.

'Now get lost,' the first man finally said. John did as he was told and hurried out as quickly as he could.

'Did you give them the money?' George asked when John walked back into the office.

'Yeah, I did. They're a couple of strange guys; quite aggressive, didn't say hello, just pointed for me to put the bag down on the floor and then told me to get lost.'

'They're the Adams family and before you ask, No, they don't get their name off the TV show. They are... how shall we put it? Gangsters. We rent some of the buildings from them and that's the rent money you took to them. I should have told you before you went why they wouldn't take the money directly from you. They don't know who's watching them. Could be the police or the taxman, so they don't touch it. Someone else will come and pick up the bag. Make sure you remember that next time. You'll probably be doing the run from now on. You don't talk to anybody about it, okay?'

'Sure, Uncle George.'

Just then Tony strolled into the office. 'Hi George, how's it all going?' he asked casually.

'Fine. Everything's going just fine,' George assured him. 'This is my nephew John; he's come to work for us.'

Tony was dressed in a smart pair of designer jeans, a short-sleeved shirt and slip-on shoes. He had an expensive watch on his left wrist and a gold bracelet on his right. He was about fifty, and looked more like a retired tennis player than a Mafioso, John thought. 'Good to meet you, John' he said. 'You'll see me around from time to time. Keep your nose clean and do as your uncle tells you and you'll do well for yourself.'

'So that's Uncle Tony,' George said after Tony had left. 'He's alright, but he doesn't suffer fools, so be on your toes when he's around. If he likes you, you can do well, but if he doesn't, you're out on your ear.'

Before John could find out more about his uncle, Nicola, one of the peep show girls, walked in wearing a skimpy leotard. 'Alright if I use the shower and sauna?' she asked, already starting to remove her clothes. John's eyes almost popped out of his head as she stepped out of the leotard without bothering to close the door. She saw him looking at her, turned to face him and gave him a friendly smile before disappearing further into the room.

George followed John's eyes and waited until he was sure Nicola couldn't hear him. 'Don't crap on your own doorstep, son. You don't mix with the girls, you hear? They're off limits. We pay them for what they do and that's as far as it goes. You fancy a bit, you go outside of where you work and find it, okay?'

'Okay Uncle, I understand.'

'Make sure you do. A lot of the girls will happily offer it if they think it will give them the best shifts. But that's where the trouble starts, so keep it in your trousers! You're doing the late shift tonight, six to around eleven thirty, over at the Erotica, where I took you yesterday. All you've got to do is sit in the kiosk and issue the two-quid tickets. If any of the punters come up complaining that you never told them to buy a drink, you just point to the sign on the wall and say, 'Didn't you read the sign when you came in, sir?' Tell them it's also printed on the back of the ticket. They'll have a good moan and amble off. If any of them look like giving you trouble, you let them see you use the intercom to call security. That's usually enough to scare them off,' George ended his brief.

John settled into the kiosk and was surprised at the number of punters happily paying their two pounds to see what they thought was going to be a live sex show. It wasn't long though before he experienced his first complaining customer who came up the stairs shouting, 'This whole thing's a blooming con! You didn't tell me I had to buy a drink!'

'It states it clearly on that sign, sir,' John said politely, 'and it's also printed on the back of your ticket.' The man studied the sign for a brief moment, huffed and stormed out.

Apart from the occasional confrontation, John found it a boring job, which he overcame by looking out through the open doors that gave him a view along Old Compton Street, the pavements bustling with all kinds of life—gay couples walking hand in hand on their way to the Admiral Duncan or the Compton; transvestites making their way to Madame JoJo's; prostitutes walking up and down trying to attract customers. It fascinated him to watch the girls walk off with a man and be back on the street within fifteen or twenty minutes. It was a constantly changing scene.

Suddenly his view was obstructed by a tall man standing in front of the kiosk. In a rather refined voice he said, 'This is an absolute scam. There was no live sex show, just a fully clothed man and a female pretending to have sex. It's a disgrace. Do you realise I'm a solicitor and I've a good mind to report this to...'

'In that case sir,' John interrupted him, 'you will have seen the sign outside that says live show, and...'

'Exactly. Live sex show, which is what I expected to see.'

'No sir, it says live show, not live sex show and you as a solicitor would know the difference. So if you want to call the police, do so, but I wonder what your colleagues and family will think of you coming to see a sex show.' John's voice was gentle and polite, but there was no mistaking the threat that lay behind it.

The man stared at John for a long moment. As he turned to walk away, he said, 'You haven't heard the last of this.' John allowed himself a smile, thinking that this same solicitor would probably be in court tomorrow prosecuting some poor guy for indecent exposure.

At the end of day Andy appeared and handed John his fifty pounds pay for the night. As he lay in bed that night he couldn't believe his luck—earning good money and living rent-free in a nice little flat in the centre of London. But then his thoughts turned to Daniel and how he had abandoned him. He resolved to have a word with Uncle George about having a weekend off to go and sort things out with Jackie and see Daniel.

John continued to learn how the business worked, and got to know the girls who worked there. He was surprised to discover that most of them were students who were doing it to supplement their income to pay for their education. Others were single mothers who had to support themselves and their children after the husbands had walked out on them. To them it was an easy way of earning good money without prostituting themselves.

There were of course the strippers who went from club to club, took their clothes off, put them back on, and moved down the road to the next club to do the same. The red lights shining in the windows in the little side streets indicated that there were prostitutes offering their services. A man would enter the building, the red light would go off and the curtains drawn. Ten minutes or so later the curtains would be opened and the red light would be switched on again.

During one of his breaks John found out while talking to Andy that not only was his mother a prostitute, but his girlfriend was one too, and he was quite proud of it, adding that she was a high class prostitute, not just a common pro.

'But what you've got to watch out for are the touts,' Andy said, wanting to change the subject.

'The touts?'

'Yeah, they're the rip-off merchants who hang around outside the hostess clubs. They try to sell tickets to the live shows, and...'

'But how can they sell tickets to our shows? Surely we're the only ones who can do that?'

'Yes, but the punters only find that out when they walk in and present their tickets which they've probably paid a fiver for.'

'So what do I say if one of them walks in?'

'Just say sorry mate, you've been conned, but you can come in, the entrance fee is only two quid. That makes them feel at least we're genuine.'

'Until of course...'

'Yeah, well that's the way the game is played. Another thing you'll see is what's called the key scam. The touts will approach someone they suspect of looking for a pro and say, "You see that pretty girl standing over there? Well, that's my girl, but she can't be seen to be openly soliciting. So if you want a good time, and I can promise she'll give it to you, you pay me twenty quid. I'll give her the nod and give you this key to her flat, which is number 26 Berwick Street. You give her time to get there, then you let yourself in and she'll be waiting for you." Of course the key is fake and doesn't fit any door anywhere. By the time the punter discovers this, the tout and the girl are long gone. Some of the girls work this kind of scheme on their own too.'

It wasn't long after Andy had told him about the touts that John spotted one outside the entrance. He rushed out, grabbed the man by the scruff of his neck, pulled him inside and set about him with some hefty blows to the head and body. 'If I ever see you hanging around here again, I'll break every bone in your body,' he said, while the man struggled to his feet, clutching his stomach and staggered out. When George and Dave got to hear about it they gave John a two hundred pound bonus.

John's reputation grew, and the hostesses often called him down at collecting time when they feared things were getting out of hand. He didn't have to resort to violence, as he now exuded an aura of fear, which was enough to scare the punters into paying.

Pleased with the way John was handling himself, his uncles agreed to give him a weekend off to go and visit Daniel and his mother.

When the weekend came, George surprised him by saying, 'You really want to rub it in and show Jackie what she's lost? Take the Range Rover and show her how well you're doing. Also, go and buy yourself a new suit and make sure you take plenty of cash with you. Let her see it so she realises what a fool she's been. Here's a couple of hundred. You've done well and you deserve it.'

John jumped at the chance and couldn't wait to pull up outside the house and see Jackie's reaction to the big car, his smart new suit and the expensive watch on his wrist. The drive up to Wigan in the Range Rover made him feel important and he craved the lifestyle his uncles were enjoying even more. He made a point of driving onto the grass verge outside the house and was pleased when some of the neighbours gave him admiring looks as he slammed the car door and walked up the path to his old house.

'I've come to collect my son,' John said to Jackie. He put his hand in his pocket and handed her a hundred pounds.

'Wow! Thanks!' she exclaimed as Daniel ran into his father's arms, holding him tightly, as if he never wanted to let go.

'I'll drop him off on Monday. By the way, that money is to pay bills and not for you or your fancy man,' John said over his shoulder as he carried his son to the car.

CHAPTER 15

FIRST BRUSH WITH THE LAW

The weekend was over too quickly, but the good news was that Jackie had agreed to let Daniel stay with Jose for another week while John headed back to work in London.

'I've got other plans for you now,' George said as he and John were walking to his office. 'I'm opening a new hostess bar and I want you to run it for me. You fancy that?'

'You mean it's going to be your own hostess bar?'

'Yep. I've rented the basement in the Phoenix from Tony. It's not as big as the Erotica but it can still be a good earner. You'll be in charge; you'll take care of security and make sure everything runs smoothly. You'll obviously be earning more money plus a percentage of the takings, and Martin will be the showman, okay?'

'Okay, thanks Uncle, I'll enjoy that.'

A week later the hostess bar was open for business. The walls and ceiling were painted black. Six tables were set in a semicircle around a bed on which the live shows would be performed. The small illuminated bar at one end was visible from the entrance. Close circuit cameras were installed for extra security. There were four hostesses, a barman and a man in the kiosk taking the entrance fees.

Everything was running smoothly, and John could not have been happier. Until one evening when a German punter became argumentative about his bill and refused to pay. He was very aggressive and started threatening the hostesses. John kept a close watch from a distance, ready to move in if the situation got worse. The man had a large camera over his shoulder, which he slipped off and gripped by the straps, ready to use it as a weapon. John swiftly moved forward to protect the girls. But without warning the man swung the camera at John, catching the side of his head and causing a four inch gash. With blood pouring from the wound, John looked at the man and said in an ice cold voice, 'You shouldn't have done that.' With that he gave the man a side kick, propelling him backwards with such force that he ended up embedded in the plasterboard wall with his legs dangling out. The hostesses joined in, using their stilettos to hit the man. Someone called the police and they responded quickly.

'So what's going on here?' the officer asked, looking at John's blood-soaked T-shirt.

'This man was getting very aggressive towards the girls and I stepped in to protect them. He smashed his camera over my head,' John explained.

'Did you do this, sir?' the officer asked, turning to the man.

'Yes I did,' he admitted in broken English. The officer put a restraining hand on the man's arm and proceeded to march him out. Two other police officers arrived and the first officer ordered them to bring everyone else to the station for witness statements.

At West End Central police station John and the girls gave their statements and were then taken to the canteen and offered tea and coffee. John's head was still bleeding and he was still wearing the blood-soaked T shirt, which prompted other police officers and staff to ask him what had happened. But things suddenly took a different turn and John was recalled to the interview room.

'Your name Lawson?' the police officer asked sombrely.

'Yes, but I already told you that,' John replied, surprised at the change in attitude.

'Right. Wait there,' the officer said and left the room. John noticed that someone was looking at him through the square glass in the door. It was an unfamiliar face, but one that he would get to know well in time—that of Inspector Ronald Atwell.

The police officer returned, resumed his seat and said, 'John Lawson, you are under arrest. You're being charged with threatening behaviour.'

'Charging me? He was the one that attacked me and I've got the wound to prove it!'

'No, you intimidated him, threatened him with his life and after you'd hit him he felt the only way to defend himself was to use whatever he had at hand.'

'No! I was the one who had to defend myself! It's all on tape from the security cameras; you can check it for yourselves.'

'We've checked the tapes, and they're all blank. That's the trouble when you install cheap crap; they never work properly, especially when you need them. I'd ask for my money back if I were you,' the officer said.

Having been formally charged, John was locked up in a cell. At one o'clock in the morning two police officers took him to Middlesex Hospital to have the wound seen to. He allowed himself a wry smile when the nurse berated the policemen for waiting so long before bringing the patient for treatment. The wound needed five stitches, after which John was taken back to the station. By now it was three o'clock in the morning and he was informed that he was being released on bail, and to report to the police station in four weeks' time.

George was very concerned about the incident, particularly as the name Lawson was being bandied about by the cops. He suggested John take a break and go and visit his family until he had to report back to the police. He gave John a mobile phone to stay in touch in case of an emergency. 'This is a Nokia Mobira Cityman. Cutting edge of technology, so we can make contact from anywhere. They're so expensive, so take care of it because they're hard to come by. If anyone sees one of these lying around they'll snatch it.'

John decided he could afford to travel first class. He phoned Jackie from the train and smiled broadly when he heard her voice clearly as she said hello. 'It's me,' he said, 'I reckon I'll be with you in half an hour,' he said.

'Where are you?' Jackie asked.

'I'm on the train.'

'Don't be daft, trains don't have telephones,' she said with an air of disbelief.

'I'm calling you on my mobile phone. You can call me back on it, but you'd better not; the calls are more expensive,' he said, liking the way he had said 'more expensive'.

Then he heard her say, 'It's your dad, he's talking on one of those new-fangled phones you can use anywhere,' and it made him smile again.

He couldn't resist calling her again from the taxi. When he'd finished, the driver looked over his shoulder and said, 'I've heard about those things; are they any good?'

'Well, you've just heard me talking on it. That ought to tell you something,' John said boastfully.

As soon as he got out of the taxi Daniel came rushing towards him. 'Daddy! Daddy!' he cried out, bristling with excitement, and John's heart swelled with pride at how his son was growing up. He looked him up and down and noticed his worn and shabby clothes. He decided he would buy him some new ones when they got to Birkenhead.

'Last time you came in a flashy car, this time you come with a flashy phone. So what's it all about?' Jackie asked as he carried Daniel back into the house.

'It's not about anything. The car is in for repairs, so I took the train,' John said, and changed the subject by asking after Craig and Stephen. He was relieved to hear that they were with their grandmother. It was heartbreaking to see their sad faces whenever he left with Daniel.

'Did you use the money I gave you to clear the bills?'

'Yes. But as soon as you get rid of one bill, another one pops up and once you've paid that, another appears out of nowhere,' Jackie said sullenly.

'So what do you owe now?'

'Two hundred.'

'How do you manage to chalk that up?'

'You forget that I've got three children to clothe and feed, plus another one on the way,' she said wearily.

'What?' John retorted angrily. 'I suppose it's that Michael's.'

'Yes, and he did a runner as soon as he found out I was pregnant,' Jackie said with a hapless shrug of her shoulders.

John dug his hand into his jacket pocket, pulled out a wad of fifty pound notes and counted off five. 'Here's two fifty. That gives you fifty to spend on you and the kids,' he said, handing her the money.

'Thanks, I can breathe again,' she said, clutching the money to her face.

'Right, now that we've got that sorted I'm going to take Daniel for a bit longer, if that's okay with you. I've got some time off.'

'Fine by me; one less to worry about for a while,' she said with a wry smile. It was a look that made John decide things had to change.

His mother was waiting at the door in Thorneycroft Street and was delighted when Daniel came rushing into her arms. 'Hello my precious darling,' she said, scooping him up into her arms and giving him a big kiss.

'Hi Mum, we've got him for as long as we like. I'm going to stay here for a few weeks; my uncles have given me some time off to spend with you and Daniel,' John said, following them into the house.

When his mother brought the tea cups out, she noticed the scar on the side of John's head. 'You been fighting again?' she asked.

'No, it was just a silly accident. I tripped and banged my head. Nothing to worry about.'

'I worry all the time, you getting mixed up in those sordid businesses.'

'Look, I'm only involved in the peep shows, and the girls are fully dressed. I just sit in the kiosk and give out change.'

'And they pay you all that money just for doing that?'

'I do some other little jobs for them too.'

'That's what worries me. They'll gradually draw you in until you get into real trouble.'

'No Mum, they're not doing anything illegal, so there's nothing for you to worry about,' John lied, not daring to tell her he had already been charged with a serious offence.

CHAPTER 16

IMMORAL AND INDECENT

George called a few weeks later to say the heat had subsided and that John should come back to work. He arrived at Euston Station and headed straight for Soho. He found his uncles in Dave's office with a rather overweight man with a bulging stomach and a mop of thick black hair. 'This is Cecil Watkins who takes care of our legal problems,' Dave announced.

'Hello sir,' John said, and offered his hand.

'You'll be pleased to know all your charges have been dropped,' Cecil Watkins said as he shook John's hand, and flakes of dandruff fell onto his pin-striped suit. 'You see,' he went on, 'there's a way of dealing with these matters that benefits everyone. To pursue this case the police would have had to keep the German tourist here, pay for his stay until the case was heard, or pay to bring him back. Either way would have been expensive. I argued that the case would have had to wait until my client—you—had fully recovered from your injuries, plus the fact that we would start proceedings against the German tourist for GBH. So in the end they dropped all charges.'

George waited until Cecil had gone before he turned to John. 'Listen, do you have any mates up North who would be interested in working for us as front men?' he asked.

'Front men, what are they?'

'The people we pay to front our businesses. They don't have to do anything and they get paid well for it. You see, on paper Uncle Dave and Uncle Tony have nothing to do with the ownership or running of the businesses. So if there's a raid they can't be touched,' George explained.

'So the front man takes the rap?'

'Not necessarily. We usually get a tip-off when there's going to be a raid, so by then front man A has sold the business to front man B, which means the police have to start all over again. Then B sells it to C and so on. Fingers is the front man at the moment, then Bullets takes over and then Diamonds.'

'Very clever! I've got so much to learn. I'm afraid I can't think of anyone to recommend at the moment,' John said pensively.

'Yes well, better to be sure than sorry. Anyway, Uncle Dave has decided to shove two fingers up the Council, so the girls in the peep shows are now going to be nude, which will draw more punters. We're still not changing the live shows because the Council will come down on us like a ton of bricks.'

'But won't the Council come down on us with the peep shows?'

'We don't know, but Cecil Watkins has worked out the difference between something that's considered immoral and something that's considered indecent. If we ran a real live sex show he reckons it would be considered immoral and would lead to prosecution, but if the girls pose naked he reckons it would be considered indecent and then it's simply a Council matter. So we're going to put up coin operated two-way mirrors that will allow the punter to see the girls for thirty seconds before the light comes back on. Then they have to put another coin in to turn the light off so they can see her again. The girls will be on a bed on a raised platform and do a slow strip. So the punters will keep putting money in to see them get completely naked. The beauty of this is there's no rip-off. The punter gets what he pays for and we reckon we'll triple our turnover.'

'I'm impressed.'

'And so you should be. Your uncle is one smart cookie. So tonight, after we've closed for business we're going to knock the booths down and rebuild them in the new style and with a new coin mechanism. Rob and Lindsey, Fingers, Bullets, Diamonds, Andy and Martin are coming to help so we should be up and running by the morning,' George enthused.

It was a hard day's night and the team worked tirelessly to get the work completed in time. The booths had been painted black and the viewing windows fitted with the new coin mechanism. The platforms were in place, with the beds angled to give each booth a good view of the performing girl. They were ready for business.

Word quickly spread that the girls in the peep shows were now posing completely naked, resulting in a continuous flow of punters from the moment they opened at nine in the morning. It never ceased to amaze John that it wasn't just the dirty old man in their macs who frequented the booths. Businessmen in smart suits would come to the kiosk, change ten or twenty pound notes for pound coins, go into the booths, coins in one hand and unzipping themselves with the other. He imagined the naive wife fussing over her husband when he got home, concerned at how tired and exhausted he looked.

One of the most unpleasant jobs for the kiosk workers was to clean up the walls and floors of the booths and to pick up the piles of discarded tissues. They also had to crawl under the platforms to replace the plastic buckets that held the pound coins. Money was coming in so fast that Dave had to buy a counting machine.

It wasn't long before the Council got wind of what was going on and decided it had to put a stop to what they considered an affront to public decency. Armed with Council workers and a pickup truck, they made their first raid soon after the Phoenix had opened for business. The Council official burst in. 'We're from Westminster City Council. This is a raid and you have three minutes to vacate the premises,' the official announced in a loud voice, tearing a formal notice from his clipboard and thrusting it towards Adam, who was manning the kiosk.

'What's all this then?' Adam asked, feigning innocence.

'The Council deems your activities to be of an indecent nature and therefore, as you can see from the notification, we're closing you down,' the official informed him pompously.

When the Council workers entered, armed with sledgehammers, girls in various stages of undress ran out onto the street, much to the delight of the passers-by. The official gave the go-ahead for the workers to start breaking up the booths and to load the broken sections onto the pickup truck.

George immediately called Cecil Watkins. 'Don't do anything to stop them, let them get on with it; they're playing right into our hands,' Cecil cautioned. 'This is a Council matter and once they've confiscated the material they'll think they've destroyed your ability to do business, they'll walk away and you can simply start up again.'

'How can we start up again? They've closed us down!' John exclaimed, looking around the room that was now just and empty shell.

'No they haven't. We knew this was likely to happen, so everything has been prefabricated, which means the booths can be rebuilt tonight and you'll be up and running again in the morning.'

John looked at George. 'But they'll just close us down again,' he said.

'Legally they can't do anything like this again for at least the next six weeks, because they have to apply for a warrant to destroy our stuff. So we can run the business as usual till then. We'll have raked in another hundred grand from this one alone and then we simply rebuild it again and again till they get fed up. We're not going to let those scumbags beat us.' George seemed unperturbed.

The next day the peep shows were up and running again, the raid not seeming to have scared away the punters. The Council's action seemed to add to the notoriety of the naked girls and simply attracted more and more people.

At times John would go behind the booths to check if the girls were okay. From there he could see the punters, but they couldn't see him until they had put their money in the slot and by then he would be out of the way. Some of the men would check their own image in the one-way glass before inserting their coins. One regular punter would take out a toothpick and meticulously pick his teeth before inserting the coin and unzipping his trousers. But the punter that fascinated him most was a very short man who brought a milk crate with him. The staff had nicknamed him 'Milk Crate Eddie'. He would take the crate into the booth, place it on the floor and stand on it so that he could see through the one-way glass without having to stand on his toes.

Everything was running smoothly, and George decided to promote John to manager of the hostess bar. 'I want you to take over as bar manager of the Erotica. You'll be under Andy's supervision to begin with, but you'll effectively be in control, particularly as far as security is concerned. You'll keep the girls in check, make sure they get the maximum number of punters in and get the maximum amount of money out of them. And you'll deal with the trouble makers who don't want to pay.'

'That's great Uncle, but I promised Daniel and my mum I'd visit them every fortnight,' John said.

'Aye son, as long as you keep bringing in the business, that's okay with me,' George assured him.

Lindsey and Rob, two brothers who had been working with the family for a couple of years, were running the porn shops. They had set up a video duplicating factory with the latest equipment, churning out hundreds of video tapes a day. John's uncles had also rented out their vacant flats to prostitutes, and their wares were being advertised in all the telephone booths around the area. The sordid side of Soho was doing all it could to meet the ever increasing demand from visitors and tourists eager to explore the darker side of London, and the money kept rolling in.

John earned the nickname of 'Sergeant' from the girls, because of his strict rules—they had to arrive on time, dress neatly and keep everything clean. Instead of being paid a hundred pounds per shift, he introduced a scheme by which they would pay the company fifty pounds to work there, and earn ten per cent of what they brought in. This meant they could earn a lot more than a hundred pounds, with the club benefitting at the same time.

Apart from the occasional difficult punter, things seemed to run relatively smoothly until one punter flatly refused to pay, and complained loudly about being ripped off. After some 'gentle persuasion' he reluctantly paid. John breathed a sigh of relief as the man stormed out.

At that exact moment Inspector Atwell happened to be doing his rounds. The disgruntled punter spotted him and rushed over to tell him what had happened. It was music to Atwell's ears and he assured the man he would look into the matter. He was so intent on dealing with the complaint that he never noticed the man turn on his heels and walk away. Bracing himself, Inspector Atwell entered the hostess bar where the girls were clearing the tables for the next round of punters. 'Can I help you officer?' John said, hurrying towards him.

'That rather depends,' Atwell said sourly.

'On what?' John stared back at him.

'I know who you are. You're a Lawson aren't you? I never forget a face. We had you in once before for beating up a tourist. I've just had a complaint from a man who said you'd threatened him with violence unless he paid you some extortionate sum of money. What do you have to say about that?'

'Have you got a search warrant to enter these premises?' John asked, his expression implacable.

Atwell seemed taken aback. 'I don't need one sonny, I'm investigating a crime. One of your customers said you ripped him off and threatened him when he refused to pay.'

'Well, we don't know of any trouble; all our customers seem to enjoy their visits and leave here happy.'

'That's not what I've heard,'

'Look Inspector, this is beginning to bore me. Where is your alleged victim? And you have no witnesses. Nobody has seen anything untoward here, so I suggest you leave. This is private property.'

'I'll leave when I'm good and ready. I've not finished my investigation into this complaint. A man has been robbed. By you!' Atwell was getting angry.

'If you don't mind, I've got a lot to do and you're delaying me,' John said, giving Atwell a gentle shove.

'Take your hands off me or I'll have you for assault!'

'Once again, you need witnesses and I can't see anyone here who could say I've assaulted you. So be sensible Inspector, and leave,' John gave him another shove towards the door.

Atwell turned and walked to the door with John following closely behind.

As they got to the street, Atwell suddenly spun around and grabbed John by the scruff of the neck, shoving him up against the wall. 'You're on my territory now, you scumbag, and I'm going to get you!' he shouted, the veins on his neck standing out and spittle flying into John's face. 'You think you lowlifes can get the better of me. Well, you've got another thing coming. I've dealt with people like you all my life. You think the law doesn't apply to you, but you're about to find out it does,' he continued, while banging John's head against the wall.

'Help!' John cried out dramatically. 'I'm being assaulted! I'm not offering any resistance!' he added, raising his hands in the air.

A passer-by approached the Inspector. 'Excuse me officer, but I don't think there's any need for this. The man is clearly not offering any resistance...'

Atwell turned to look at the man without relaxing his grip on John. 'I would ask you to mind your own business, sir. This is a police matter and I'm dealing with it.'

'That may be so, but I don't care for the way you're dealing with it,' the man said. He took a cigarette packet out of his pocket, tore off the lid and wrote his name and phone number on it. 'Here, take this if you need a witness,' he said to John. The Inspector tried to snatch it from him, but John got hold of it and shoved it into his pocket. As the man walked off Atwell took out his two-way radio and called for backup. Within minutes a squad car arrived, John was bundled into it and driven to West End Central police station, where he was ushered into an interviewing room.

'I'm going to throw the book at you, Lawson! Assaulting a senior police officer and threatening a member of the public!' he shouted before storming out, leaving John wondering if he should have had handled the matter differently.

'The inspector seems in a right old mood and he's not nice to be around when he's like that,' the duty constable said, looking at John's troubled face.

'Yeah well, I'd like to see the duty sergeant. I wish to make a complaint. It was the Inspector who actually assaulted me, not the other way around and I have a witness to prove it,' John told him.

Atwell came back into the room. 'Right Lawson, empty your pockets.'

John placed the contents of his pockets, including the lid of the cigarette packet, on the bare table. Atwell snatched it, tore it up and tossed it into the waste bin. 'So where's your evidence now Lawson?' he said with a malevolent grin.

At the front desk the duty sergeant said, 'You are being charged with assaulting a police officer and demanding money with menace. Anything you say may be used against you in a court of law, but if you don't mention something you might later rely on in court, it could harm your defence. Do you understand?'

'I understand that you've refused to listen to my complaint. I'm the one who's been assaulted and that officer making the charge has destroyed the evidence I had to prove it by tearing it up and throwing it in the waste bin.'

'I see,' the duty sergeant said, not sure what to do next. 'Well, I suppose we'd better go and have a look. But if you're playing games you'll be in even more trouble,' he warned.

In the interview room the duty sergeant placed the waste basket on the table. 'What exactly are we looking for?' he asked, and he began to rummage through it.

'A torn off lid of a cigarette packet. It has the name and phone number of the witness, which is why the Inspector tore it up,' John explained.

'Is this what you're on about?' the duty sergeant asked, holding up a piece of the torn lid with part of a name on it.

'Yes, if you find the other pieces you'll have the name and the contact number of the witness, like I said.'

The duty sergeant laid the pieces out on the table and pieced them together. 'Right, you wait here,' he said, picked up the pieces and left the room. A feeling of relief swept over John as he waited.

Back in the room the duty sergeant said with an indulgent smile, 'It has been decided not to proceed with charges against you, but should we receive any further complaints against you, you could be in serious trouble. Now get out of here.'

CHAPTER 17

THE JAMAICAN YARDIES

'How good are you with a gun?'

John stared curiously back at his uncle George. 'Dad taught me to shoot.' The thought stirred his childhood memories. 'So I guess I'm pretty good, why?'

'Good, because there are drug gangs trying to move in on our territory and it's scaring the punters away. So we're going to have to deal with them, or the prostitutes will move out and we'll be left with a lot of empty flats. You'll need a weapon.'

'I don't know Uncle, what if I get caught with it? That Inspector is out to get me.'

'You won't need to carry it all the time. We'll keep it locked up here until you need it. Any special gun you like?'

'A Browning 9mm would be my preference; that's what Dad trained me on.'

'Well, as it happens my man has one for sale,' George said. 'So if you're ever called on to bring 'your little friend' you know what to bring, okay?'

A few days later John got an urgent call from Andy to come to the video shop in Berwick Street. Waiting for him were his uncles, Andy, Martin, Bullets, Fingers, Diamonds, Lindsey and Rob, as well as some of the Maltese heavies.

'Right, we've got trouble with the Yardies. They're starting to operate in this street and they're scaring the punters; so much so that the girls did hardly any business last night. So we're going to have to sort them out, teach them a lesson. This is our territory and they're not going to encroach on it,' George said.

'What have you got in mind?' John asked.

'A few cracks over their heads should do it,' Andy suggested before Dave butted in.

'Have you got any idea who we're dealing with? The power these people wield is phenomenal. They're into everything, gun crime, drug trafficking, marijuana, crack cocaine, the lot. They're trying to take complete control of the drug trade. They think they're better than us; they are ruthless and they kill anyone who gets in their way. They use machetes, Uzis and the Ingran Mach10. Most of the other gangs won't go up against them.'

John was impressed with his uncle's knowledge. 'If they've got all those weapons, it'll turn into a bloodbath if we go up against them. And the place will be swarming with police,' he said. 'Can't we try talking to them? Show them some respect and explain that we're not into drugs and we're not here to take over their business? We just want them to find another place to conduct their trade.'

Dave looked bemused, but George said, 'Well, if you're willing to go and talk to them, John, we'll give it a try. But if it doesn't work, we'll have to think of something else pretty damn quickly.'

'Give me a few days to suss them out and come up with a plan,' John said, putting on a brave face.

John used one of the empty flats above the video shop in Berwick Street to observe how the Yardies operated. It gradually became clear there were two main men, one of whom had lookouts and runners around the area touting for the regulars and new customers. He was a tall Rasta with a mass of dreadlocks. A scar ran from his temple across his right eye to the tip of his nose. He displayed a fair amount of gold—a heavy bracelet on his right wrist, a gold watch on the left, a gold chain around his neck and a mouth full of gold teeth.

The other man would stand in the shadows of a doorway across the street, closely watching everything that was taking place. Before any of the drugs were handed over by the Rasta, the man in the shadows would give a nod of approval. This man wore no conspicuous jewellery, was clean shaven, of medium build, and yet he exuded such confidence that John was sure this was the man he would have to talk to if he was going to achieve anything. He went back to his uncles and explained what he proposed to do. They agreed to his plan and they met up with the others at the Intrepid Fox to put it into action.

Heading through the alleyway between Wardour and Berwick Streets, the rest of the group held back. John tapped the Browning concealed in his waistband under his coat. He made his way towards the man in the shadows and was immediately surrounded by the look-outs.

'Wha you wan, English man?' one of the look-outs demanded, his wide eyes glinting dangerously.

'I want to speak to your boss,' John replied, meeting his stare.

'Den speak to da Rasta man across da street,' the lookout said menacingly.

'I want to speak to the real boss,' John said without flinching.

'Why you wan speak to me, bwoy?' the boss interjected.

'I'd like to speak to you about a business arrangement.'

'Wha kind of business arrangement? Wha you got that would interest me, rude bwoy?'

'My family own most of the buildings in this street and the girls that work in them.'

'You mean you wan sell me the business?'

'No, I want to come to a business arrangement that could be lucrative for both of us,' John persisted. 'But it wouldn't be sensible to discuss it here on the street. Would you come to my office so we can talk privately?'

'Rude bwoy wanna talk business, so Denzil, you take care of tings till I be back,' he told the Rasta dripping with gold. 'If I not be back soon y'all come lookin for me, okay?'

'Sure ting, Winston,' Denzil acknowledged.

John took him to one of the empty flats above the shops in Berwick Street. The room contained only a small table and two chairs. Once in the room John unbuttoned his coat and purposely let the boss man see the gun tucked into his waistband. Winston's smile froze and he stepped back, reaching for the door handle with one hand while effortlessly grabbing hold of a machete concealed in his jacket with the other.

'Hold it!' John said.

'Blood clot man, you gonna shoot me or is you a bagga mouth?' he said after an endless silence. John realised he could shoot the man well before he had half raised the machete, but if he shot him, he also knew all hell would break loose and there would be killing on a massive scale.

'I don't like being dissed with a gun. I'm outta here. So go ahead bumbaclaat, shoot me in me back and my bredren will find you, rape you in front of your family and then cut your head off,' Winston said, turning to leave.

John knew from what he had read about the Yardies that the threat was very real and now had to make the biggest decision of his life. If he wasn't going to shoot him, he would have to show respect by laying down his gun. 'Wait!' he called out. 'If I was going to shoot you you'd be dead by now.' He carefully removed the gun from his waistband, pressed the clip to release the magazine, and it dropped into his open hand. Then he ejected the bullet from the chamber and placed the gun, magazine and bullet on the table with the butt facing him. If necessary, he could grab it and reload it within seconds.

'Nuh duh dat, it could be de most stupid ting you do, English man,' Winston said, still uncertain, waiting to see what John was going to do next.

'I've done that to show respect so that we can talk sensibly without any threats.'

'Okay, so you don't wanna shoot me man, so wha this lucrative deal you offering, English man? You wan in on the action? We don't deal with white bwoys,' Winston said, recovering his confidence, tucking the machete back into his waistband and pulling up one of the chairs.

'This is how it is,' John began. 'My family and the Maltese Mafia own these buildings and the girls that work in them and what you're doing is beginning to interfere with our business and that is starting to upset the bosses.'

'How wha we do interfere in your business?'

'We've been watching you. Your guys are scaring away our customers by hanging around the entrances to our flats. We don't want to interfere in your business; we're not into drugs, and we have no intention of ever being. So here's the lucrative part I'm offering. If you move your activities further up the street, away from our business, then...'

'Are you trettening me, English man?'

'Let me put it this way: We're also involved with the Adams family,' John paused as he saw a flicker of recognition on Winston's face. 'So you know who else you could be dealing with. Quite simply, if you don't move, you'll be taken out. If you think you're the only ones carrying weapons and willing to kill, you're misjudging us. If you want all-out war, keep operating where you are and you'll get it. But like I said, it will be much more lucrative for you to move.'

'So if we move up the street, there be no problem?'

'No problem; you can deal, do what you like. I told you we're not interested in drugs.'

'Tell me someting English man. Would you have shot me if I given you trouble?'

'Right between the eyes,' John said. He saw the fear in Winston's eyes and hoped he could not read the fear in his own.

'Okay English man, everyting cool, you show respec, so we move. I don't wan no trouble,' Winston said, getting to his feet. 'But one more ting—next time you wan talk business I be packing a Uzi,' Winston said menacingly and headed out the door.

John picked up his Browning, quickly reassembled it and followed Winston out, breathing a silent sigh of relief. As they walked out of the building John's whole team and a few of the Maltese heavies emerged from the alleyway as arranged, and lined up on the opposite side of the street as a show of force.

'Winston, whag wan!' Denzil shouted across at him as he recognised the Maltese heavies.

'Nuttin' ah gwan bredren, all cool,' Winston assured him.

'You see that lot standing there? Well, that's how close you came. They're all packing and would have taken out the lot of you if you'd given us any trouble,' John said coldly.

'Respec, English man,' Winston said, gesturing towards John's uncles and the Maltese Mafia.

'Respect to you, Rasta man. By the way, I'm Scottish, not English,' John said before crossing over to join the others.

George slapped John on the shoulder as they made their way back through the alleyway to the Intrepid Fox for a well-earned pint. 'I didn't think it was going to be that easy,' Dave said when they reached the private room on the first floor.

All the suppressed fear suddenly seemed to flood up in John's throat. George read the look on his face. 'It took some guts to do what you did, but you pulled it off without a shot being fired. Here, son,' he said, handing John a thick wad of notes. 'You just saved the business. We're proud of you. What would you like to drink?'

One morning George called John to his office. 'You were warned, but you don't seem to have taken any notice,' George said, his voice devoid of emotion.

John stared at his uncle trying to work out what he had been warned about.

'Dinnae look so innocent. You've been having it off with a peep show girl, and I warned you not to get involved there. I know it's difficult with naked girls running around all over the place, but it only leads to trouble. You start to favour them, and next thing you're telling them about what goes on here. And if they get nicked they'll grass you up without another thought if it's going to get them off the hook. So if you can't keep it in your trousers, make sure I don't find out, because nephew or not, I'll damn well fire you. Understood?'

'Understood,' John said piously. What his uncle didn't know, however, was that John was sleeping with Nicola as well as three Czechoslovakian girls from the hostess bar, although he felt quite confident none of them knew about the others.

But as invariably happens, the girls found out about each other, had a fall-out and walked out of the hostess bar. John's uncles were so infuriated that John's heroism with the Yardies was forgotten and he was ordered to pack his things and head off back to Birkenhead for a month to cool his ardour.

John was happy to be back in Birkenhead and doubly pleased when Jackie agreed to let him keep Daniel for a whole month. By now she had had her baby and was involved with yet another man. John was finding it increasingly hard to let Daniel go back to her, and it broke his heart to see his son cry when he had to hand him over. It made him determined to apply for custody.

Having found a good solicitor, John's application for full custody of Daniel was filed, together with the divorce proceedings, and a plan was put in place for social services to visit both parents' homes to prepare a report for the court.

The days turned into weeks and as much as John enjoyed being home, he was beginning to miss the excitement of the big city and was pleased when George called.

CHAPTER 18

THE LOVE OF MONEY

1988

'Good to have you back, son. I hope you've learnt your lesson; no messing on your doorstep, okay?'

'It won't happen again, Uncle, I promise.'

'We're closing down the video shops,' George said after John had told him all about his conversation with his solicitor and the social services' visit.

'Why? They were doing alright, weren't they?' John asked.

'Nah, there's too many of them opening up. They're all starting to set up their own duplicating machines, so by the time we've paid the rent and done the duplicating, it's not worth the aggro. We're going to flog the videos for ten quid each and close the shops. The porn business is changing, son.'

The closing down signs were put up and to everyone's amazement the shops were invaded and the entire stock of videos was sold within hours. The whole idea of getting rid of the stock turned into such a roaring business that some of the other video shops had to close down. George and Dave snapped them up, stuck the same closing down signs in the windows, and sales continued to go through the roof, with thousands of videos being sold every week.

As John walked back to the office one day with the takings from the hostess bar, he noticed a security van used to transfer large sums of money parked outside their building. Inside, George stopped him in the corridor. 'Do you know what a million pounds looks like?' he asked with a broad smile.

'I can't begin to imagine.'

'Okay, close your eyes and don't open them till I say so,' George said, taking him by the hand and guiding him into Dave's office.

'Okay, open.'

John's eyes bulged as he stared at the twenty pound notes stacked in neat piles on the table. 'I've never seen so much money,' he mumbled, almost unable to speak.

'There are fifty thousand twenty pound notes weighing 54.5 kilos,' his uncle said proudly. 'Don't you think it's an amazing sight? Take a good look, John, you'll never see anything like it again in your life.'

'What are you going to do with it?' John couldn't help asking.

'I'm not going to do anything with it. I just wanted to see what a million pounds in cash looked like. It's going straight back to the bank with these guys,' George said, pointing at the two security guards at the back of the room. 'This whole exercise has cost me twelve grand but it's been worth every penny. Okay guys, you can take it away now.' He turned back to John. 'If you can't visualise what a million pounds look like, you'll never make a million. If you have no money, you have no power, so keep that image in your head and who knows, maybe one day.'

The image of a million pounds laid out on the table embedded itself in John's mind and he couldn't shake it off. It was like a carrot dangling in front of his eyes, and it made him determined to work harder, be harder and make as much money as he could. The love of money was now his motivation.

The test came sooner than expected, when a tall young American walked into the bar. He had long hair and was wearing a black leather coat. 'Hey man, when's the show starting?' he asked John in a loud voice.

'One of the hostesses will attend to you sir, if you care to take a seat at one of the tables,' John answered politely. As it happened there was an American hostess on duty. Linzy was tall and blonde and very shapely. John thought she would be perfect for a fellow American and told her to take his order.

'What would you like to drink, sir?' she asked demurely, accentuating her American accent.

'No, I don't want a drink, I just want to see the show. What time does it start?'

'Didn't you see the sign on the door as you entered, sir? All customers have to buy a drink. It's also printed on the back of your ticket. What would you like, beer, spirits or a cocktail?'

'Ah damn it, just give me a coke,' he said irritably.

Linzy returned with a glass of coke on a silver tray. She bent over and placed it on the table, giving him a good view of her ample bosom. 'You're obviously American, as I am. Would you like me to join you, sir?'

'Yeah sure, why not?' he said, gesturing for her to sit down.

'Are you going to be a gentleman and buy a lady a drink?' she asked demurely.

'Sure, what would you like?'

Linzy picked up the menu and pretended to peruse it as one of the other scantily clad hostesses came over with a notepad to take the order.

'I'll have a sex on the beach,' Linzy said.

'Sex on the beach? What kind of a drink is that?' the American asked.

'Oh, it's a seductively delicious drink,' she explained, pouting her lips.

'I must remember that,' he said, feeling a stirring in his loins.

The American was becoming impatient. 'When is the damn show going to start?' he demanded.

'Any minute now sir; as soon as all the bills have been paid,' she explained. Just then one of the hostesses approached and placed his bill in front of him.

He was reaching for his wallet when he saw the amount on the bill and exclaimed, 'A hundred and six pounds! How the hell do you get that? I only had one damn coke!'

'Please sir, keep your voice down,' Linzy said, picking up the menu. 'The charges are all here. You had a coke that as you can see is twelve pounds, the cocktail you bought me is forty four pounds and the hostess fee for sitting with you is fifty pounds, which totals a hundred and six pounds.'

'This is outrageous!' The American leapt to his feet, sending the tray flying. Linzy got up, but he pushed her away and she fell backwards over a table. Then he ran towards the exit, shoving aside anyone who got in his way. John moved swiftly from behind the bar and waited for him to get close enough to give him his trademark side kick to the chest. This sent the American flying into one of the tables and collapsing on the floor.

John bent over him, grabbed him by the collar and dragged him across to the bar, where he slammed his head down on the counter. 'I don't like men who manhandle women,' he said. 'I can have you for assault. Now are you going to pay your bill or do I have to get really rough?'

The man's face crumpled in pain. 'Look, I'm sorry man, I panicked. I was just so surprised at the bill. I didn't expect it to be so high. I haven't got that kind of money on me,' he pleaded. The other punters saw what was going on, and quickly paid and fled.

'So what have you got?' John asked, still holding him, ready to bang his head on the bar again.

'I've only got thirty of your English pounds.'

'So what else have you got?'

'I've got American Express traveller's cheques.'

'That'll do,' John said with a smile, releasing his grip, but ready to grab him if he tried to make a run for it, which he didn't. He just looked nervously at John, slipped his hand into his coat pocket, tore off four fifty dollar cheques and handed them over.

'I think another one of those will ease the lady's hurt feelings,' John said, making sure he signed each one.

'Well, you sorted that one out good and proper,' Linzy said once the American had beaten a hasty retreat.

'Stupid Yank, thought he could get one over on me. No one does that; people mess with me at their own risk. You alright?' John asked Linzy.

'Yes, I'm okay, just laddered my stockings, that's all. But I always have a spare pair for when they get laddered by a groper,' she said.

'He finally paid, so you'll get your percentage,' John said with an air of pride. 'Right people, move your arses and get the place straightened out for the next lot.'

'Yes Sergeant,' the girls mockingly saluted as they set about righting the tables and clearing up the mess.

'Lawson!' Inspector Atwell called out loudly, and everybody looked up as he entered the bar, followed by several policemen. 'He described you well,' Atwell continued, approaching the bar. 'You're in real trouble this time. I've got a witness, alive as he could be after the beating you gave him. And he's going to give a detailed statement as soon as his injuries have been seen to. I'm arresting you on a charge of demanding money with menace, assault, causing grievous bodily harm and robbery. You don't have to say anything, but anything you do say may be used against you as evidence in court. Do you understand?'

John nodded. 'Cuff him,' Atwell ordered two of the policemen. They grabbed John's arms and tried to force them behind his back, but he resisted, clamping his arms tightly to his side.

'Don't force my arms...'

'Resisting arrest; there's another charge I can add to the book,' Atwell cut in, enjoying the moment.

'I was just trying to say, if they let go of my arms I'll voluntarily put them behind my back so they can cuff me.'

'Then do it!' Atwell shouted. The two policemen cuffed John and escorted him out of the bar.

'Right, all you ladies will be required to come to the station to give statements. So if you have something decent to cover yourselves, I suggest you get it on, or you'll be taken as you are,' Atwell said with an air of distaste.

John looked relieved when Cecil Watkins finally walked into the interview room at West End Central police station.

'Sorry, couldn't get here earlier,' Cecil said as he sat down at the table across from John. 'This one is not going to be so easy. It looks as if Inspector Atwell is determined to get you a prison sentence. Because this is your first offence, I've managed to get you bailed. But there are conditions. You can't work or frequent any of the bars, peepshows or video shops in Soho. If you do, your bail will be withdrawn. It can take anything up to twelve months for the case to come to trial, but I'll do all I can to delay it, because if it goes over the twelve months it will have to be dropped. Don't hold your breath, though. The American you allegedly assaulted is willing to come back from the States to give evidence. The thing to do now is go back to Birkenhead, lay low and above all stay out of trouble,' Cecil advised.

Back at the office the news was no better. 'I know you thought you were doing the right thing,' George said, 'but I'm afraid you're finished here. You're still family, but you're too much of a risk to be seen around us. If there's any way the case can be dropped, you can be sure Cecil will find it.' He reached into his pocket and pulled out a thick wad of notes. 'Here's two grand to keep you going and make sure you stay out of trouble. We don't want the Lawson name all over the papers. Now give our love to Jose and Alex and make sure you take care of them.'

As John walked back along Old Compton Street to collect his belongings, he took one last look at the Phoenix and the bars that were beginning to fill with the early evening crowd. He paused for a moment, realising he may never walk there again or feel that atmosphere, the energy and vitality, the buzz that was so unlike anything else he knew.

CHAPTER 19

TRIALS AND TRIBULATIONS
1989

'We're here to meet your barrister, Mr. John Stanford QC, who will be handling your defence,' Cecil explained.

'But I thought you were defending me,' John said, somewhat surprised.

'No, the trial is being held in the Crown Court and this is how it works: You instruct the firm, and we instruct the barrister to conduct your defence in court. They're the ones who wear the wigs. So the purpose of this meeting is to go through everything so the barrister can prepare your defence.'

'So,' John Stanford began, and gestured for them to sit down, 'we have a difficult case. The charge is robbery; they've dropped the other charges of extortion, grievous bodily harm, etcetera.' He waved a piece of paper at John. 'The Crown is paying for the witness to fly out from America, and for his hotel expenses. This is the basis of his statement: He walked into the bar expecting to see a live sex show. He got upset when he was presented with a bill for a hundred and six pounds for a glass of coke. He never attacked the hostesses, rather he claims they attacked him and as he tried to leave you did a double-footed drop kick catching him full in the chest. You then dragged him to the bar and threatened him with a gun or a knife. He also states he felt something hard pressed against his head and thought you were going to kill him.' The barrister put the paper down and looked at John. 'The problem is that he stated he paid the money because he thought you had a knife or a gun, which the prosecution will argue is the same as actually having a knife or a gun in the eyes of the law. They also have the traveller's cheques he says he was forced to sign, even claiming his signature is shaky due to his nervousness. The good news is the medical report shows no signs of any injury to his chest. The witness has clearly been briefed as to what to put in his statement and it does look serious. I have to say, you could be looking at five years if the jury believe his account of what happened.'

'The two hostesses will tell you that's not what happened; he..."

The barrister held up his hand. 'We've been trying to contact them but they seem to have disappeared off the face of the earth. So I'm going to put forward that the witness lives in Hollywood Boulevard where there's an abundance of strip clubs and hostess bars, so he can't claim he didn't know what he was walking into; that he attacked you and tried to leave without paying. That's an offence in itself. It's not the best defence I could have wished for, but the fact that you don't have a criminal record will hold you in good stead. Let's just hope we have a sympathetic jury and a lenient judge,' he said judiciously, getting to his feet, indicating that the meeting was over.

'You'd be surprised the people he's got off for me,' Cecil said as they walked along Chancery Lane.

'I can't understand why the girls wouldn't come and give evidence on my behalf after all I did for them,' John said with an air of despair.

Cecil stopped and turned to face him. 'They didn't just disappear, they were paid to disappear.'

'You mean the police paid them to disappear?'

'No, we did. Your uncles couldn't allow them to give evidence because the prosecution would have made them say things about the organisation that would not only have done you damage but would have caused immense damage to your uncles. Even if we hadn't called them as witnesses the prosecution would have made them compellable witnesses. Then the proverbial crap would truly have hit the fan,' Cecil explained.

'I'll never understand the law,' John sighed.

'You don't have to, that's what I'm paid for.'

'Will my uncles be coming to the court?'

'No, they can't be seen to have any association with you or the case. So I suggest you go straight back home and the next time I see you is with the barrister at Southwark Crown Court. Come prepared you might go to prison. In the meantime make sure you keep out of trouble,' Cecil added, and turned to wave down a taxi.

John was exhausted by the time he got back from London, but to his delight the date for the custody hearing had been set and he attended the hearing with his solicitor, Mr Angilvy. It was held in the judge's chambers at the family court in a rather informal manner. John and his solicitor sat on one side of the table, Jackie and her solicitor on the other and the judge at the head of the table.

'This hearing is to determine what is in the best interests of the child,' the Judge addressed both parents. 'I have studied the reports presented by the social services and they make interesting reading. It is very unusual for the father to be granted full custody of a child. However,' he continued, 'the report shows Mr Lawson has a genuine love for the child and the child wishes to stay with his father. The house was found to be clean and well maintained and Mr Lawson does have the support of his mother in taking care of the child. The former Mrs. Lawson has four other children from four different fathers and is pregnant with a fifth from yet another father. According to the report she is finding it difficult to cope with her circumstances. It is therefore my judgement, after considering all the evidence before me, that the interests of the child, Daniel Lee Lawson, would be best served by granting the father full custody...'

'No, you can't do that! He's my son and I won't give him up!' Jackie shouted, leaping to her feet. 'I carried him for nine months; I nursed him and took care of him! What more can a mother be expected to do?' she added before being restrained by her solicitor.

The judge looked at her sternly. 'Madam, if you do not resume your seat and remain silent I will have you removed from this room. In granting full custody to the father,' he continued, 'you will of course have full non-residential access and visiting rights to the child, which I hope can be mutually agreed upon between the two of you without further recourse to this court. I'm sure your solicitor will advise you of those rights.'

'Rights? What rights? You've taken my kid away after all I've done for him! What's he ever done for him except come and visit him occasionally? Ask him that before you make such a judgement!' she shouted.

'This court is adjourned,' the judge announced, got to his feet and left the chamber, followed by the clerk.

Jackie started to bang the table and shouting, 'It's not fair, it's not fair! I don't deserve this!' She collapsed into her chair and burst into tears.

John was over the moon with the judgment, and so was his mother. He had spent all the money his uncle had given him, mainly on the solicitor, but he felt it was money well spent. He happily agreed to the arrangements that were put in place for Jackie to see Daniel, but after the second visit she made no further attempt to see him. It seemed she had just walked away from everything in the same way his father had done.

With the unpleasantness over, John knew he had to do something to make a better life for himself and Daniel. But the next hurdle arrived by way of a letter informing him that his trial was set to take place in London in nine months' time. *How could I have been so selfish, so stupid?* He cursed himself. *But I won't go to prison; they've got me the best lawyer and they're paying him a lot of money*. But still the thought that he might go to prison rose like bile in his throat.

Nine months later the verdict read: We cannot allow the unscrupulous to contaminate and destroy the good in our society. I hope this case will serve to warn people of the methods you and others employ to prey on unsuspecting tourists. We will not tolerate this kind of behaviour, and therefore I sentence you to nine months imprisonment. Take him down.

CHAPTER 20

BUSTER AND A PAT OF BUTTER

After sharing a cell with Alfie for just over a month, John was sad to say goodbye to him. 'I 'ope yer learned somefink from what I've told yer, boy,' Alfie chirped cheerfully. 'Remember, keep yer 'ead down, do yer time, and don't worry, Wandsworth will be a doddle compared to this place.' It upset John that Alfie seemed so casual, but he realised it was his way of hiding his emotions.

As John sat in the confines of the sweat box he reflected on the times he'd driven past the prison and vowed he would never end up there. And here he was, about to enter the gates of Wandsworth as a prisoner.

The warden took delight in guiding the prisoners along the E wing where the execution chamber was situated. He paused and opened the door for them to see inside. There was a huge beam from which hung three chain adjusting blocks, with a noose hanging in the centre. There was a three by two metre trapdoor in the floor, with an operating lever on the side.

'Down below is the pit where the man drops and there's a gate to the yard where the body is taken out. They test the system every six months because there's still a death penalty for treason, piracy with violence, or mutiny in the armed forces. So as long as none of you fit into those categories you won't be falling into that trap,' the warden chuckled at his own pun. 'There've been some interesting people hanged here. There was William Joyce, better known as Lord Haw Haw; there was a double execution when Edward Smith and Joseph Brown stood on the gallows together; John George Haigh, the acid bath murderer; Timothy Evans and John Christie. Francis Forsyth was only eighteen when he was hanged in 1960, and the last execution was Henryk Niemaszin September 1961,' he related, showing off his gruesome knowledge.

John was guided to the middle cell on the top landing of D wing. Instead of friendly old Alfie, a scruffy convict, a junkie by the look of it, awaited him. The cell had the smell of urine, excrement and stale tobacco, which seemed to delight the warden as he shoved John in and relocked the cell door. Paint was peeling off the walls, cockroaches crawled around in the corners and the floor was splattered with cigarette stubs and ash. To one side the cause of the dreadful smell was clearly visible in a bucket.

'What you in for then?' his cell mate asked, slouching back on his bunk.

John took an instant dislike to the man and realised he would have to show some force if he was to improve conditions in the cell. 'Robbery with violence,' he said, and it seemed to have the desired effect. 'And what are you in for?'

'Breaking into a few homes and that,' the man said casually.

'What's your name?' John asked.

'Michael, what's yours?'

'John,' he replied. 'I tell you one thing Michael, you're going to clean up your act or there's going to be trouble in here. And if you ever crap in that bucket again...'

'You're joking, aren't you? Where else can you crap when you're locked up for the night?'

'You take some newspaper or one of your old socks, crap in it and toss it out the window, or better still, you learn to control your bowels so you can crap in the toilets before lock-up. You crap in that bucket again, I'll make you eat it, understand?'

John was obviously the bigger and stronger and Michael knew

he was no match for him. 'You know who's across the landing?' he asked, wanting to change the subject.

'How the hell would I know? I've just arrived, you idiot.'

Michael winced. 'James Hussey,' he said with aplomb.

'Who's he?'

'None other than one of the great train robbers.'

'They were all released ages ago, except for Ronnie Biggs who's still in Brazil,' John said, looking at Michael as if he was mad.

'Oh, he's here alright. He was only out a few months and now he's doing a seven year stretch for cocaine smuggling. You know he was the one who bashed the train driver over the head with an iron bar?' There was a strange admiration in Michael's voice. 'You interested in going to the movie on Wednesday afternoon then?'

'What movie?' John asked surprised.

'This'll make you laugh, talking about Hussey; they're only going to be showing Buster.'

'You mean the Phil Collins movie about Buster Edwards and the great train robbery?'

'That's the one.'

Just then they heard the key turning in the lock and the cell door opened. 'Right, move yourselves, it's mealtime,' the warden barked.

They both grabbed their plates and hurried out, John having determined he was going to keep his nose clean and not do anything to antagonise the wardens, particularly as they seemed stricter and more aggressive than those at Pentonville or Brixton.

They went down several flights of enclosed stairs to the ground floor where other prisoners served the food. With a dollop of potatoes and soggy vegetables piled onto their trays, the inmates moved to the end of the row of food trolleys to where they received pats of butter before heading over to the tea urns and bread trays. As John stood waiting for his butter, the black inmate who was serving took no notice of him, and the queue started building up behind him. John picked up the pallet knife and helped himself, but as he moved on, the inmate called out, 'What ya tink you're doin' man? That's my job!'

'Oh shut up, dickhead,' John said and moved on to the urn to fill his mug with tea.

'No man talks to me like that, I'm going to do you, English man!' he shouted at John.

'You and who else?' John said, turning around to face him, but one of the wardens stepped in and blocked his path.

'None of that, you've got your food, now get back to your cell before there's trouble.'

Sitting in the cell, trying to eat his meal with the stink permeating everything around him, John looked across at Michael shovelling the food down as if it was his last meal. *It would be if I had my way*, he thought as he pushed his food around on the plate.

'What was all that about with the black guy?' Michael asked, swallowing the last fork full of food.

'Oh nothing really, the dickhead got upset over a pat of butter.'

'Yeah, but I heard him threaten you.'

'So what, all talk to impress his mates.'

'Yeah, but the fact that he said it out loud means he's going to have to do something otherwise he'll lose face.'

'So who cares?'

'You don't understand. It's happened before. An inmate threatened one of those guys and later that night he was rushed to hospital with a gash down the side of his face. If they don't carry out their threats they're picked on and called big mouths with no guts. So watch your back; that guy will sure as hell come after you,' Michael warned.

'So what do I do? Sit and wait for it to happen?'

'You look like you could stand up to him, so get him first.'

'I'm only in here for nine months, which means I'll only do four and a half, and I've done half of that already, so I don't want to cause any trouble.'

'You haven't got much choice, he's going to come for you whether you like it or not. He's probably a lifer, so it won't make any difference to him.'

'Then I'm going to have to think of something to get myself out of this,' John said, puffing up his shoulders to hide his worry.

Every day during the exercise period John would walk around with Michael and see the black man strolling with his mates and pointing a finger at him.

'You see, he's marked you; he's going to have to do you soon,' Michael warned him.

The usual boring routine continued and John was relieved when Wednesday afternoon came and they were all ushered down to the gym to watch the movie. The inmates were not allowed to talk to anyone in the row in front of or behind them. They watched in silence until one of the inmates shouted out, pointing his finger at the screen, 'That's him, that's Buster Edwards!' The real Buster Edwards was shown arriving at the airport in Mexico, walking with Phil Collins's wife Jill.

'Whose stupid idea was it to show them this film?' John heard one of the senior wardens say to a colleague.

'I think the Governor thought it would be good to show them crime doesn't pay,' the colleague said.

'Well, the way Buster's living it up is hardly an example of crime not paying. I wouldn't have minded some of that myself,' the senior warden said.

The inmates remained quiet throughout the rest of the film, but as the credits rolled, they started a slow hand clap, chanting, 'Jim... meee! Jim...meee!' applauding James Hussey, who was sitting in the audience with them—something the authorities had obviously overlooked.

'Damn, I knew this was a bad idea; now there's going to be trouble. Let's hope we can keep it under control,' the senior warden said as the clapping and shouting increased. The rest of the wardens looked towards the senior warden, not sure what he wanted them to do. Some of them had already drawn their batons. The senior warden tried to quieten the prisoners down, but to no avail. James

Hussey stood up, took a bow and a great cheer went up as he raised his hand to acknowledge it. It was a euphoric expression of defiance against authority.

The following day at lunchtime nobody was surprised to hear that further screenings of the movie had been cancelled. As John got to the end of the line to collect his bread, the butter guy was standing waiting for him. 'I'm still going to do you man, that's for sure,' he said, and slapped a pat of butter onto John's plate.

'What are you going to do, smother me in butter and give me a massage?' John said, wiping some butter off his shirt.

'No man, I'm going to cut you. You remember your face while you can, because it ain't goin' to look the same when I cut you up, batty bwoy.'

'You don't scare me, butter boy. Carry on serving your pats of butter, but be careful you don't strain yourself,' John retorted with heavy sarcasm.

After lunch John's nerves started playing up and he felt a flush of panic grip his chest. He suddenly felt an intense need to go to the toilet, and the thought of doing it in the cell made his stomach protest even more. He got up and pressed the bell.

'What you do that for?' Michael asked.

'I need a crap and there's no way I'm using the bucket, and neither are you,' John said, rubbing his stomach.

A warden appeared. 'What is it?' he asked gruffly.

'Sorry Boss, my stomach's upset and I need to go to the toilet and I don't like the idea of doing it in the bucket. Is there any way you can let me go to the toilet? I would really appreciate it, Boss,' John said in his most subservient manner.

'Alright Lawson, but don't make a habit of it. I'll leave the cell on the latch and I want to hear it slam shut when you get back. Don't make me come looking for you, okay?' the warden said, letting him out.

All the cubicle doors were open and an inmate was on his knees cleaning one of the toilet bowls, singing away to himself. As John got closer he recognised the butter guy. He couldn't believe his luck. There was stillness about him as he assessed the scene. Then, acting on pure adrenaline, a grim look on his face, he crept up behind the man, raised his leg and brought his boot down hard on the back of his head. The man's face pounded into the toilet bowl, smashing his teeth, cracking the bowl and rendering him unconscious. There was blood everywhere. John pulled the chain. 'Maybe that'll flush some of the arrogance out of you,' he said, and hurried out, the need to use the toilet having somehow evaporated.

'I'm done, Boss!' he called as he got back to the cell and slammed the door shut.

That night John hardly slept, not knowing whether he had killed the guy and if at any moment he would hear footsteps approaching to haul him out and accuse him of murder. He thought about the execution chamber, and wondered if the death penalty still existed for killing a prisoner.

As John got ready to go down to breakfast, the warden unlocking the cell door surprised him by saying, 'After breakfast, pack your stuff Lawson, you're being moved.'

'Whereto this time, Boss?'

'You're going to Stanford Hill open prison on the Isle of Sheppey. You're lucky to be moving, there's going to be a clampdown, someone was beaten up in the toilets yesterday and the Governor is peed off about it.' the warden replied.

After breakfast John asked the warden, 'Boss, can I make a quick phone call so I can let my mum know I'm moving?'

'Alright Lawson, you've got five minutes, then make your way down to the PO's office.'

When John heard his mother answer after the usual telephone procedure, he said, 'Mum, I haven't got long, just to tell you the good news. I'm being moved to an open prison and I'll have loads of time to talk to you and Daniel from there.'

'Oh, son, that's such good news, you must have been behaving yourself to be moved there,' Jose said, fighting back the tears. 'Have a quick word with Daniel, he's standing right here.'

'Daddy, Daddy, when are you coming home?' Daniel cried excitedly. John's chest tightened with emotion at the sound of his son's voice.

'I don't know Son, but it won't be too long now.'

'How many sleeps, Dad?'

'Dad's got to work a bit longer, but it won't be too many sleeps. You be a good boy for your nan.'

As John replaced the receiver his shoulders slumped. He was missing Daniel terribly but he still had two and a half months to serve.

CHAPTER 21

VENGANCE IS MINE

1989

When John got off the train at Liverpool Station, Daniel and his mother were waiting for him at the barriers. 'Daddy! Daddy!' Daniel cried out and rushed into his arms.

In the taxi on the way home, Jose asked, 'So how long are you planning on staying?'

'I'm not going anywhere. I'm back for good.'

'Wonderful! At least you won't be mixing with those unsavoury people anymore. So the first thing you can do is look for a job here.'

'I know Ma, I'll go down to the job centre first thing tomorrow. What about Jackie, has she been in touch?'

'Not a word, it would seem she's lost all interest.'

'Does she know about me being away?'

'Not that I'm aware of. Let's keep our fingers crossed that it stays that way,' Jose said, the sunlight temporarily blinding them as the taxi emerged from the Mersey tunnel into Birkenhead.

John was pleased to see Alex, but noticed he didn't seem to be his usual chatty self.

'What's the matter, kid?' John asked, walking into the bedroom where Alex was sitting on the edge of the bed staring into space.

'You know that girl I met while you were inside?'

'Yeah, Samantha, isn't it?'

'Yeah well, Sam... she's up the duff and I haven't told Ma yet.'

'Oh boy, you'll have to man up and tell her before it's too late.'

'Yeah, but that's not the only problem. The foreman's got it in for me at work,' Alex said, and John could see the sadness in his eyes. 'All of a sudden I can't do anything right. He tells me to do one thing and then he comes back and asks why I'm doing that instead of something else.'

'Well, just hang in there kiddo, you've been there a long time and you've almost served your time. Won't be long before they have to triple your wages.'

John was up early the next morning and headed down to the local Department of Social Security. Depression washed over him when he saw the mishmash of people sitting awaiting their turn in quiet desperation. When his turn came he hurried to the counter and explained his situation.

'So does that mean you're on probation?' the assistant asked.

'No, it means I'm on parole,' he said, unsure of the implication.

'What's the difference?'

'The difference is I'm a free man and I don't have to report to anyone,' John explained, sounding a little irritated.

'I see. Well, we have your details on record and because you're a single parent we'll reinstate your benefits as from today. It will of course help if you start looking for a job to get yourself off benefits,' the assistant said with an air of superiority.

'I'll start on it right away,' he said, wanting to smash his fist through the glass screen between him and the assistant.

After having been back for only a week, a letter arrived from the Methodist Housing Association informing John that he had been allocated a two-bedroomed end of terrace house in Elm Street. It was well positioned, near the shops, the market and Birkenhead town centre. He wasn't able to buy new furniture, but around the corner from his new house the Charles Thompson Mission church was selling second hand furniture.

When John approached the entrance to the building he looked up at the words on the overhanging sign: 'It is appointed unto men to die once and after this the judgement.'

He wasn't sure how to interpret it. Once inside the large hall he looked around at a scraggly group of people lining up to be served a hot meal by a small group of smartly dressed women.

A friendly looking man in his early fifties came out of the kitchen area and noticed John standing there. 'Hello, I'm Rob Jeffs; I'm the pastor here. What can I do for you?' he said, a smile spreading across his kind face.

'I was just passing and wondered if you might know where I can buy some cheap furniture. You see, I've just come out of prison and I'm a single parent. My son and I have moved into number 2 Elm Street,' John explained, playing heavily on the situation.

'Oh, we must see what we can do for you,' the pastor said. 'That is what the mission is here for,' he added and led John to a door at the back of the hall, and ushered him inside. 'Will any of this be of use to you?' he asked, pointing to a stack of furniture piled up to the ceiling.

'Where do you get all this from?' John was amazed at how much there was.

'We do house clearances. We dispose of the rubbish and hold onto the good stuff. So choose what you need and we'll arrange to get it to you.'

'Thank you, but I need to know how much it's going to cost.'

'My dear boy, there is no charge, these are God's gifts to those in need,' the pastor said with a benevolent sweep of his arms.

There was another stroke of luck when John was offered his job back as barman at The Jimmy's over weekends. This was not exactly what he had wanted, as he still wanted to work as a bouncer, but it was a job and that's what he needed.

John started visiting his old friend Flemmo again, and on one of his visits Flemmo's sister Lynn was there. She was just as beautiful as he had remembered her from seven years earlier. He had always admired her lovely blonde hair and beautiful light green eyes. She was dressed casually, and it showed off her shapely figure. John had had a crush on Lynn in those days, but back then fourteen year old girls were not interested in fourteen year old boys. Lynn had brought her son with her.

'So you're married now and you have a son?' John remarked.

'Was married,' she said. 'This is Michael, he's four. He's Phil's son, you remember the guitar player in the Beatles tribute band? Well anyway, after we split up I got married to a guy called David but we're divorced now, thank goodness. I had to get out, I was afraid for our safety,' she said, her voice quivering.

'I have a son too. His name's Daniel and he's also four.'

'Who fancies a drink?' Flemmo suggested as he walked to the kitchen.

'You know, I used to fancy you,' John said when Flemmo had left the room.

'I know you did,' she said coyly.

'We're both single, so what would you say if I was to ask you out?'

The question caught her by surprise. 'You won't know unless you ask,' she said with a smile that made her eyes sparkle.

John did ask her out. Their relationship grew and after a while Lynn moved in with John. Flemmo's mother wasn't happy about it as she had always looked on John as a bad boy. Flemmo himself was not sure how he felt about the arrangement, but didn't want to fall out with John or his sister, so he kept his thoughts to himself. Daniel and Michael got on well, but Lynn soon started resenting the lonely weekends with John working and coming home in the early hours of the morning and sleeping all day.

Soon the Methodist Housing Association offered John a more modern, three-bedroomed house in Wood Close, which meant the two boys could have their own bedrooms, and he happily accepted the offer.

Early one Saturday morning Lynn woke John to tell him his mother had phoned and said that her house had been burgled in the night and she needed to speak to him. He leapt out of bed. 'I must get there,' he said, grabbing his clothes and hurriedly putting them on.

'So what the hell happened?' he asked his mother when she opened the door.

'We never heard them, we were all asleep,' she explained as she led him to the kitchen and put the kettle on.

'So that's how whoever got in,' John said, looking across at the broken window of the back door. 'What did they take?'

'The television and video recorder, some of my jewellery and Alex's pay packet, which he'd left on the mantelpiece. They even took Daniel's little leather jacket and a pair of his trainers.' Jose's voice was trembling, her hands shaking as she put the mugs of tea down on the table. 'I've called the police.'

'I've got a good idea it might be one of the local druggies around here. They'll steal anything to get a fix; even that little crap Lee across the road could have done it.'

'Don't talk like that, the Henrys are a nice family and they're my friends,' Jose said.

'If it wasn't him, I bet he knows who did it, so I'll have a quiet word with him.'

'Yeah well, we all know what having a quiet word means to you,' Alex said, coming into the kitchen.

'So what do you suggest, bruv?'

'Let the police handle it,' Jose said, her face pale and anxious.

'I'm going to have a look outside to see if they've left any clues,' John said, getting up from the table.

While looking around outside, John spotted Lee coming out of his house and scamper off down the street. He waited until Lee had turned into one of the narrow alleyways near the bus depot on Laird Street before chasing after him. It was easy to catch up with him, and John grabbed him by the scruff of the neck. 'You broke into my mother's house last night, didn't you, you little toe rag?'

'No, I didn't, honest.'

'Honest! Everything that comes out your drugged filled mouth is a lie. So tell me what you've done with the stuff, or...'

'I didn't do it, I swear on my mother's life,' Lee squealed, his body beginning to shake as John squeezed his throat.

'You'd swear on anything, but I tell you this, if I don't find out by tomorrow who did this, I'm coming after you, and Lee, if I have to make you disappear, then so be it,' John said, relaxing his grip on Lee's throat before punching him in the stomach.

Later that evening Jose received a phone call from the local police to say that someone had phoned in and given the name of a possible suspect and that they were looking into it. John decided to visit the police station to find out more.

Laird Street police station was one of those old fashioned buildings that looked more like a single garage and was manned by only a handful of officers at any one time. At the counter the sergeant smiled at John indulgently and said, 'We get a lot of people phoning in with names, some for revenge, others for mischief, so I'm afraid we can't just run off and arrest every person whose name is given to us.'

'I wonder if you could give me the name. I have a sneaking feeling I know who might have phoned you,' John pleaded.

'I'm afraid I can't do that, sir,' the sergeant said, 'and if you'll excuse me, I've got work to do.' He left the folder on the desk in front of John and as he got to the door that led to the offices, he turned around and gave John a meaningful wink.

John took the hint, flipped the file around, opened it and quickly scanned the pages. His smile broadened as he read the name Michael Atherton and it broadened even more when he read the address—21 Tees Street, one of the river streets in the North End.

Just then the sergeant came back into the room. 'Forgot the file,' he said, picking it up. 'If there is any further information forthcoming, we will of course let you know,' he added.

'Thank you sergeant,' John said appreciatively.

'One more thing, if I happen to hear about a certain individual in the river streets having an unfortunate accident, it won't have had anything to do with you, will it, Mr. Lawson?' the sergeant said with a wry grin.

'No sergeant, absolutely not,' John replied, matching his grin.

At least there are still some good cops, John thought as he walked out of the station.

While putting on his crisp white shirt, black trousers and shiny black shoes for the night's stint at The Jimmy's, John thought of what to do about Michael Atherton. By the time his shift was over, his desire for revenge was so overwhelming that he couldn't wait any longer. He went home, quietly let himself in so as not to wake anyone and crept silently out to the backyard shed to dig out the truncheon he had hidden away. It was made of solid wood, about fourteen inches long, with a leather strap handle attached to it.

At six that morning John got up, slipped on his black leather jacket, shoved the truncheon up his left sleeve and quietly left the house. When he got to 21 Tees Street he was relieved to see there was no one about and all the curtains of the neighbouring houses were still drawn. With adrenaline coursing through his veins he started hammering on the door. 'Michael Atherton, open this door!' he shouted.

After a few bangs a top window opened and a man's head poked out. He looked a mess, his face dirty and his hair scraggly. Before John could say a word he ducked back in, the window slammed shut and John heard him shout, 'It's the bizzies!' John smiled when he realised the way he was dressed made him look like a policeman.

'Open this door now or we'll be forced to break it down!' he shouted in a formal voice. He heard footsteps hurrying down the stairs and the door chain being slipped on. Slowly the door opened as far as the chain would allow. 'Where's you search warrant?' a face behind the door asked.

'Here!' John raised his foot and kicked the door, snapping the chain. The door opened and trapped the man against the wall.

At that moment a woman came down the stairs shouting, 'You can't do that!'

'Stay out of this, it's this scumbag I've come to see,' John said, closing the door behind him. He grabbed Atherton by the scruff of the neck and dragged him across the room. As Atherton struggled to get to his feet, John drew the truncheon and hit him over the head, sending him reeling over the back of the sofa. 'You can't do that, that's police brutality!' the woman screamed.

John turned around and shoved her down into an armchair, waving the truncheon in her face. 'I don't like hitting women, but if you don't shut that mouth of yours I'll be forced to. I'm not a copper and this scumbag broke into my mother's house and stole her stuff.'

'It wasn't me,' Atherton pleaded, his gaping mouth revealing a row of chipped yellow teeth.

John raised the truncheon threateningly. He looked around the room and spotted Daniel's jacket on one of the chairs. 'So it wasn't you,' he said, picking up the jacket. 'This is my son's jacket!' He loomed over Atherton and waved the jacket in his face. 'So where's the rest of the stuff and the wage packet you stole? You listen to me—I don't care how you do it, but I want everything returned to my mother's house by tomorrow night. If it's not there, I'll come back and I promise you, you'll wish you'd never come near us.' John hit Atherton in the face with a thud, splattering the truncheon with blood. 'You've got until tomorrow,' he said, and stormed out.

The next evening there was a knock on the front door and when Jose opened it she found her television and video recorder and an envelope filled with cash on the front step.

'How did you manage that?' Jose asked John, but guessing the answer.

'Let's just say he was full of remorse and wanted to make amends,' John said with a sheepish grin.

'How did you get to be so devious? I remember your uncles talking exactly like that when they caught the guy who'd stolen the stuff from the trunk,' Jose said ruefully.

'The one thing my uncles taught me was not to rely on the law. If you want justice, you have to go out and get it for yourself,' John said with a savage grin.

John saw an advertisement for taxi drivers and thought it would be a more exciting job, but he needed to get a medical certificate before he could be granted a licence.

'Don't worry,' one of the cabbies said. 'Go and see this Indian doctor, bung him forty quid and he'll give you a clean bill of health.' He handed John a piece of paper with the name and address of the doctor.

True to the cabby's word, once John had slipped the doctor the forty pounds, he started filling in the form without any physical examination. 'Any criminal convictions?' the doctor asked without looking up from the form.

'None,' John lied and watched as the doctor completed the form, scribbled his signature and handed it to him.

John left his job at The Jimmy's and leased a Ford Mondeo and a radio from the taxi firm. He was allowed to keep what was left over of the fare after he'd paid for the fuel. He chose to work nights, when the takings were better, especially over weekends.

One Friday night Lynn went to a girlfriend's birthday party, and John had arranged to pick her up from the Fishermans Wharf in Seacombe after his shift.

When he arrived, Lynn seemed upset. 'What's wrong, what's happened?' he asked.

'It's my ex, he's in there and he came over and grabbed hold of me and insisted I dance with him. I tried to pull away, but he's so strong. I was scared, so I had one dance with him and thought that was it, but he kept on. They tried to stop him, but he wasn't having any of it and he tried to grab me again, so we all left and I've been waiting in the manager's office for you to come,' she explained tearfully.

'Why the hell didn't you call the office and let me know? I would have come straight away,' John said, looking at the red marks on her wrists.

'You were working and I didn't want you to lose any money by packing up early.'

'Is he still in there?'

'Yes.'

'Right, you wait here.'

Lynn's ex-husband David was standing at the bar with a group of men when he saw John enter. He casually placed his glass on the bar, turned to face him and puffed himself up in the way that body builders have a habit of doing.

John charged at him, kicked him full in the chest, propelling him backwards into the people sitting at the tables, drinks spilling everywhere. He lay on the floor and looked up at John, his eyes wide with disbelief. John gave him two heavy punches to the face, putting any thought of a fight out of his mind as he slumped into a state of near unconsciousness.

'If you ever touch Lynn again I'll kill you,' John said, turned around and walked out of the club.

Lynn looked up anxiously as John got back in the car. 'What did you say to him?' she asked.

'Oh, just that if he touched you again I'd kill him,' John said calmly.

The next day, on a call-out to pick up a passenger in Harrowby Road, Birkenhead, a smartly dressed but decidedly angry looking man came storming out of the front door to where John was waiting in his taxi. John jumped out and opened the rear door for him. 'Where to?' he asked as he settled back in the driver's seat.

'The Queen's Arms pub in Oxton Village and don't you take any crafty detours,' the man said gruffly.

John said nothing, but studied the man's brooding face in the rear view mirror. 'You alright mate?' he asked.

'Fine, as long as keep your mouth shut and mind your own damn business,' the man snapped.

It took all John's self control not to stop the car, haul the man out and give him a good thumping, but he put his foot down, wanting to get to the destination as fast as he could.

They remained silent for the rest of the journey.

'Right, stop here!' the man shouted as they approached the pub.

'That'll be five pounds please,' John said, and turned around to face the man.

'You're getting nothing. I don't like you or this poxy car,' the man said, opening the door to get out.

'Hey dickhead, you owe me for the fare!' John called out and hurried after him.

The man stopped and turned to face John. 'I'm not paying you anything, so just get back in that car and get stuffed,' he said.

'You owe me the fare and I want it,' John said, trying to control his temper.

'And what are you going to do about it?' the man shouted as he moved aggressively towards John, who gave him a side kick in the chest, sending him reeling into a bush. As John turned back to the car, the man scrambled to his feet and called out, 'Is that the best you can do, dickhead?'

John stopped. It was only a few pounds and certainly not worth the risk of getting into trouble, so he continued walking back to the car, but as he did so the man charged after him and repeated, 'I said, is that the best you can do, dickhead?'

Whatever control John had, disappeared, and as the man got to him, he gave him a roundhouse kick to the head and the man went down like a ton of bricks, unconscious before he hit the pavement.

'No mate, *that's* the best I can do,' John said, and walked back to the car.

'Do you realise the uncle of the man you attacked last night sits on the licensing committee?' the owner of the taxi company said to John the following morning.

'Hang on, it was he who attacked me and refused to pay the fare,' John cut in.

'Yeah I know, that lad's trouble, but you know the rules.'

'You mean, if a customer refuses to pay, you have to just sit there and take it?' John glared at the owner in disbelief.

'What you don't do is get out of the car and knock the person unconscious. You're lucky the uncle has decided not to report the matter to the police,' the owner said.

'Yeah well, that doesn't surprise me, the way his nephew was behaving; a right dickhead he was.'

'That's as may be, but the fact of the matter is, you left him lying unconscious on the pavement. So you're fired and your licence is revoked,' the owner said, holding out his hand for John to hand over his ID badge.

CHAPTER 22

A BOARDROOM SCUFFLE
1993

John was helping Lynn around the house when his mother phoned and asked him to come round as something had happened to Alex. When he got there he found Alex slumped in one of the armchairs and he immediately knew something was very wrong.

'What's the matter kid, why aren't you at work?' John asked.

'They've... sacked... me,' Alex struggled to get the words out.

'But you only needed two more weeks to complete your five year apprenticeship!'

'I think that's why they did it; I think I was set up.' Alex clasped his hands to stop them from shaking. 'I had to cut some metal bars to a hundred and forty millimetres, which I did. Then the foreman accused me of cutting them the wrong length. He said he'd told me to make them a hundred and forty four millimetres long. I told him he'd seen me set the machine before he signed the job off. He denied it, of course, and he reported me to the bosses, who said I'd been negligent and that I'd cost them a lot of money and that I needn't come back to work again.'

'Where was the union in all this?'

'What union? If you want to become a member of a union you have to inform the management and they'd sack you before you've joined. With all the unemployment the bosses can do what they like. And it's not only me, they've sacked other apprentices before they'd completed their apprenticeship so they don't have to pay them full rates.'

'The nerve of them! I'm going to have a word, they can't get away with this.' John was ready to cause trouble.

'No, please bruv, you'll only make matters worse,' Alex pleaded. 'Samantha and I have split for good this time and now I'll have to go through all the crap you went through to see my son. Where am I going to get the money to pay for that?'

'Well, I'm not having it,' John said and stormed out.

No one attempted to stop him when he charged through the factory demanding to know where the MD's office was. Finding it, he burst in, causing the secretary to almost fall off her chair. 'Excuse me! Excuse me! You can't go in there, they're having a meeting!' She jumped up to try to block him as he made for the boardroom door.

'If I was you I'd shut up and sit down,' John snapped and gave the door a kick.

The five directors sitting around the boardroom table looked up simultaneously. John stood glaring at them, his body almost filling the door frame. 'Which one of you scumbags sacked my brother?'

'Just a minute,' one of the directors said in a controlled voice. 'I don't know who you are and how you got in here, but I suggest you leave before we call the police.'

Ignoring him, John said, 'Alex Lawson has been working here for the past five years. He had only two weeks to go to get his qualifications and your twisted foreman sacks him for no reason. Where is he? Bring him up here, let's see what he has to say for himself.'

The director at the far end of the table spoke up. 'I don't know where he is, but if your brother is anything like you, I suspect he deserved to get sacked.'

John's face became incandescent with anger and he kicked the edge of the table with such force that it shot back and pinned the man against the far wall. 'My brother put his life and soul into this job. He's never taken a day off, ate his lunch at the machines and often worked late without any extra pay. If he doesn't receive his time served documents in the next two weeks I'll burn this factory down with the lot of you in it!'

'I'll have you arrested for...'

John reached over and grabbed the man by his tie, pulled him across the table and spat, 'Go on then, why don't you? But I tell you, the newspapers would love a story like this; exploitation of cheap labour and all that. So if I was you, I'd do the decent thing and there'll be no more trouble.' Then he turned and walked out.

'There you are, as you can see I didn't need an appointment,' he said as he stormed past the bemused secretary.

Two weeks later Alex received his qualifying certificates together with two weeks' back pay.

CHAPTER 23

ALONG CAME JENNY

1995

John was still struggling to find a decent job and his relationship with Lynn had run its course. They decided to go their separate ways with no bitterness or ill-will, and Lynn moved out and left John to get on with his life.

John and Alex were getting on with their lives and with both of them out of the house Jose felt lost and depressed. Life had dealt her many blows, and they were beginning to leave their mark on her tough exterior. Her bouts of depression were increasing and she turned to drink to ease the pain. Sleeping pills only delayed each night's anxieties, and she reached a point where she wanted to fall asleep and not wake up again.

In despair she cried out to the heavens, 'God, if you're up there, if you're real then you'd better show up because I've had enough of this life!' Emotionally exhausted and in floods of tears she fell asleep on the sofa.

There was a gentle tapping on the front door, which roused her to near consciousness. *'Is that God speaking to me, telling me He's here and that He's heard my prayers?'* she thought.

'It's the gasman!' she heard a voice shout, and her hope disappeared.

'How silly of me,' she sighed as she heaved herself off the sofa to let the gasman in.

'Are you alright?' he asked, looking at her troubled face. 'I can come back later if you prefer.'

'Not really. Everything just seems to be getting on top of me and I don't know which way to turn.'

'I know the feeling. I've been there myself, but I learned that no one can store up immunity from disaster or tragedy. All we can control is how we respond to it. When you feel life is falling apart it could actually be falling together. I've been through some rough times in my life, and it was Jesus who helped me overcome my circumstances. I'm also a pastor now. In fact, we're having a gathering at our house tomorrow night and you're welcome to join us,' he invited.

There was something about the compassion in the way the man spoke that made Jose think about going. The following night she braved her anxieties and went to the pastor's house. A woman opened the door and greeted Jose as if she'd been expecting her. She introduced herself as Angie, Pastor Mike's wife.

Jose started attending their church meetings and she often thought of what had happened back in South Africa when Ronnie McGregor became a reborn Christian. And here she was, all those years later, inviting Jesus into her life too.

Jose changed as if from night to day. John and Alex thought their mother had gone mad, and they began to worry that she might have got caught up in a cult.

John was restless. He missed the stimulation of Soho, the excitement, the danger, the cosmopolitan atmosphere and the money. He tried to push the feelings aside, but they kept coming back to haunt him. It was like a deep underlying vacuum sucking at his brain, like a drug he had no fix for.

Thankfully he got a call from the manager of a Bon Marché store in Birkenhead to tell him his application for a job as store detective had been successful. It was exciting work, but it never came close to the excitement he found in Soho.

One day John was chasing a shoplifter up Grange Road when a man came around the corner and accidentally tripped the thief up, landing on top of him and pinning him to the ground.

'Thanks man, this guy would have outrun me if you hadn't jumped in,' John said when he caught up with them. 'John Lawson,' he introduced himself.

'Anytime, mate. Colin Crowley,' the man replied sheepishly.

'Tell you what, Colin, you fancy grabbing a beer after work? I owe you one,' John offered.

'Hey lads, I'll buy you both a drink if you let me off,' the bedraggled shoplifter butted in.

'Just give me the clothes you stole and get lost.' John was in a forgiving mood.

Colin Crowley's sister Sue owned the hardware shop Contraband, situated in the basement of Bon Marché. Colin was a single father with two boys, Alan and Paul, whose mother had walked out on them a few years earlier, and he and John became good friends, often meeting up for a pint.

It wasn't long before Sue asked John to come and work for her as their store detective. John accepted, and arranged for Alex to take over his job at Bon Marché.

'I was thinking of taking my boys to Butlins Holiday Camp in Wales, why don't you and Daniel come too?' Colin suggested as they sat having a drink in the Charing Cross pub after work one day.

It could not have come at a better time. John was getting bored and felt stifled by the dreary daily routine. 'Sounds like a good idea. I need to get away from this damn place for a while.'

Butlins Pwllheli holiday camp in North Wales had all the ingredients for a fun-packed couple of weeks for the kids. It had a funfair, indoor and outdoor swimming pools, a ballroom, a boating lake, sports fields, an amusement arcade, shops, and a miniature railway, as well as the famous redcoats to make sure everyone enjoyed themselves.

Jenny, a petite blonde with an innocent looking face, was also holidaying there with her daughter Siobhan. Jenny was from Musselburgh, known as the Honest Town, just outside Edinburgh. She had an intoxicating smile and a soft Scottish accent.

John was surprised when Jenny told him she worked as a

bus driver; he could not imagine her sitting behind the wheel of a double-decker bus. He became smitten with her, and a romance soon blossomed between them.

Within a short time Jenny and Siobhan moved from Scotland into Wood Close with John and Daniel. It seemed the perfect arrangement and John was contented.

But John's happiness was marred by news from his mother that his Gran Lawson had died. He was overwhelmed with shock and sadness. 'What happened?' he asked. 'She was so fit. She was still doing high kicks the last time I was there.'

'If it's any comfort, son, she died peacefully in her sleep. She would have told you not to cry for her, she's been called home by God.'

John travelled to Scotland with his mother and Alex to attend the funeral, where there was a multitude of aunts, uncles, cousins and friends, for Mrs. Kathleen Lawson was well respected. Even George and Dave had made the effort to come all the way from London. All her children were there, except for John's father. Nothing was said about Lex's absence, but once again John felt betrayed that he had not even made the effort to attend his mother's funeral.

Back in Birkenhead the following week, John, Jenny and the children were driving along Shrewsbury Road when a speeding car came out of a side street and smashed into their car. John's spine was fractured, the driver was arrested and charged, and John was awarded £10,000 in compensation. But the money was soon spent on a new kitchen and a custom motorcycle, which didn't please Jenny one bit.

CHAPTER 24

NICK'S NIGHTCLUB

1996

Soon after getting back to work at Contraband, Sue informed John that the store detective he had been standing in for was returning from sick leave and that she would have to let him go. Jenny suggested that John should come and work with her at the pub, where they were in need of a barman. It seemed like a good idea, as it could serve as a training ground for opening their own pub one day.

But John's inability to draw a curtain over the past, over the loss of his beloved grandmother and the excitement of working for his uncle George, made him feel as if life was passing him by.

The opportunity he had been waiting for came via Alex, who was now working for Leisure Security as a bouncer at a club called Nick's in Oldham. The club had a reputation as a haunt for drug dealers and general trouble makers, but that didn't bother John, who craved the excitement. His experience at the hostess bars soon proved his ability to handle difficult customers and it wasn't long before the manager offered him the job as head doorman.

The first test of John's supervisory skills came when he spotted a couple who appeared to have had far too much to drink. The man passed out and fell off his chair, while the woman remained slumped over the bar. John asked two of the bouncers to escort them off the premises. But that was easier said than done. As one of the bouncers, Tony, bent over to help the man up, the woman grabbed a glass from the bar and shoved it into his face, almost severing his upper lip. Tony shouted for help while trying to hold the loose flesh together. It took three men to manoeuvre the man to the entrance and out onto the street while Tony made his way to the manager's office for the first aid kit.

John and two other bouncers tried to tackle the woman, but she seemed to have the strength of ten men and started punching and biting them as they tried to get her to the exit. One of the bouncers punched her in the face when she started biting his nose, but she just carried on fighting. 'I don't believe it, I've just punched her so hard that she should have been knocked clean out, but look at her, she looks like she hasn't felt a thing,' he said.

'I reckon they must be on speedballs, you can hit them as hard as you like, but they don't feel it. I saw that at The Jimmy's in Birkenhead,' John said when they had finally managed to get the couple out onto the pavement. Just then the man turned around and kicked Alex full on the shin, snapping the bone just below the knee. Alex let out a blood curdling scream. As John rushed to help his brother, the man broke free, grabbed the woman by the hand and ran off.

Tony and Alex were rapidly taken off in an ambulance and when the police arrived, John joined them in their search for the couple. It wasn't long before they spotted them and set off in hot pursuit. The man was running incredibly fast, but the fact that this man had broken his brother's leg spurred John on, and he eventually caught up with him. With a flying rugby tackle he brought him down and laid into him with heavy punches. When the police officer caught up with them, they cuffed the man and hauled him into the van. Heading back to the main street, they found the police officer who had followed the woman lying on the ground, his uniform in tatters, and saw the woman getting into a taxi. The police van managed to block it, and she too was shoved into the van, screaming blue murder.

The man turned out to be a big-time drug dealer who was out on bail for attempted murder.

The following night John and the rest of the staff left the club earlier than usual, having managed to get the last few customers out by 2:30am. As they got into their cars in the car park they saw a small convoy of 4x4 jeeps draw up outside the club and watched as a group of men wearing balaclavas and carrying shotguns, jumped out and stormed the main entrance. Realising it was closed, they got back into their vehicles and sped off.

'Someone up there must be looking after us,' John said to his passengers. 'Let's get out of here while we still can.'

With Alex still in hospital and the ever increasing danger from the local drug dealers, the team at Nick's was reinforced with two new men—Jay, a British ex paratrooper, and Rico, a South African ex special forces soldier and professional wrestler. With John in charge, the team had a formidable reputation and word soon spread that Nick's nightclub was not a place to look for trouble.

About a month later the case was due in court and the team headed to Oldham for the trial. But the same men who had appeared outside the club with shotguns were there to offer them a deal—five thousand pounds in compensation for Alex if they agreed not to press charges against the drug dealer and his wife. The deal was struck and the case never came to trial.

CHAPTER 25

PRIME SUSPECT

There was ever increasing violence at the club doors, with some of the gangs turning up armed to the teeth. Jez, one of the new doormen from Birkenhead, suggested they take up some weapons training. He told John he knew an ex SAS guy who had permission to use the army firing range at Altcar on the outskirts of Liverpool and regularly trained bodyguards, and a meeting was arranged.

Because of his SAS connections, 'Mack' would not reveal his real name when they met him at his house in Liverpool. As they were introduced, the first thing that struck John was how much he looked like Sean Connery. 'You know, you don't half look like...'

'Sean Connery. Yeah, I've been told many times, but that's where the resemblance ends. I can shoot a lot better than he ever can.' Mack's handshake almost crushed John's fingers. He exuded an aura of power, even though John guessed him to be well into his sixties.

'I do basic bodyguard and firearm training, how to handle a weapon, how to strip it down, clean it and put it back together again, how to draw and fire from the hip and walk in correct formation with your principal. I'll teach you about firing arcs so you don't end up shooting each other instead of the attackers, and some basic CQB—that's short for Close Quarter Combat. So if you're up for it, we'll meet here tomorrow and I'll take you to the army firing range.'

Four weeks later, after intensive training, Mack approached John and Jez and asked if they were interested in doing film work.

'What kind of filming?' John wanted to know.

'A television company's stunt co-ordinator occasionally gets in touch with me when he needs people who are experienced in handling weapons to do some authentic film scenes. In this case it's for a production called 'Prime Suspect' with Helen Mirren. It's going to be shot around a disused railway station in Manchester. You'll be considered as extras with action, so you'll be paid ninety pounds a day and you'll be on set for three days. What do you think, you up for it?'

'Sounds great, I'm up for it,' John eagerly agreed.

'Me too,' Jez offered excitedly. 'So what exactly will we be doing?'

'They want three guys, so I'm one short, but as far as I know you'll be acting as armed police wearing all the protective gear; you'll be armed with real live rifles and hand guns that have been modified to fire pellets that look like real bullets,' Mack explained.

'What are we going to be shooting at?' Jez asked.

'You shoot the bad guy when he raises his gun to shoot Helen Mirren.'

'One of our team, Jay, was in the paras, I'm sure he'll be up for it too,' John offered.

'Sounds good. I was in the paras myself before I joined the two-two's, so get your friend to meet us on location and I'll have a quick chat with him,' Mack said.

Came the day, John, Jez, Jay and the other extras were walking around the disused railway station in Manchester, dressed in their police costumes, waiting to be called.

'They think we're real police,' Jay said, as curious crowds began to gather.

'Hang on a minute, I want to try something,' Jez said, and moved towards the crowd. 'Right people, move back to a safer distance,' he instructed them, and they immediately obeyed.

'Just shows what effect a uniform has on people,' John said.

'What's happening?' one of the crowd called out.

'I'm afraid I'm not at liberty to tell you,' Jez replied and hurried away.

The moment came when John was positioned on the railway track with three men in supportive positions behind him. Jez and his team were positioned in one of the old ticket offices.

'Right, the scene is this,' the director Philip Davies began. 'You'll be down there on the track with your sniper rifle. Open your bipod and support your weapon on the platform edge and take aim at the target. When the signal is given, you open fire, then jump up onto the platform and rush forward, directly towards the camera, weapons still at the ready, okay?'

'Sure,' they acknowledged.

'The others in the ticket office will do the same, fire their weapons and then rush forward at the same time, got that?'

'No problem,' John said with an element of arrogance.

'I'm told you're experts,' Philip said, looking at John who had been issued with a sniper rifle, 'but be careful where you point them. As you can see, the crew are wearing protective glasses just in case of an accident. I'm told those pellets burst into flames as they blast out,' Philip advised them.

'Just one thing, sir,' John spoke up. 'This sniper rifle has a bipod attached. In ordinary circumstances the sniper would stay in position and let the others run forward.'

'Well, this is television and it looks more dramatic if you're running with it,' Philip Davies said, more interested in the overall picture than in the detail.

The cameras were lined up and the scene was set. John positioned himself, his feet firmly planted, the sniper rifle lined up and ready to fire, just waiting for the director to give the cue by dropping his arm.

Philip dropped his arm and everyone opened fire, the shots reverberating around the station. As John made his move to leap onto the platform, his foot caught the edge and he fell backwards onto the track, nearly crushing the men behind him.

'CUT!' Philip shouted. 'I thought you guys were supposed to be good at this. You only had to jump onto the blooming platform and run,' he said scornfully.

'I told you, you wouldn't normally run with a fixed bipod, but don't worry, I'll do it right next time.' John felt miffed for screwing up.

The scene was re-set, the rifles reloaded, everybody in first position again, ready for the cameras to roll. The director lowered his arm, everyone opened fire, and the volley of shots reverberated once again around the area as John swiftly leapt onto the platform and made a perfect run past the cameras.

'CUT! Okay lads, we got it. Looked great.' This time Philip Davies had a satisfied smile on his face.

Riding on this success, Mack got a call from SianelPedwarCymru (Channel Four Wales), who were producing a cop drama series entitled A41. In this sequence a group of armed terrorists had taken hostages and were holed up in a café, threatening to blow it up if anyone came near. Dressed again as armed police, John and his team had to drive up in a police car, jump out, grab their weapons and surround the café. John had to take out an MP4 sub-machinegun, insert the magazine and pull back the safety catch while the cameras moved in close to capture the action.

After completing their sequence, they were held in position as the big moment came when the café was blown up. The set was surrounded by fire engines, ambulances, first aid personnel, explosives experts and real policemen; so much so that it was impossible to work out who were extras and who not.

The explosion was spectacular and the café was razed to the ground. 'I know a few buildings in Birkenhead I'd like to do that to,' Jez said, staring at the smouldering remains.

'Yeah, and I know a few buildings in Drumchapel I'd like to do that to as well,' John said reflectively.

They earned a hundred pounds each for the day's work, which pleased everybody.

Mack was very pleased with the work that was coming in from the television companies, but he was planning to move abroad in a few weeks' time. Before he left, there was one more filming job. Christopher Eccleston was to play the lead role in the controversial documentary drama about the Hillsborough tragedy in which 96

Liverpool football fans lost their lives. This time the team were to be normal police officers with no weapons, and Mack was asked to find more extras to make up numbers. John roped in a couple of real police officers he knew, and together they travelled to the football ground that had been set up as Hillsborough stadium. They got kitted out in police uniforms and took up their places in the stadium. The show attracted a huge audience, especially from the people of Merseyside who had been affected by the tragedy.

The day after the show was aired, John picked Daniel up from school as usual, and much to his delight several of the parents told him they had seen him on telly the previous night.

During this time, unbeknown to John, Jenny had auditioned for the television show 'Blankety Blank' which was hosted by the female impersonator of Paul O'Grady's character, Lilly Savage.

Jenny persuaded John to come with her and he ended up being auditioned as well. He was selected to be a contestant in their Christmas Special edition, to be aired on Boxing Day.

The show was recorded in London in November and John and Jenny stayed over at the Sherlock Holmes Hotel in Baker Street. John got through to the final round, and won a digital camera and the famous 'Blankety Blank' cheque book and pen. After the show they met up with his uncle George and his girlfriend Yasmin and went to a show together before heading back to Merseyside. It was John's first time back in Soho after a couple of years and once more the yearning to be back there started resurfacing.

CHAPTER 26

SHOTGUN AND MARRIAGE

1997

John was surprised when Jay, the new bouncer, contacted him with an interesting proposition to earn big money. He explained that he was having a problem with an ex bouncer nicknamed Pedro because he looked Spanish. Pedro was a drug dealer with a vile reputation for inflicting pain and torture on anyone who crossed him. Jay had had a run-in with Pedro in a pub one night, after he and his small gang of followers had threatened him. Jay had to make a hasty retreat, but swore that one day he would exact revenge for being made to look a fool.

'So what have you got in mind?' John was curious to know.

Jay explained that he had done some surveillance on Pedro and knew where and when he bought his drugs. 'He stocks up on a Thursday, so the best time to hit him would be on Wednesday night when he's ready with the cash to stock up again on the Thursday. There'll be thousands in his house, so I want us to break in and take the lot, plus anything else that's worth money. So, you interested?' He didn't have to ask, he could read the answer on John's face.

'It's going to take three of us; know anyone who might be interested?' Jay asked.

'Yes, I think our new lad Darren will be up for it,' John said..

John and Darren drove up to Kirkham to meet Jay and were surprised to find him with a sawn off shotgun, cartridges and a tub of salt laid out on a table, and were mystified to see Jay emptying the cartridges.

'What are you doing that for?' John asked.

'It's an old trick I learned in the army. If you want to really shock someone, but you don't want to kill them, you take out the bearings and refill the cartridges with rock salt, which will knock them off their feet,' Jay explained. 'We'll go to his house in the early hours of the morning and bang on the door as if we're from the police. I've done a recce; his house is at the end of a country lane and it's detached, so nobody will hear us. We can approach the house through a hedge at the back. I've tested the police response time with a fake call and I reckon we've got a good eight minutes to do the job and get away if anyone did call the police.'

John knew the risk he was taking and what the consequences would be if it went wrong, but chances like this didn't come along often and the reward was going to be worth the risk. He needed to prove to Jenny he could still bring in the money and take care of them.

Pedro was awakened by heavy banging on the door and wondered what lunatic would want to wake him up at that time of the morning. His second thought was that it had to be the police, but that didn't worry him much; he could take care of them as he usually did—bung them a few grand and they would happily get lost, reporting they'd found nothing. The banging persisted and he hurried down the stairs to the front door, slipped the chain on before cautiously opening it and peeping out. The first thing he saw was the barrel of a sawn-off shotgun, and he tried to slam the door shut. But Jay was ready; he jammed a crow bar between the frame and the door. Pedro panicked and ran back up the stairs. John and Darren put their shoulders to the door and the chain quickly gave way under their pressure. All three chased up the stairs after him, but Pedro had managed to get into the bedroom and wedged the double bed against the door.

It didn't take them long to force the bed back far enough to squeeze through. Pedro was wielding a machete, and his wife was screaming her head off. Jay was in no mood to argue and blasted him with the shotgun, propelling him back about a metre before crashing to the floor. His wife became hysterical, screaming that they had killed him. Jay grabbed her by the throat and shoved her hard against the wall telling her to shut up or she'd get the same. She stopped screaming and slumped to the floor, sobbing.

'Right, let's get him downstairs,' Jay said to John and Darren, who grabbed hold of Pedro as he began to recover.

'I'll have you killed. Do you know who I am? You'll regret this. No one does this and gets away with it,' Pedro gasped as they dragged him into the kitchen and plonked him down on a chair.

'Shut it,' Jay said, and whacked him with the butt of the shotgun, blood now covering his head. 'Tie him up,' he told Darren, 'and see what you can find in the drawer,' he said to John, indicating the cutlery drawer.

While Darren tied the still protesting Pedro to the chair, John searched the drawer and found a long carving knife. 'You're going to tell us where the money is?' John said, pressing the tip of the blade to Pedro's throat.

Pedro stared at him in a show of bravado.

'Maybe another blast from that shotgun will help persuade him,' John suggested.

Jay smiled as he re-cocked the shotgun and pushed it between Pedro's legs, into his crotch. 'I'm telling you now, you're going to lose your crown jewels if you don't tell us where the money is.'

'In there! In there!' Pedro screamed, nodding his head towards one of the kitchen cupboards. John crossed to the cupboard and found a large Quality Street tin crammed full of money.

'Right, keep an eye on him while I have a look around to see what else I can find,' Jay told them and moved off to the other room.

'Who are you lot?' Pedro said, struggling to free himself.

'Just keep it shut!' John told him as he pulled him to his feet, but Pedro had more strength than they had realised and managed to break the cable ties around his wrists. He made a dash to get away, barging past Jay as he came back carrying a stash of drugs he had found.

Pedro knew he was fighting for his life and showed incredible strength for his size.

John managed to get a stranglehold around his neck, squeezing it until he passed out.

As Pedro came to, Jay put the shotgun to his head. 'You've been encroaching on our territory, so you've got three days to pack up and move. If you don't and we have to come back, we'll kill you and the missus. Right lads, let's get the hell out of here.' he ordered, and picked up the Quality Street tin.

John's reward was two and a half thousand pounds. *Not bad for a night's work; Jenny should be pleased with me*, he thought as he made his way home.

The money came in useful, as John and Jenny both felt it was time to tie the knot and they set the date for the 11th of June 1997. Jenny wanted a romantic wedding and they decided on the Dominican Republic, at a resort called Playa Dorada in Puerto Plata. John's mother had happily agreed to look after Daniel and Siobhan. They chose a two week holiday package to comply with the Dominican Republic's regulations that they had to be resident in the country for a full week before the marriage ceremony could take place.

John wore the full regalia of a Scotsman—a Bonnie Prince Charlie Tartan kilt with sporran, black jacket and waistcoat, the Scottish dagger, the Sgian-dubh, tucked into white socks, and traditional black brogues. Jenny looked radiant, her hair set with ringlets and a sparkling tiara. Her long white silk dress moulded the slim curves of her body beautifully. She held a bouquet of tropical flowers of the Dominican Republic. After the ceremony they posed for photographs on the sun-drenched beach, and when they got back to the hotel, they found their room filled with a beautiful array of colourful flowers that exuded an exotic bouquet of fragrances.

Back home, his mother arranged a reception party at the Conservative Club in Birkenhead, which was attended by all the family and friends. To John's delight even his uncle George attended.

A few weeks later Jenny announced that she was pregnant, much to everyone's delight. John was jubilant—he was married and his beautiful wife was pregnant with their first child. He felt as if nothing could go wrong.

CHAPTER 27

MEETING THE WARRIOR

Mick Powells had always loved motorcycles and decided to leave Leisure Security, the company he, John and the other bouncers were working for, to start a biker gang on the Wirral with his right hand man, Martin. They called themselves the Nomads and found premises in the New Ferry area to turn into a clubhouse. Keen to have John as a member, they quickly initiated him into the Nomads.

Mick and Martin also set up a new security company with two friends—Mike Ahearne, one of the stars of the television show 'The Gladiators', where he went under the name of Warrior, and Gary Sandland, a world champion kick boxer. They called the company 'Ahearne and Sandland' and put together a team to send into various nightclubs where the local bouncers were no longer able to handle the gangster problem. The task was to get the club back under control, establish a new team of bouncers, and then move on to the next trouble spot.

John and the other bouncers from Nick's were keen to join the new company. They knew that Mike Ahearne's celebrity status would open doors to lucrative contracts. Mike enjoyed the high life that fame had brought him; he liked the lavish lifestyle, gambling and he loved the ladies. But it came at a price, and he soon found himself in financial difficulty and knew that the security business would provide him with a good source of income. At the time he was sharing an apartment with Elmore Davies, a high-ranking Merseyside police officer, who was later found to have been selling information on drug dealers operating in Merseyside to the notorious drug baron, Curtis Warren, who at the time was serving a long prison sentence in Holland.

Because of his relationship with Elmore Davies, Mike Ahearne had connections in the Merseyside police force, and was able to arrange for some of the officers to train John and the other bouncers during their off duty time on how to deal with difficult situations and violent customers, while remaining within the law.

Their first job was at the Northern Lights nightclub in Blackburn. It was close to Blackburn Rovers Football Club and there was always a strong police presence in the road opposite the club on match days. Adam, one of the previous doormen, had been badly beaten up in a fight with a gang of drug dealers when he refused to let them in, and his arm was badly broken. He agreed to join Ahearne and Sandland as soon as his arm had healed and came up to the club to help John identify the trouble makers.

The following week, the drug dealers who had beaten Adam up decided to visit the club again, to test the new security. This was the moment John and the team had been waiting for and John told the two bouncers at the door to be polite and to let them in without arousing suspicion.

The gang, believing their reputation was the reason they were being treated with such respect, made their way to their usual spot behind the DJ's desk, near the emergency exit. Once they had settled in and had been served their drinks, John instructed the bouncers to get into position, ready to move in when he gave the signal.

'Excuse me sir, I'd like a quick word with you,' John said, tapping the gang leader on the shoulder. This was the sign for the bouncers to move in. They started beating the gang up with truncheons and knuckle dusters, eventually driving them out through the emergency exit into the yard, where they continued to beat them to a pulp.

John grabbed hold of the leader. 'I believe you like breaking arms,' he said. A bloody face stared back at John. 'I don't know what you mean,' the man said.

'You broke our doorman's arm, and this is to remind you that we don't take kindly to people who do that.' John dragged him across to a pile of wooden crates and stretched his right arm over a gap between the crates. He shouted back at Adam, 'Do you want to do the honours, mate?'

'Too right!' Adam's eyes glinted dangerously. He grabbed hold of a stainless steel bar stool and brought it crashing down on the man's arm with such force they could hear the bone snap above the gang leader's screams.

Through Mick Powells' association with Mike Ahearne, the company was becoming well known in nightclub circles, gaining a reputation as the team to call on when a club was experiencing trouble. Mick was very pleased with the way John was handling things as head doorman and doubled his salary so that he was now earning thirty pounds an hour. John had put a strong team together—his brother Alex, Jay, Andy, Jez, Darren and Phil, all Birkenhead boys. Rico had left to pursue his wrestling career in Mexico.

Violence in the nightclubs was on the increase, and in some clubs John and his team had to wear bullet proof vests, shin and elbow pads, and arm themselves with collapsible truncheons and knuckledusters.

Sacha's nightclub was in the basement of the Britannia Hotel in Manchester's Piccadilly. They were having problems with gangs who would storm into the club, refuse to pay and help themselves to drinks and whatever else they could lay their hands on.

On their first night there, one of the local gangsters again attempted to get in to help himself without paying. John blocked his way and told him he wasn't allowed in. The gangster—a black man with short dreadlocks, sporting a heavy gold chain around his neck and wearing a red baseball cap turned the wrong way round—threatened John with all kinds of violence if he didn't step out of the way and let him in.

John slapped him hard across the face with what was termed a 'bitch slap' in Manchester. The gangster tumbled backwards and fell to the ground. John grabbed hold of him, dragged him a through a puddle of water, pulled him back onto his feet and sent him on his way with a solid kick up the backside.

A local doorman who had watched the scene, said to John, 'You're crazy. You shouldn't have done that. You have no idea what you're up against. I don't want to be around when he comes back with his mates. They'll kill the lot of you; I'm out of here.'

Satisfied that the matter had been settled, John took out his mobile to phone Jenny, but as he turned around, the gangster was back, this time with the rest of his mob. 'What you going to do now, slap me again?' he challenged, his cheeks still flaring an angry colour.

John flipped the mobile back into his pocket. It was quite clear that they were tooled up, their weapons bulging inside their coats. 'Like I told you, I'm not letting you in, so find someplace else,' John said defiantly, remembering how he had confronted the Yardies in Soho.

'Listen to him; he thinks he's ten men. You got a death wish or summit?' the gang leader grinned.

'No, but some of you might have, so bring it on,' John challenged, and reached into his jacket as if he was reaching for a gun.

'Nah, nah, it's okay mate, we'll find somewhere else,' the gang leader said, turned and began to move off.

John watched them walk off, not quite believing how well his bluff had worked and how easily he had scared them off. But as he turned around, his complacency evaporated. Mick Powells came up to him and introduced a stocky bald man surrounded by a group of black men. 'This is Brian Phillips. He is, shall we say, well connected in the Salford area, and this is his team,' Mick said. 'With the reputation this place has, I thought you might need a little back-up, so I rang me old mucker here and asked if he would mind helping out.'

'So that's why they turned turtle and ran off. There was I thinking I'd scared them off,' John said.

Brian Phillips stood five feet ten inches tall and was thick-set. His head was completely shaved, and his eyes were hard and dark.

'Listen, you were good, kiddo. It took a lot of balls to take them on, but you're in Manchester now, and its different here. The gangs go around proper tooled up and you'd better watch your back now. You'd have taken a bullet if we hadn't been around,' Brian said.

John took note of what Brian had said but still had an air of confidence in his own abilities. The team did a good job at Sacha's and soon brought in a new squad to take over while they focused on what was coming next.

Carl Ince, who operated Elite Security that ran many of the clubs in the Preston area, was running short of manpower and called on his old pal Mick Powells for help at a club called Cheeky Monkeys. The club was mainly frequented by students out for a good time, but drug-dealing gangs from Manchester had started moving in, and the local gangs didn't like the idea of outsiders on their territory.

The Italian owners of the club didn't know how to deal with the situation and desperately needed help. Mick Powells gave the task to John, who made up the team with his brother Alex, Jay, Michael, Darren, Jez, Phil and Michael.

John had placed his men strategically around the club to be on the lookout for any trouble, but the club's dance area created a problem—it was painted jet black, and with its flashing lights and smoke machine, visibility was reduced to a bare minimum.

On the second night all seemed to be going as well, as it had on the first, until the team caught two black guys selling drugs and threw them out. John was pleased with the way they handled the situation. 'Good, that'll teach them not to operate here,' he said.

Suddenly the warning light in reception began flashing—a signal from the DJ that there was trouble brewing. 'You boys had better go and see what's going on. I'll bolt the doors here and be right there,' John told the others.

Back in the bar area John and Jay found tables and chairs knocked over and scattered to one side. Innocent customers were standing with their backs against the walls. The rest of the team were standing in a line facing a group of about fifteen black men, ready to pounce and egging the bouncers on to make the first move.

John stepped forward, reached into the pouch he had strapped to his belt and pulled out a collapsible nunchaku that telescoped out with a whoosh. He began spinning it around in his practiced style, the metal tips making a swishing sound as they spun through the air.

The gang started throwing bottles as John closed in on them, but he caught the guy nearest to him with a whack to the head and he fell down as John hit the next guy across the knees, sweeping his legs out from under him. 'Come on then, who's next?' he shouted, still swirling the nunchaku.

The gang decided they didn't want any of it, turned and rushed out through the emergency exit. John looked down at the two dazed guys trying to get to their feet. 'Throw these two out and lock the emergency exit,' he instructed. 'I don't think we'll see them around here again.'

When he walked back to the reception area and looked out through the reinforced glass window in the door, he saw the whole group gathered in the street, some of them talking on their mobile phones. 'What do we do now?' Alex asked apprehensively

'I'm going to tell them to get stuffed,' John said. He stepped out and walked across to the gang. 'I don't know who you lot think you are, but we're used to dealing with dickheads like you, all full of it when you're together, but on your own you're nothing. You're from Manchester, so you should know better. We're with Brian Phillips, and if you don't know who he is, you'd better get on your phones and find out before you get seriously hurt.'

There was a moment's hesitation before the group exchanged glances and decided it would be better to leave.

The news of the Manchester drug gang being thrown out of the club spread far and wide, but there was one gang that didn't like the idea of guys from Liverpool—Scousers, as they were known—

coming into their territory and telling them where they could go and where not. So they hatched a plan to filter into Cheeky Monkeys one by one, bringing their girlfriends along and quietly mingling with the students and other customers.

By midnight they had all gathered together and were ready to cause trouble. Some of them were already high on Temazepam, a prescription drug that is used as a substitute for heroin. Hyped up and further fuelled by alcohol, they waited for their moment to attack the Scousers. Jez was the trigger when he walked up to one of them and asked politely, 'Do you mind taking your glass off the dance floor?' The man ignored Jez and carried on dancing. 'I said, would you mind taking your glass off the floor?' Jez repeated firmly.

The man stopped dancing and turned to Jez. 'Why don't you Scousers stuff off back to Liverpool and leave us alone? We don't like you and we don't want you here,' he said, spitting out the words.

'We're not Scousers, we're from Birkenhead and you still need to take that glass off the dance floor.'

'Birkenhead, Liverpool, just go back to wherever it is you came from,' the man said and carried on dancing.

'In that case I have no choice but to ask you to leave, or you'll be forcibly removed from the premises.' Jez was doing his best to keep his calm.

'You and who else?' the man said, as his mates began to gather around him. Jez pressed the alarm button on his walkie-talkie and in no time John and the others joined him. They quickly set about the gang, who in their drugged and drunken state were no match for the team.

Having bundled them out through the fire exit without too much trouble, things returned to normal, with the music starting up again and customers coming back onto the dance floor.

As John returned to the reception he noticed a group of the girls hurrying out. He guessed they must have come with members of the gang, and that was confirmed when he saw them joining up with them in the street outside the club.

'They're still hanging around; what do you think they're up to?' Jay asked when he joined John.

'I think they were just waiting for their girlfriends to come out,' John said pensively.

'What any woman sees in the likes of them is a mystery to me,' Jay remarked.

John was about to turn his back when he heard one gang member call out. 'Hey, doesn't the eye-tie who owns the club own that restaurant as well?'

'Yeah, you're right. Why don't we go there and help ourselves to some bevvies?' another member suggested.

Realising he had to do something fast, John stepped out and shouted at the top of his voice, 'don't you lot go anywhere near there!'

The gang stopped and the leader shouted back, 'Who's going to stop us? We're on the streets now, our territory, so if you want a fight, bring it on.'

By then the rest of the team had joined John and were standing shoulder to shoulder with him. 'What do think lads, shall we go for it?' he asked.

'Yeah, let's show the Mancs we don't like being called Scousers,' Alex said.

As they moved forward they pulled the brass knuckle dusters out of their pockets, slipped them on and began laying into the gang. The girls scurried off to avoid being caught up in the fray.

It wasn't long before the combined skills of the team, even though they were outnumbered two to one, got the upper hand and bodies began to litter the ground.

Jay had picked up one of the gang members and tossed him into the air, his body flying over John's head before landing on the concrete pavement with a heavy thud. Jez had wrestled one of the gang to the ground and was straddled over him, pounding him in the head. Phil and Darren, standing side by side, took on three of the gang members; Phil laid into two others and soon there was only one of them still on his feet. He picked up a beer bottle, smashed the end off and came charging at John, just as Jay got to his side. Without exchanging a word they let the man come at them, then at the last moment John lowered his body and leg-swept him. He was flung into the air, giving Jay the perfect chance to catch him with an elbow in the face, his lips exploding and his teeth bursting out of his mouth. He was unconscious before he hit the ground.

The street looked like a battlefield with bodies lying everywhere. John looked around at the blood-stained pavement and realised that they could be in serious trouble. 'Right lads, turn them all over and put them in the recovery position; we don't want any of these scumbags dying on us,' he said without any emotion. 'Then get back inside, get rid of your weapons and put them in a bin bag with any of your clothes that are blood-stained or torn. Hide it in the bottle skip in the backyard. Wash your hands and faces and change into your spare shirts. You can bet your arse the bizzies will be here soon.'

The ambulances arrived, soon followed by the police, whose presence was heralded by heavy banging on the front door. 'What the heck's been going on here?' a chief inspector in uniform demanded, forcing himself inside as soon as John had opened the door, followed by several of his constables.

'Been going on where?' John asked.

The officer raised his eyes to the ceiling in exasperation, then fixed his gaze on John. 'Don't try fooling with me. Does it look like I've got mug stamped across my forehead? I want to know what's been going on here,' he said, jabbing John with his forefinger.

'What do you think's been going on? It's a club and there's been dancing and drinking like any other licensed club,' John said.

'I don't mean in here, you idiot. I mean out there in the street where the paramedics are treating some seriously injured people!' the inspector shouted.

'Why, has there been a car accident?' John asked, knowing it was a useless thing to say; he could see it in the officer's face.

'Accident, my arse; that lot out there have taken a terrible beating and I want to know what you lot had to do with it.'

'Look officer, there was someone in here earlier trying to push drugs, but we don't stand for that nonsense in this club and we escorted him off the premises, keeping everything peaceful, just the way it should be.' John informed him, doing his best to keep his expression composed.

The officer frowned in annoyance. 'Oh, really; if you think I believe that crap, you're the one with mug written across your forehead. I'll get to the bottom of this. Get your team out here now,' he demanded. 'If any of you have any cuts or bruises, I'll nick the lot of you.'

The team was lined up and the chief inspector examined them one by one, looking for any tell-tale swelling or bruising on the knuckles, then examined their clothing for any rips or bloodstains.

Andy was last in the line and the officer had still not found a single blemish on any of them. 'I don't know what's been going on, but I tell you, when those guys wake up in the Royal Preston, you can be sure I'll be the first face they see and I'll interview every single one of them and then I'll be back,' he said, and turned to leave, looking like a man worn out by defeat. But he stopped in his tracks when John and the team burst out laughing. 'What's so funny?' he asked, the anger back in his voice.

'Sorry officer, it's more like if they wake up!' John said, doing his best to suppress his laughter.

'Yes well, you'll be laughing on the other side of your faces when I get to the bottom of this.'

'Let's hope those guys don't remember a thing when they come round,' John said as soon as the officer had left.

'They shouldn't have been so stupid to try and take us on in the first place, should they?' Alex said, patting his brother on the back.

'Right, let's round up the stragglers and get them out of here, and then I think we all deserve a blooming good drink,' John said, and led them back to the bar.

Not one of the gang members could remember a thing about what had happened that night—thanks to Temazepam.

CHAPTER 28

AN EXPLOSIVE REVELATION

1998

On the 3rd of March Jenny began to have contractions and called John to come home quickly. They rushed to Arrowe Park hospital that evening and in the early hours of the next morning Jenny gave birth to a baby boy. Tears of joy streamed down John's face as he watch his son being born, but it soon turned to panic when the nurses rushed the baby to a table on the other side of the room. An exhausted Jenny reached for John and cried, 'What's the matter? Why have they taken him over there?'

A nurse came over to explain that the baby had not yet taken his first breath and they were going to clear his airways. 'Don't worry, everything will be okay,' she consoled them.

The tense few moments seemed like hours before the baby let out a cry, and the nurses brought him over and handed him gently to Jenny, who was now crying tears of relief, as was John. The proud parents named him Arran, after one of the Scottish Isles.

After the success at Cheeky Monkeys, there was yet another club with similar problems. JFK's was an American themed nightclub, situated on Washway Road in Sale, Manchester. It had been converted from the Pyramid cinema, which had a unique frontage of Egyptian themed mouldings and tall fluted pillars. It was set well back from the main road, with a large pavement area in front. The interior had retained the Egyptian theme and consisted of the main area on the ground floor, with a large dance floor and long bar at the far end, behind which were housed the kitchens. The first floor contained rooms reserved for private parties and special occasions, leading onto a balcony. The stairway from the reception area to the first floor was sealed off by a metal gate.

The club was having a lot of trouble with gangs running riot. There had been a drive-by shooting a few weeks earlier, with one of the gangs trying to kill a doorman with a submachine gun. The front door was still riddled with bullet holes. Not quite sure what they were in for, John and his team, together with Mick Powells, set off in two cars for JFK's.

On arrival it became clear that the manager of the club had not given the doormen notice that a new team would be taking over. 'Wait here,' Mick said. 'I'll have to go and tell them their services are no longer required.'

While they were waiting, Mike Ahearne said, 'Mick's got a unique way of dealing with these situations. It won't be the first time he's had to sack someone.'

Soon the doormen came storming out, shouting obscenities and slamming the doors behind them. As they came past the team's cars, they gave them the V sign. Mick appeared in the doorway and beckoned them to come in.

Alarms started blaring as the team entered the club—their knuckledusters and other weaponry had set off the metal detectors. 'Just shows you, you can't walk in here carrying, although the gangs have been doing it without the doormen making any effort to stop them,' Mick said once they were gathered in the reception area. 'This is Billy McIntosh, the manager; you'll be working closely with him.'

'Hi guys, hope you're gonnae bring some order back to this place, 'cause it's got out of hand and it's driving the customers away.' Billy spoke in a broad Glaswegian accent.

Mick explained that he was keeping on two of the regular doormen, Damon and Tony, who would be able to point out the trouble makers to the team. John studied the two men—Damon was a tall, well-groomed black man who looked like he could handle himself, and Tony was short and stocky and strong looking too.

The club opened with the new team in place and word soon got around that 'Warrior' Mike Ahearne was in attendance. Everybody wanted to be photographed with him, particularly the ladies.

Alex was manning the metal detectors when he noticed a very attractive girl eager to have her picture taken with Mike Ahearne. 'Aren't I good enough to be photographed with you then?' he asked jokingly. The girl looked at him with a glint in her piercing blue eyes. She had short blonde hair and sported a golden tan. She told Alex her name was Vicci and happily agreed to be photographed with him. It was love at first sight. She was beautiful and everything Alex had ever hoped for in a woman.

John had the local guys, Damon and Tony, with him on the main door so they could spot the troublemakers as they arrived, but they said nothing when three big black limousines with blacked-out windows pulled up outside. 'Do you know this lot?' John asked them, feeling something was about to kick off.

'Don't recognise any of them,' Damon said, as a number of black men emerged from the cars and began scanning the area.

'Better get the rest of the boys, this looks like it could be heavy stuff,' John said. He watched one of the men open the rear door, and broke into a smile of relief when he saw Brian Philips step out.

'Alright kiddo, how you doing?' Brian greeted John as he walked into the club, closely guarded by four of his men.

'Fine, relieved to see it was you getting out of that car,' John said with a hint of nervousness.

'I 'eard the people who provided the club with the previous doormen are a bit upset and they're planning some kind of retribution, so I thought I'd come and show support,' Brian said with a wink, tapping the gun under his coat.

'Well, I don't think they'd be stupid enough to try something if they know you're here,' John said.

'No, I don't think so either, but if there's a problem, you call me, kiddo.' Brian said, and walked back out, with his men following him closely.

On the second night John saw a heavily built man with dreadlocks walking purposefully towards the entrance. 'That's James; he's banned,' Damon advised him.

'Why?' John asked, studying the man.

'He smashed a bottle over a girl's head just because she wouldn't dance with him. He's skitso and he hadn't taken his medication.' John sensed an element of fear in Damon's voice.

'Okay, I'll take care of it,' John said, moving swiftly onto the pavement.

'What you want man?' James said when John stopped directly in front of him.

'I'm the new head doorman and you're barred. You hit a girl with a bottle.'

'I didn't hit no girl with a bottle, I just pushed her away because she dissed me, man.'

'I'm not going to argue with you, you're barred and that's the end of it.'

'You think you can stop me?' James said, and tried to sidestep John. 'I'm not having you Scousers coming up 'ere and chucking us out of our clubs.'

'We're not Scousers and you're not getting in, mate,' John said and started walking back to the entrance. Behind him James shouted into his mobile, 'I'm going to shoot these Scousers, put a team together 'cause we can't allow this lot to come up here and disrespect us!'

Back inside, Damon said to John, 'We're going to have trouble.'

'Oh, I've had those kinds of threats before, but nobody's shot me yet.'

'Yeah, but this is Manchester.'

The thought was enough to worry John and he decided to call Brian, who said he would take care of it.

The following night James approached the club again, but John was already on the pavement, prepared for a confrontation.

'Hey man,' James said, raising his hands as if in surrender. 'I've come to say I'm sorry I dissed you, I didn't know you were working with Mr Philips,' he said, offering his hand.

'Okay, so now you know. I'll have a word with the management and maybe we'll let you back in next week, but one thing, make sure you've taken your meds, behave yourself and cause no trouble, okay?' John shook his hand.

'Sure man, I respect that,' James said and walked off.

'That's something I thought I'd never see,' Damon said when John came back inside.

It seemed the word had got round that the new doormen were not standing for any nonsense and that trouble makers would be swiftly shown the door. But Manchester being Manchester, it was inevitable that a local gang member would decide to test the doormen's power and try to enter armed with a gun. The metal detectors picked it up and the alarm went off.

Alex was working the main door that night, and before anyone was able to react, he walked up to the man and said in a quiet voice, 'Look, I don't know who you are, but we know you're carrying. So this is the situation.' By now he had guided the man to the entrance of the dance floor. 'You see those two men in smart suits at the bar? They're Five O, CID; they've got this place under surveillance. So if you're stupid enough to walk in there carrying that thing, you're going to get nicked.'

The man looked at Alex, his face softened and he said, 'Nice one, man.'

'Now go and put the thing in the car and then we'll let you in,' Alex told him.

John waited until the man had left and said to Alex. 'How the heck did you manage that? Those two fellas you pointed out are just ordinary punters.'

'We know that, but he doesn't. The point is, we avoided a confrontation,' Alex said philosophically.

'I'm impressed kiddo, I would never have thought of that.'

'No you wouldn't; you'd have just tried to bundle him out or smash his face in, and if he'd pulled the gun, anyone of us could have been killed.'

In the early hours of one morning, after the club had closed, Jay took John aside for a quiet word. 'Listen, when I was in the paras, we were on exercise one weekend and I ended up taking home some plastic explosives and boosters and mercury tilt switches and stuff like that; inadvertently, you know? Now it's lying there in my backpack. Do you know anything about explosives?'

'No, nothing,' John said. 'What is a mercury tilt switch in any case?'

'You put it on a car and wire it up to the detonator, and as soon as someone gets in the car it tilts and the mercury rolls down to the switch and BOOM!'

'Blooming heck, Jay! What are you going to do with it?'

'That's what I wanted to talk to you about. There's no way I can hand it back to the army; I'll end up back in the glasshouse.'

'Where's the stuff now?'

'I've got it stashed in the garden shed.'

'Okay, I'll figure something out,' John said, already thinking it could be a nice little earner.

The first person John approached was Brian Philips, who he knew had a connection with the UDA in Northern Ireland. 'You're out of your mind if you think I'd touch that stuff, and neither should you. You could get life for handling those kinds of explosives. Don't ever talk to me about anything like that again. If you do, I'll chop your legs off, understood?' Brian was adamant. 'Take my advice and stay well away from it.'

John didn't take his advice and approached Mick Powells at one of the Nomads meetings. Mick seemed interested, and told John he would think about it and let him know.

After the meeting John went to his local pub for a pint, and bumped into an old biker friend whom he trusted. This friend was even more outspoken than Brian about the dangers of dealing with explosives, and John made up his mind not to have anything to do with it. 'I've been thinking about the situation, Jay, and it's not worth the risk mate, we're talking life here if I were to get caught. You'll just have to get rid of it.'

'Yeah, I understand, but where? I can't just dump it.'

'Well, you're going to have to do something. You can't just leave it in the garden shed.'

'I know, I know, I'll think of something,' Jay said, a cloud of concern darkening his face.

When John read a newspaper report about a bomb scare at a care home near Preston, he immediately made the connection with Jay's explosive dilemma. It turned out he had taken the sticks of plastic explosive, carefully wrapped them in cling film and together with the boosters, detonators, tilt switches and the two live hand grenades, stuffed them into a backpack and asked his mother to store it for him, not daring to tell her what was inside.

His mother decided to store the backpack in her personal locker at the care home where she worked. Then she fell ill and in the three weeks of her absence the plastic explosives began to sweat, producing a liquid that seeped through the backpack, and eventually out under the door of the locker. The manager was alerted and when they discovered the contents, called the emergency services. In no time the police and a bomb disposal unit were on site. Fearing the explosives could go off at any minute, they evacuated the care home with the disabled being hurried out in their wheelchairs, not knowing what all the fuss was about.

Jay's mother was arrested, but released without charge, while Jay was arrested and charged with possession of explosives. He was lucky—the court was lenient and he made bail. The army did not want it made public that a soldier could to walk out of the barracks with explosives and the means to detonate them.

The incident made John rethink his lifestyle, and he decided it was time to change. 'Listen Mick, I'm sick of this gang life,' he announced when he saw him at the Nomads' clubhouse.

'What's brought that on?' Mick looked stunned.

'It's all becoming too much. The Outlaws in Liverpool barely tolerate us and I can see a war looming.'

'I never thought I'd hear this from you, John; you turned yellow or something?'

'No, it's just that I'm more of a loner, mate.'

Mick's expression changed. 'Well, let me tell you. You don't just decide to give up your patch and your loyalty to your brothers in arms. Oh no, we decide when you leave and your patch is ripped from you by us, by force, and then you're cast out for your disloyalty,' he explained.

John squared up to Mick. 'I don't like being threatened, Mick, you should know that. So let's understand each other, I'm walking away from this clean, and for your sake I hope that's the end of it.'

CHAPTER 29

WITHOUT CERTIFICATION

1998

Four months after Arran's birth, Jenny was pregnant again, and John had become fed-up with driving to Manchester four nights a week, so he was delighted when he got a call from his uncle George, who told him they were planning to open an adult video shop in Birkenhead and they wanted him to run it. They still had a massive stock of tapes and DVDs to get rid of. George said he would front all the costs of leasing a shop and split the proceeds fifty-fifty. It seemed a great opportunity to 'get off the doors' and to make more money. Jenny took some gentle persuasion, but soon she was happy at the prospect.

John found the ideal shop in Grange Road West, next door to the Cavendish Pub, and he signed the lease. He painted the interior black, put up shelves for the stock and installed security cameras and an entrance buzzer. He needed two assistants—one for day the shift and one for the night. His first choice was Alex for weeknights. Within three weeks John was ready for business. An old school friend, Michael Edge, known as Edgy, had walked in while John was putting the finishing touches to the shop front, and John had offered him the day shift job, which he eagerly accepted.

By the second day of trading the shelves were almost empty. John went back to the lock-up he had rented to get more stock, but on his return he found the shop full of police and Trading Standards officers from Birkenhead Council.

'You're nicked,' a sergeant informed him, taking hold of the heavy carrier bags and handing them to one of the constables.

'What's the charge?' John asked, knowing what the answer would be.

'You and your accomplice here, Mr. Edge, will find out when you get to the station,' the sergeant informed him.

At that moment Alex arrived for his shift and found his brother being handcuffed. 'What's going on here?' he wanted to know.

'It's a police raid, so you need to leave sir,' one of the constables replied.

'Oh, okay, none of my business.' Alex hurried out of the shop.

But the sergeant had been studying the shop surveillance video, and just as Alex was leaving, he called out, 'Hold it right there! You look like the man in this video. Please step over here and let me have a closer look at you.'

Alex obediently stepped over towards the sergeant, his head bowed sheepishly. The sergeant smiled triumphantly and said, 'You're nicked too.'

Edgy was released, as it was clear that John had duped him, but John and Alex were both charged. To their surprise they were not charged with possessing and selling pornography, or with piracy, but with 'Certification'—unlawfully selling tapes and DVDs without the British Board of Film Censors classification certificates. The shop was closed down, which didn't please Uncle George, and John had to go back to working the doors in Manchester while awaiting trial.

The case came up in the Liverpool Crown Court and the judge's closing statement read:

'I have viewed five of these videos and have to state, they are the most hardcore pornographic films it has been my displeasure to have to view. It is pornography at its worst. Alexander Lawson, I find you not guilty, you may step down, but as for you John Lawson, I find you guilty as charged. Is there anything you wish to say in mitigation before I pass sentence?'

'Yes, your Honour,' John said, rising to his feet. 'I understand the charge against me is for selling videos without displaying the proper certification. Why then was it necessary to view all five videos that were such a displeasure to watch?'

A collective intake of breath could be heard, and then sniggers started reverberating around the courtroom. John's lawyer tugged at his sleeve and whispered, 'For goodness sake, sit down before he doubles the sentence.'

The judge hammered his mallet for silence, but John was not to be stopped. 'I would also like to know what the contents of the tapes have to do with the charge I'm facing.'

'You have been found guilty of selling videos without the proper certification and I am sentencing you to four months imprisonment. Take him down,' the judge ordered, ignoring John's questions.

CHAPTER 30

HMP WALTON, LIVERPOOL

John was not as perturbed as before when he was being driven to Walton Prison in the sweatbox. He would only be doing eight weeks of the four months, and he knew all the procedures. As long as he kept his nose clean it would be a cat walk.

The large reception cell where the prisoners were assessed was much the same as Brixton, stinking of body odour and stale tobacco. It was filled with the usual mixture of common criminals, drug addicts and a few first-timers. While John awaited his turn, he suddenly heard his name being called. The voice sounded threatening and the stare from the prison officer was so intense it raised the hairs on the back of his neck—the man was huge, very muscular and had eyes that seemed to dare you to challenge him.

'Don't just stand there Lawson, get your arse over here!' he shouted across the room. John hurried to the desk and to his surprise the prison officer leaned over and whispered, 'You alright, John?' John looked at him with shock. 'Don't you recognise me? It's Gary, I sometimes work on the doors with Gary Sandland. You worked with us at one of the clubs in Southport.'

John tried to recall it, but before he could say anything, Gary shouted, 'In my office now, Lawson. MOVE!' John meekly followed him into the office.

The door slammed shut, and John sighed with relief when Gary smiled and said, 'Want to phone the missus?'

'Can I?'

'Sure, but make it quick. I'll make sure you get a cell to yourself. There's a lot of smackheads in here and you don't want to be mixing with them.' John couldn't believe his luck, and he called Jenny. The call went through without the usual instructions that precede calls from the cell blocks. He was careful not to mention Gary to Jenny, and asked her to call his mother and let her know he was okay.

'Right, outside Lawson!' Gary shouted at the top of his voice. 'Let's get you kitted out and into your cell; and watch yourself, I'll be keeping an eye on you.'

True to his word Gary put him in a cell on his own. There was the usual slopping out and the proverbial run to collect his meals, but John managed to settle into the routine with Gary keeping an eye on him.

But four days later he was moved to Kirkham open prison. It had originally been a Royal Air Force base, and became the main armament training centre before being taken over by the Home Office and converted into an open prison.

The billets consisted of sixteen beds, eight along each side, each with a bedside table and locker. At the end of the billet was a toilet and shower room. There was a recreation room as well as a television room. John was allocated bed one in billet two. This time he discovered that Jay's father, Alan, was working there. Alan was a civilian employee in charge of the canteen and lived no more than three hundred yards from the prison.

The inmates were offered educational courses such as woodworking, painting and decorating and horticulture, none of which appealed to John. But as luck would have it he was offered the job of wing runner, which meant sitting outside the chief prison officer's office waiting to be called to take messages to other prison officers, or to tell an inmate to report somewhere or other. The beauty was that it allowed him to roam around the prison without being constantly checked. When he was checked, he would simply say, 'Wing runner, on my way to deliver a message, boss.'

Jay was still working at JFK's while awaiting trial, and sometimes helped his father with prison deliveries. During one such a delivery he managed to steal a load of phone cards and arranged to drop some off for John. He got a message through to John that he would pack them into a crushed Coca Cola can and toss it over the fence of the sports field at midnight when security was most relaxed. All John had to do was to get up very early the next morning, pretend to go for some running exercises and retrieve the can, which he did. He tucked the can into his shirt and made his way back to the billet.

There were twenty phone cards in the tin, and John was rich. Not only could he make as many calls as he wanted, it wasn't long before he was selling cards and buying whatever he wanted, including a Sony Walkman for two phone cards.

The chief prison officer decided he needed another wing runner and a new inmate appeared when John arrived for duty in the morning. He was a huge black man, with muscles seeming to bulge from every part of his body. His head was shaved smooth and shone in the light. 'Alright mate, I'm Robbie,' he said, in a Northern accent, offering his massive hand.

'Hi, I'm John.' There was no mistaking the power in Robbie's hand.

'So what you in for?' Robbie asked, settling his heavy frame into the seat next to John.

'Bit blooming silly, really. I was running a video shop and got four months; not for selling pornography but for selling porn without it being certificated. What about you, what you in for?'

'Oh, a bit of wheeling and dealing that went wrong. Finished up getting six months.'

'You look seriously fit. You do a lot of training?'

'Yeah, I try to. Karate. I represented Britain a few times, but now I'm into property; buying, selling and renting out anything to make a few bob. What about you, you still going to run the video shop when you get out?'

'Nope. They closed it down and seized most of the stock. We'd only been open a couple of days.'

'So what are you thinking of doing?'

'Well, before opening the shop I was a bouncer. Had a hard crew that was sent in to sort out clubs where the local bouncers couldn't keep trouble makers out.'

'LAWSON!' John suddenly heard his name being shouted out by the chief prison officer.

'Listen, I know some people who could use you and your mates. We'll talk more when we get a chance,' Robbie said, and John hurried into the office.

It was John's birthday on the 28th of October, and unbeknown to him Jay had set up a collection at JFK's to buy some booze to smuggle into the prison. He planned to sneak in and drop the parcel in the bushes behind a bench in the garden area that was used for the horticultural courses. It was beautifully laid out with flower beds, stone patios with benches and several clumps of bushes—the ideal place to stash booty.

There was an amazing selection of whisky, vodka and brandy, as well as some beer. The problem now was getting the booze to his room, and having built up a trusting relationship with Robbie, John decided he was the one to help him. John donned his donkey jacket with large pockets, and while Robbie kept a lookout he stuffed the beer bottles into the pockets before tucking two bottles of whisky down the front of his jeans, and a bottle of brandy for Robbie. Loaded up, they carefully made their way back up the garden, but stopped in their tracks when they saw one of the prison wardens walking straight towards them.

'Oh boy, we're in for it,' John said, as he felt one of the whisky bottles slipping down the front of his jeans and making the zip of his flies slide down.

'And what are you two up to, wandering around out here?' the warden demanded.

'We're wing runners and we've been delivering messages for the CPO; we're just on our way back, boss,' John answered, feeling the bottle pressing harder and causing the zip to slide further down. He noticed the warden glance at his groin with a curious look on his face. The bottom of the bottle was just peeking out, as if John's privates were about to pop out. The warden, aware that John saw what he was staring at, quickly raised his eyes, not wanting to be accused of inappropriate behaviour.

'Sorry boss, I've just been to the toilet, forgot to do myself up,' John said, pushing the bottle in and quickly pulling up the zip.

'Right lad, next time make sure you're tidy before you leave the toilet,' the warden said, and walked on.

As they walked off, the zipper started opening again and this time the bottle slipped right out, but John managed to catch it just before it hit the ground.

Robbie looked at him in horror. 'Don't you ever do that to me again; we could have got nicked big time.'

'Well we weren't, and just think, we can have ourselves a nice little drink tonight and for several nights after.'

With a good supply of booze and the luxuries bought with the phone cards, the rest of John's short stay went smoothly.

John became fascinated by what Robbie told him about VAT swindles that crooked businesses were perpetrating on a massive scale. He explained how they would set up a group of companies in Europe and then one company would order a million pounds worth of electrical goods from another; that company would then export the goods in a large container and claim the VAT back. The trick was that the container would be empty. They earned millions this way, elevating them to gangster status, until Her Majesty's Customs found out about it and closed the loophole. But some of the crooks became greedy and started cheating on their partners in crime, and the result was that enforcers were sent in to try and retrieve the stolen millions.

Robbie saw John's interest; he warned him that it was a dangerous business, but that the rewards more than compensated for the risks.

'Listen Robbie, I'm out next week and you'll be out a few weeks later. Let's meet up and sort out some serious business,' John said, exhilarated by the thought of the millions up for grabs.

CHAPTER 31

A ROLLING STONE GATHERS JOHN

1999

It saddened John to learn that Jay got three years in Manchester's Strangeways prison in the same week he was released from Kirkham, but he knew that if Jay kept his nose clean he would only do eighteen months. He resolved to go and visit Jay once he'd got his own life sorted out.

Soon after his release John was on his way home from the shops one day, when he saw Daniel and Siobhan playing with their neighbours' children, which pleased him. But the smile drained from his face when one of the boys started chasing a girl with a stick and shouting in the foulest and most obscene language what he was going to do to her when he caught her. The girl was no better, using the same obscenities while running away from him. John rushed to his children, took them both by the hand and dragged them back indoors before they could protest. By the time he got to the kitchen where Jenny was preparing dinner, Siobhan was crying and struggling to free herself. 'What on earth is going on?' Jenny asked, and John released his grip on them.

'I'm not having my children swearing and behaving like the kids around here! You should've heard the language, it was disgusting! It was worse than what I've heard the heavies use.'

'That's the one thing I've always admired about you; with all the things you get up to—and I'm sure I don't know the half of it—you don't swear. So what do you propose we do about it? We can't live in isolation.' Jenny continued preparing the dinner.

'But we can get the heck away from here and move somewhere a little more decent.'

'Such as?'

'Such as Scotland. I've always wanted to go back there; I hate Birkenhead. There's nothing for us here, and it's riddled with crime and drugs.'

Jenny looked gloomy. 'But we've spent a small fortune doing this place up. You want us to just walk out and leave it?'

John took both her hands and looked into her eyes. 'Yes, let's go; let's start all over. You like Scotland as much as I do. I love you and the kids and I don't want anything ever to happen to any of you. We have Daniel, Siobhan and Arran to think about, and the one on the way. I don't like the idea of them being brought up here.' John's voice was warm and tinged with sadness.

A look of sympathy flashed across Jenny's face and she broke into a smile. 'You're right, but if we're going to do it, let's do it before I'm too far gone and not able to cope with a move.'

After dinner they went online in search of rental properties. 'This one looks good,' Jenny eventually said, pointing at an advertisement of a three-bedroomed house in Wallyford near Musselburgh. 'I know the area and it's nice.'

John contacted the landlord and in February 1999 they moved, leaving Birkenhead well behind.

Arran celebrated his first birthday in March 2000 and a month later John had to rush Jenny to the Edinburgh maternity hospital in the early hours of the morning. She gave birth to a healthy boy and like Arran, Lewis was also named after a Scottish isle.

'Well, that's Arran and Lewis; what's the next one, Skye?' John quipped, overjoyed at the birth of another son.

'You've got to be joking. That's it, no more,' Jenny said emphatically.

Once they had settled in and the children's schooling arranged, John set about looking for work. He found a job with Rock Steady Security, a company that handled many of the doors in Edinburgh, as well as providing security at rock concerts.

His first job was at Club Thirty in Frederick Street, Edinburgh. It was fairly routine work, with very little trouble. Then the area manager called John in and explained that they had been contracted to provide security for a Rolling Stones concert at Murrayfield Stadium, the home of the Scottish Rugby Union. He wanted John in the team to bodyguard the Stones at the Balmoral Hotel on Princes Street when they came up in June. He was paired with Achi, a tough Israeli ex-soldier trained in the skills of Krav Maga, an unarmed combat technique developed by the Israeli military. Achi was a man you wouldn't want to pick an argument with.

John was assigned to Keith Richards' suite and Achi to Ronnie Wood's. It was a boring job—twelve hour shifts, mainly sitting in the corridor outside the suite to ensure that no unauthorised person came anywhere near. There was always the threat of crazed female fans or the press trying to sneak in.

On the third night the fire alarm went off and everyone was ordered to evacuate the hotel. John banged on Keith Richards' door and led him and his PA down the stairs towards the fire exit. He was about to take them outside when he spotted a group of paparazzi, all waiting with their cameras at the ready. 'I think this is a ruse to get you out onto the street. You'll be much safer in here,' John said, hustling them into a small corridor and keeping them there until the all clear sounded.

One reporter managed to sneak in, but before he could take a picture, John spun him around and pushed him out through the fire exit, slamming it shut and guiding Keith and his PA back to their rooms.

The following morning John McCallum, head of the Rolling Stones' security team, invited John to breakfast, having been told how he had prevented the paparazzi from getting to Keith. Big John, as McCallum was known, offered John a permanent job on the security team. But having just settled in Scotland, and with a new baby, John knew Jenny wouldn't take kindly to him touring around the country and abroad, and he reluctantly turned down the offer.

So now John and Jenny had four children, which meant they needed a bigger house. By chance John was introduced to a mortgage adviser who told him he could arrange a mortgage for a fee of £500. He would produce false pay slips and bank statements, and all John had to do was to come up with the deposit.

The pay slips and bank statements were good forgeries, but the deposit wasn't going to be that easy. The sporadic work John was getting on the doors wasn't even enough to cover their domestic expenses. But, as always seemed to happen when John was in need, opportunity came out of the blue. While he was working the door at Club Thirty, one of the drug dealers told John one night that he was having a run-in with another drug dealer who worked for his rival, Mikey McGraw. He had started encroaching on his territory and needed to be taught a lesson.

'I can take care of him if you like,' John offered, remembering how Jay had dealt with Pedro and walked away with a tidy sum of money. 'But whatever money I take is mine,' he added.

'You're welcome to it,' the dealer agreed. 'I'm not interested in the money, I just want him given a good hiding.'

The target lived on the notorious Niddrie Housing Estate, where the film *Trainspotting* had been shot. It was one of the worst, most drug-riddled communities in Scotland. The man had two bull terriers at his house, as burglaries and car thefts were rife on the estate, so John thought it wiser to wait for him at the club once he had done his night's dealings. It also meant he would have a good stash of money on him.

The chance came on a Saturday night when the dealer slipped out through the rear exit into the courtyard. 'I've got to make a quick phone call,' John said to the doorman working with him, and hurried to the rear exit.

The drug dealer was scrolling through his mobile, unaware of John creeping up on him. Suddenly he became aware of movement behind him, turned and looked up, and John caught him with a solid right to the jaw. He collapsed unconscious to the ground. John quickly relieved him of all the notes crammed into his pockets, hurried to the front of the club and casually strolled back to his position at the door.

John went home that night several thousand pounds richer—enough for the deposit. All he had to do now was to find the house.

CHAPTER 32

TRAFFICKERS AND PIMPS

John found the perfect house in Port Seton on the coast of the Firth of Forth, four miles north east of Musselburgh. It cost ninety three thousand pounds and with the back hand payment to the dodgy mortgage broker John was able to obtain a ninety percent mortgage.

Jenny was delighted to be living in a more respectable neighbourhood. The house had four bedrooms, with an en suite master bedroom. There was a spacious living area on the ground floor, a large and fully fitted kitchen, and an integral garage where John could store his beloved chopper motorbike.

What little financial resources John had in the bank had been used up in the move to Port Seton. They were now living in a posh area, but John had to earn enough to pay the £650 monthly mortgage instalment as well as to feed and clothe his family. To help cover the costs, Jenny went back to working as a bus driver. Despite his security job at Rock Steady and working the doors at local nightclubs, John needed to find more ways to supplement their income.

It came in the form of a call from Uncle George, who told him he had sacked Gary, who had been managing the massage parlour. 'I need someone quick and the only person I feel I can trust is you,' George explained. It was an exciting offer, for John still had the urge for something bigger, something challenging and with more money. But having just moved home, he felt he couldn't accept it without at least discussing it with Jenny.

Jenny knew full well that massage parlour was a euphemism for a brothel, but John explained that his uncle would provide him with a rent-free apartment and that he would come home every weekend. The £1,100 cash was more than he could ever hope to earn locally. It also meant Jenny would be able to give up her job. Reluctantly she agreed, having extracted a promise from John that there would be no monkey business with the girls.

Steam & Sun was situated around the corner from Euston Station in London. It was in a dreadful state—the rooms were filthy and the girls—mainly Albanians and Ukrainians—were almost all on drugs and paying scant attention to their personal hygiene. To compound the problems, his uncle was drinking heavily and smoking vast amounts of hash, leaving John to make all the decisions.

He started by refurbishing the rooms, replacing the sauna and showers and creating a friendlier, sexier interior. The next step was to get rid of all the girls who worked for pimps.

The pimps would wait outside in the early hours of the morning to collect the money their girls had earned, and there would always be shouting and fighting when this happened.

John discovered the pimps had been paying Gary fifty pounds a night for each of their girls to work there, earning Gary a good five hundred pounds a night over and above his wages.

The pimps were obviously furious when John sacked their girls and tried to negotiate a deal with him, even offering him a share of their income as they had done with Gary, but he turned them down, as he was determined to go upmarket and bring in a better class of girl, not controlled by pimps.

From experience John knew the pimps could cause a lot of trouble and he felt he needed his old friend, his 9 mm Browning with him as a precaution, as well as fifty rounds of ammunition.

His instincts were right, and around midnight one night there was heavy banging on the front door. John looked through his window, which was directly above the front door, and saw the group of Albanian pimps shouting for him to come out. He tucked his gun into the back of his jeans and went out to confront them.

'We not happy. You listen good, we cut you up if you don't let girls back!' one of the pimps called out, waving a large knife.

John met his glare and said in a low voice, 'You don't bring a knife to a gunfight.'

'You try be funny. I can cut you to pieces with this,' the pimp threatened. 'This is London not Albania, you don't have gun,' he challenged, flicking the knife threateningly from one hand to the other.

John reached behind him, pulled out the gun, cocked it and aimed it at the pimp. 'Drop the knife NOW!' John said as he walked towards the pimp with the gun pointing directly at his face. The rest of the men turned and ran away and the pimp's knife clattered onto the pavement. John walked up to him and smashed him on the nose with the butt of the Browning. Blood splattered across his face. 'You're right, this is not Albania, it's London. Now get lost before I put a bullet through that thick skull of yours.'

The showdown was over—the pimp turned and walked away without another word.

Every girl at the massage parlour had a story. Nikita was a beautiful blonde with an innocent face and a well shaped body. She came from a small village in the Ukraine. She told John that she was from a poor family and her boyfriend, who had promised to marry her, ran off when she fell pregnant. Desperate to find a job to support her son, she found an employment agency that offered jobs as au pairs in the UK. Soon she was on her way to St. Petersburg, where the agency arranged her passport and paid her air fare.

When she arrived in the UK, she was herded into a room with some other girls and told she would have to work as a prostitute to pay back the thousands of pounds they had spent on her. When she refused, she was beaten, raped, locked up and refused food until she complied.

Something pricked at John's conscience, and he heard himself say, 'I'd like to help you.'

'No, you can't; nobody can,' she said, looking up at him for a moment, before burying her face back in her hands. 'They said they would kill my family and my son if I try to escape. They know where my family lives.'

This is the story of her life and in some ways it mirrors in my own, John thought. Terrible images of girls being beaten and raped flashed through his mind and struck him like little electric shocks. He was running a brothel; he was a link in this chain, so how could he claim to worry about their plight?

It's not my problem. My problem is to make sure they turn up on time and satisfy the clients. This is a business, a means of making money, he thought. He had to be strong, otherwise everything could be taken away from him, and he wasn't prepared to have that happen. He straightened up, determined to get on with the business of running a brothel.

One Friday evening a couple of smartly dressed Eastern European men walked into the club's reception area with a strange request. The receptionist buzzed John, who could see the men on the CCTV, and he rushed downstairs. One of the men introduced himself as Nicos and explained that his friend Luka was desperately looking for his wife who had run off after an argument, and he feared she might have got herself involved in prostitution and was possibly working there.

Luka took a photograph from his pocket and showed it to John. 'There's no one here that looks anything like her,' John assured him.

'Would it be possible to have a look around and speak to some of the girls who perhaps may have seen her?' Nicos asked. 'She could have changed her appearance that you perhaps wouldn't notice, but Luka would.'

John hesitated. To him they looked like men with a military background, turned gangster. They were dressed in smart Armani suits, expensive shoes and wore gold Rolex watches, but there was a harshness about them that put him on his guard.

'Okay, as long as you're quick about it,' John agreed, thinking it would be better to let them see that the girl was not there, rather than refusing and having trouble.

While they were talking to the girls and showing the photograph around, John noticed that the two men seemed to adopt a more aggressive manner, which caused some of the girls to become agitated.

'Right, that's enough, you've seen the girl is not here, so time's up,' John said, starting to usher then out.

As they got to the front door, Nicos turned to John and said, 'We don't believe you.'

'I don't care what you believe. You've seen she's not here, so be on your way.' John watched them get into a black Mercedes with blacked out windows and drive off.

When John asked the girls why they had been nervous, they explained that the men were not looking for a wife, but for one of their girls who had run off and started working independently. They said the men were part of a Croatian Mafia gang, which gave John the uncomfortable feeling that he would be hearing from them again.

It happened sooner than John had anticipated, when two hours later a fleet of five black Mercedes Benzes turned in to Charlton Street. Nicos and Luka got out of the first car, quickly followed by ten more men, all well dressed. One of them stood out as the boss, having had the car door opened for him, and the other men forming a protective shield around him.

They're coming to break the place apart, to teach me a lesson, John thought, then suddenly remembered what he had done with the Yardies.

He took the Browning from its hiding place. *'If I go down I'll take a few of them with me,'* he said to himself as he filled the magazine, stuck the gun in the back of his jeans and made his way out.

There was an uneasy silence as he strode towards Nicos and Luka. Some of the men with them reached for their guns inside their coats. 'Let's go inside and sort this out,' John said calmly. He turned around and walked inside.

Once in the office, he said, 'Look, whatever you think is going on, I want to assure you we are no threat to your operations. And to prove it I'm going to take my gun out and put it on the...'

'You're carrying?' Nicos was obviously surprised.

'Of course, you don't think I'd go out there naked, do you?'John pressed the clip to release the magazine and laid it all on the coffee table. 'Listen, you might not know it, but we're a major outfit; we're connected with the Smith family, I guess you know who they are. We run the brothel, the sex clubs, the peep shows and the hostess bars; you run the girls, so there's no conflict. You came in here with a bullcrap story about a wife when you were in fact looking for one of your runaways. You saw that she's not here. She's never worked here and if you leave me your details I'll happily let you know if she turns up looking for work.'

'Okay, we'll take your word for it,' Nicos said, turning to leave.

John followed them out, leaving the gun and ammunition on the table. He watched as Nicos and Luka walked to the boss, obviously explaining what had taken place. The boss looked across at John and beckoned him with his finger. Up close John thought that he looked a lot like Marlon Brando in *The Godfather*.

'I respect you for the way you behaved and I see you're not a threat to our business, so this matter is ended. Omogućuje dobiti odavde,' he said to his men. He turned, waited for the car door to be opened and got in.

Once back in his office John stood staring down at the gun and ammunition on the table, amazed that he had managed to pacify a gang that was way out of his league.

The incident enhanced his reputation considerably, and the girls in particular were feeling a lot safer.

'O sole mio, sta' nfronte a te! O sole, o sole mio, sta' nfronte a te, sta' nfronte a te!' Giovanni's voice bellowed out, echoing in the stairway as he made his way up to his room. Giovanni had been a thorn in John's side since becoming manager. He had been a tenant in the flats before the place was taken over and simply refused to move out. George had tried to oust him several times, but he didn't want to upset the Italian Mafia that ran a series of lucrative cons in Oxford Street on unsuspecting tourists and Giovanni was one of their drivers. The truth was that they disliked him as much as George did and would have been happy to get rid of him anyway.

Hearing him singing away as if he didn't have a care in the world aggravated John more than usual, particularly because it was so soon after the confrontation with the Croatians. He grabbed his gun from the table, loaded the magazine and stormed downstairs to the Italian's room. He hammered on the door and shouted, 'Giovanni! I want you out of here today!'

Giovanni opened the door and snarled at John in broken English, 'You anda 'o elsa? I'ma going nowhere, I'ma connected with...'

John raised the gun and said, 'Yes you are, and you're going to be connected permanently with the lead in this gun if you don't get the heck out of here today.'

'You willa needa lawyer to getta me outta here,' Giovanni said, and slammed the door.

'I've got the best lawyer there is; his name is Browning,' John said, firing five shots into the framework above the door. 'You'd be better off getting a funeral director, you stupid wop!'

'Okay, okay! I'a move, I'a go tonight, I'a promise,' Giovanni shouted from inside the room.

John walked off, feeling a little calmer. He would now have a room to accommodate the extra security person he knew he was going to need.

On his next weekend at home John met up with Chris, who had worked the doors with him. Chris was a decent guy and reliable enough. He and his girlfriend Lauren were both biker types and into heavy rock. Lauren's blonde hair and good looks belied her toughness, and John offered her a job as receptionist, knowing that Chris would be more inclined to move to London if she could go along.

Chris and Lauren moved into the flat that Giovanni had vacated, and settled into the operation very quickly. John was now able to concentrate on running the business instead of having to check on security around the clock.

One evening Lauren buzzed John to tell him there was trouble at reception. John rushed down to find an arrogant young guy with a cockney accent shouting about being ripped off, claiming to have paid a taxi driver for his evening's entertainment at the club.

John tried to explain that the cab driver had nothing to do with the parlour and it was the cabbie who had ripped him off, but the man would have none of it and was getting more aggressive.

The ease with which John had dealt with the Croatian gang, combined with his frustration at having to work so far away from home, made him deal with the man in a very different way. He hit him with such force that he spun around, his face catching the door frame and breaking two teeth. Then John grabbed hold of him and threw him out into the street.

To make sure that he wouldn't attempt to come back in, John watched him on the CCTV and saw him get to his feet, wrench up a loose paving stone and hurl it at one of the windows, shattering it.

John ran upstairs, grabbed his gun, rushed outside and pointed it at the man's head. 'If you don't get away from here now I'm going to blow your head off!' he shouted. The man ran off, but stopped further up the street and took out his mobile. A spark of fear hit John as he realised the man could be phoning the police. He rushed back to his room, wiped his fingerprints off the gun and threw it out of the window, into the alley behind the building. By now he could hear the wailing of sirens approaching.

The police quickly sealed the street off before bursting into the massage parlour. 'Where's the gun?' the policeman demanded, as he and the rest of the armed response unit charged in.

'There aren't any guns around here,' John said calmly.

'There's been a report that you threatened a man with a gun...'

'No officer, I only pointed this at him,' John cut in, holding up his walkie talkie. 'He's drunk and obviously thought it was a gun.'

'Well, that may be, but we have to carry out a search,' the officer insisted.

'Help yourselves, but you won't find anything,' John said with an air of confidence.

They didn't find the gun, but they did find an old replica gun case on top of the wardrobe that belonged to the previous manager, and John was arrested.

What an idiot I've been. I just hope Cecil can get me off of this one, John thought as he was driven off to Camden police station.

'We've got the gun case, and it's being examined by...' the detective constable began, but Cecil Watkins cut in angrily, shaking his head and causing the usual dandruff to settle on the shoulders of his crumpled suit. 'And that's all you have, an old replica case, no gun, no bullets. I guarantee that you will not find my client's prints on that case; it belonged to the previous tenant.'

'We have a detailed statement from the victim that your client threatened him with a gun,' the detective constable persisted.

'Victim? The man was drunk and high on cocaine! He smashed a window, and when my client tried to calm him, he simply mistook his walkie talkie for a gun. You have no reason to hold my client and I demand he be released!'

The detective looked at Cecil and then at John, knowing he had to let John go.

'Thanks Cecil,' John said as they drove off in a taxi.

'Blooming fool, what were you thinking, brandishing a gun in the street?'

'I just lost my rag; he was behaving like an idiot.'

'And so were you! You have to report back in a week, so let's just hope the idiot doesn't want to pursue the allegations.'

Three days later John received a phone call and immediately recognised the voice. He instinctively switched the phone to speaker, took the voice recorder from the drawer and switched it on. 'What do you want?' he asked.

'Just thought I'd let you know I'm going to have my day in court. You broke two of my teeth, you scum.' The man's voice was thick with rage.

'Fine by me. I hope your wife enjoys it. I'm sure she'll be very interested to learn you'd come to a brothel all drugged up and looking for a prostitute.'

John heard a faint intake of breath and then a pause. 'Okay, I tell you what,' the man said, 'you bung me five grand and I won't give evidence.'

John gave a little laugh. 'I tell you what, you don't give evidence and I won't play this recording to the police of you trying to bribe me.'

This time there was a louder intake of breath. 'You telling me you've been recording this conversation?'

'Yes, listen to yourself, you plonker. You think you can get one over on me?' John said, and pressed the playback button. After a few seconds the phone went dead.

A few days later Cecil phoned to say the man had withdrawn his allegations, admitting he could have been mistaken in thinking it was a gun.

CHAPTER 33

DISHONOUR AMONG THIEVES

2000

In their bid to close down the peep shows and hostess bars in Soho, the Council used a compulsory purchase order to buy the building on the corner of Wardour and Brewer Streets where the Erotica club was situated. They also bought the ground floor and basement of the Phoenix in Moor Street. They paid millions for the properties, but still got them well below their market value. Tony and Dave were not too pleased, but it did make them a small fortune. They still owned the apartments upstairs and decided to rent them out to prostitutes, which provided them with a steady income.

But George was drinking more and more and increasing his drug use, which made him very difficult to deal with. Totally out of his mind on skunk weed and fuelled by whiskey, he dropped off a carrier bag containing twelve grand for John to look after. He came back the next day and said he had lost the money, but when John explained he had put it in the safe, and called his uncle a drunk, an argument developed. The situation got out of control and John realised one of them was going to get seriously hurt if he stayed on any longer. So he packed his bags and left, bringing an abrupt and sad end to their relationship.

Back in Scotland, John needed to find work again. He got his old job back at Mad Dogs, where he met up with Michael Chamberlain, a South African ex-Special Forces soldier, now living in Scotland with his wife Cara. Michael looked like a Samurai warrior, which was quite apt, as he was skilled in Aikido.

Once again John contacted Robbie, who said he had a job John might be interested in. He explained that there was a businessman, simply referred to as 'the German', who was very wealthy, with a fleet of expensive cars and his own helicopter, who was into VAT fraud in a big way. Like many others he had found a loophole in the law and had set up a most sophisticated scam that was known as the Carousel Fraud, involving millions of pounds worth of goods, mainly mobile phones and computer chips. Purchased free of VAT on the Continent, they were then sold on in the UK with the VAT added, which was then claimed back from Inland Revenue. But the goods were never sold for consumption in the UK, and simply passed through a series of companies before being exported back out of the UK. The same goods were then re-imported, and so the goods went round and round, repeating the fraud many times over. The goods were circulated as many as thirty five times before the company at the centre of the transactions disappeared from the records, having by then claimed millions of pounds in VAT.

The problem, Robbie went on to explain, was that the German had been working with a local gangster in the North East, known as Spider, who got greedy and decided to go on his own. He had started up companies using the German's identity and made a few million before running off to Benidorm in Spain with the proceeds. But he left a trail that Customs and Excise caught on to, with the result that the loophole was firmly closed. Robbie further explained that Lloyd, a bouncer friend of his, who was the principal contact man for the German, had been to Spider's apartment in Benidorm and said the place was full of shoe boxes stuffed with fifty pound notes. It was impossible to guess how much money was stashed in each box, let alone how many boxes there were, but he estimated at least a hundred or more.

The deal the German was offering was that he was more interested in teaching Spider a lesson than in the money, and he was happy to split it with whoever was willing to carry out the job.

This was music to John's ears and he immediately contacted Jay, who was now out of prison and looking for work. He also spoke to Michael Chamberlain to find out if they were interested in a profitable trip to Spain. They said yes and went with John to meet Robbie and Lloyd at a restaurant at a service station on the M6 in Staffordshire.

Lloyd was a big black guy with a tough, expressive face. He explained that there were more people who owed the German millions of pounds. One in particular had already been questioned by the police and the German was worried that his assets might be frozen before he got his money back.

John was intrigued. 'When are we going to meet this German?' he asked.

'Actually, he's been watching you from the other side of the restaurant,' Lloyd said, motioning the German to come over. A smart looking, middle aged man slowly made his way to their table. He was clean shaven and wearing an expensive suit with a white silk shirt, the cuffs displaying solid gold cufflinks. On his right wrist he wore a Rolex Oyster.

'Guten Tag Meine Herren,' he greeted them. 'Please don't get up, there's no need for formalities. Let us get on with the business at hand.' He studied each one of them as he pulled up a chair and sat down. He turned his gaze to John, reached into his jacket pocket and handed him a slip of paper. 'Here is the man's address and this is the code number to a Swiss bank account. Guard it with your life. You will force der dieb, sorry I mean the thief, who you only need to know as David, to transfer thirteen million pounds from his bank accounts in South Africa. Anything you find in the house—jewellery, silverware or cash—you may keep. Also, I will pay you ten per cent of the thirteen million pounds once it has been successfully transferred to the Swiss bank account.'

'Make it twenty percent and we'll get the job done,' John said with a confident smile.

'Agreed, as I anticipated,' the German said with a smug smile.

John looked at the others to gauge their reaction and was quickly assured by the looks on their faces they were all up for it. The fact that the job was in the North East, much nearer to home, was an added incentive and if successful they could then take down Spider and the others.

The team headed off to the address the German had given them to start planning the operation. It was a large mansion set in vast grounds, surrounded on three sides by security fencing and on the fourth side there was a low brick wall bordering a churchyard. The large back garden had a rear gate leading to a narrow lane, which was covered by CCTV. The main entrance had an electronically operated iron gate and the entire area was also covered by cameras. In the driveway was an array of expensive cars, including a Lamborghini, a Ferrari, a Bentley, a Rolls Royce and two Range Rovers.

Because this was a big job, John felt they would need an extra pair of hands, so he got in touch with Darren, the bouncer from Birkenhead, who was very happy to join the team.

Next they started working on the most effective way of getting into the house unnoticed. Jay reminded John of the time they had worked as extras on the TV show *Prime Suspect*, when the public took them to be policemen, and suggested they dress up like police doing a raid. It was decided that only Jay would dress in uniform and the others would dress like plain clothes detectives and carry fake IDs. They would also all carry walkie talkies.

One week later the job was on. John, Jay and Michael hid in a disused building a few miles away and waited for the all clear call from the surveillance guy Darren, who was hiding in the field next to the house. But Darren couldn't get a signal on his mobile which forced him to break protocol and move to where he could tell John that the early morning would be the best time to make the raid, as David, his girlfriend and two friends had been partying all night had now crashed out.

John, Jay and Michael headed down to the churchyard next to the house. Darren was told to go to the motorway service station to monitor police radio signals and to let them know if any of them were coming their way.

Jay put on the police uniform while John and Michael, dressed in plain clothes, pulled stockings over their heads and kept them hidden under the baseball caps they were wearing. They carefully made their way over the churchyard wall to the back entrance, avoiding the security cameras. To their surprise the back door was unlocked and they were able to move in without a sound, not even having to pretend it was a police raid. *This is going to be easy*, John thought as they slipped silently into the hallway. But then he heard the sounds of a television, and he raised his hand to stop the others from moving forward. John recognised the voices of the Teletubbies and the sound of children laughing. His shock turned to horror when he spotted children's shoes and little suitcases standing at the bottom of a staircase, as if the kids were ready to travel somewhere.

John froze for a moment, then turned to the others and ran his hand across his throat as a silent indication to stop what they were doing. 'Stand down,' he whispered, and they turned around and made their way quietly back to the churchyard.

'What the heck was that all about?' Jay demanded.

'It's one thing beating up a man and holding him and his friends hostage, but it's another thing if children are involved. How the heck did Darren not spot the kids?' John said, anger and disappointment written all over his face.

'So what now?' Jay asked, frustration sounding in his voice.

'We'll try again, only this time we'll make sure there are no children around.'

Jay was incensed. 'I don't understand you going soft over a bunch of kids,' he said.

'Children in this situation are trouble. I've seen children hurt and I want no part of it. We'll do the job another time and this time we'll replace Darren with Tam Kelly.'

'Yeah, but will the German understand? He still hasn't got his money and we've got nothing out of it either.' Jay said, still exasperated.

Michael, who hadn't said anything, tried to appease Jay. 'John's right, we'll just have to try again. And don't forget there are still the other jobs the German wants done.'

Two weeks later the team were back on the job and John had decided this time they should all do the surveillance and take turns to keep watch. With a pair of high powered binoculars they were able to look in through the windows and were relieved to see David, a woman and two other men once again happily sipping champagne and sniffing cocaine until the early hours of the morning before stumbling off to their rooms.

While the team waited for them to settle down and fall asleep, they donned their outfits and hung their fake police badges around their necks. They made their way into the grounds the same way as before, but this time the door was locked and they had to force it open. The noise woke David, who came tearing down the stairs armed with an air rifle.

'Armed police, put the weapon down!' Jay shouted, raising a pistol. David stood frozen to the spot, staring at the 'police officer' who was aiming a weapon at him. 'This is a police raid, drop the weapon and get down on your knees,' Jay ordered him.

David slowly lowered the air rifle and sank to his knees, allowing John and Michael to move in and cuff him.

'You were arrested and questioned a few weeks ago regarding our investigation into VAT fraud and we're here to follow up on that. And the fact that you now threatened a police officer with a weapon will not help your situation,' John informed him, keeping his voice calm and formal.

'Right, you hold him here while we search the house,' Jay said to John, and the rest of the team moved up the staircase to check the bedrooms.

The pretty brunette in David's bed sat up and grabbed the duvet to cover her nakedness as Jay burst in. 'Oh thank goodness, I thought for a moment you were some gangsters that had broken in,' she exclaimed, and smiled at the policeman standing in front of her.

'It's alright Madam, we're here as part of an investigation and I would like you to remain here until we've completed our work. If you don't, you may find yourself being charged with interfering with an investigation. Do you understand?' Jay said gently.

'Yes, I understand officer, but I need to go to the toilet,' she said, shuffling to the edge of the bed.

'Right, hurry up, I'll wait for you,' Jay said, and watched her slip out of bed, dragging the duvet behind her. *Another time, another place*, he thought at the sight of her neat little bottom as she disappeared into the bathroom.

Michael and Tam found the two guests dead to the world. It took some time to wake them from their drunken stupor, handcuff them and drag them onto the landing where they made them lie face down and told them not to move or look up.

'The bird upstairs thinks we're real police and I've locked her in the toilet,' Jay said as he came back downstairs.

David strained his neck to look up. 'What do you mean she thinks you're real police?'"

'Keep your mouth shut,' John said, giving him a hefty kick in the ribs to emphasise the point before telling Jay to check the security system to see if they had been picked up by any of the cameras.

Jay found a bank of monitors and VHS video recorders in a small room that used to be a pantry, and discovered to his joy that none of the machines were running. 'Great security system you've got here, except the recorders aren't running,' he said when he got back to the hall.

'So you lot are not police, you're robbers!' David shouted. 'Well, you won't find any money here. All your efforts will be for nothing.'

'We've actually been sent by the German, and I guess you know what he wants,' John said, taking out his Browning and pressing it to David's head. 'We've come to collect the thirteen million pounds you owe him, so let's not waste any time. Where's your computer?' John pressed the barrel harder against his skin, and the man looked positively stricken.

'In the study at the end of the hallway,' David said, his voice trembling. Jay quickly found the laptop and brought it back to the hallway where John now had David on his knees on the floor.

'You're going to do a fast track transfer from your account in South Africa to this number in Switzerland. Here are the details,' John explained, and placed the laptop on the floor next to David.

'You've got to be kidding! I can't transfer that kind of money just like that. I'd have to speak to my dad in South Africa before I can do something like that.'

'Then speak to your dad, because understand this. We've gone to a lot of trouble to get this far and if you're going to be difficult, just remember, your bird and your two mates are upstairs and we won't hesitate to hurt them if we have to. So be sensible and phone your dear dad and be very careful what you say to him. One wrong word and your girlfriend will be the first to get it.'

David reached over and picked up the receiver, but as he started to tap in the number, a buzzer sounded.

'What the heck's that?' John asked.

David's face relaxed into a brief smile. 'That's someone at the main gate, so what are you going to do now?'

Jay hurried off to check the monitors. 'There's a guy with a white van at the main gate, what's he want?' he said as he rushed back in.

'We're having the place redecorated; he must be the painter,' David said while the buzzer kept sounding.

'How the heck didn't we spot that?' Jay asked nobody in particular.

'Because they're only starting today,' David said cockily. 'How are you going to explain your little escapade to him? I tell you what, why don't you lot just slip out and I promise I won't say anything to anyone.'

'Well, if the place is being redecorated it won't matter if there's blood splattered on the walls. So keep your mouth shut while I go and deal with him. Shoot him if he tries anything stupid,' John said, kicking David in the stomach before hurrying out and rolling the stocking back up under his cap.

John slipped his earpiece in as he approached the main gate, 'Bravo two, just checking, suspect at main gate, over,' he said out loud, pretending to be speaking into the walkie talkie and flashing his fake ID badge as he got to the gate.

The man glanced at the badge and asked, 'What's happening officer?'

'You must be the decorator scheduled for this week,' John said, ignoring the man's question.

'Yes, yes, that's right, I've come to start with the prep work, I always like getting an early...'

'Well, I'm afraid you won't be able to do anything today,' John interrupted him. 'There's a police operation in progress and the place is sealed off. Just wait here while I radio in your vehicle's registration number,' John said and read the number into his radio. While doing this he heard Michael's muffled voice talking anxiously to Jay.

'Right, your vehicle checks out, so turn around and be on your way and I suggest you check whether it will be okay for you to come back tomorrow.' John turned on his heels. As soon as he was out of sight, he pulled the stocking back over his face and drew his gun before making his way back to the house to find out what Michael's problem was.

Michael was talking about two women who had arrived at the back gate, and finding it locked, they climbed over it and were making their way up to the house. Michael wanted to know what to do. Jay, being the one wearing the uniform, confronted the ladies just as they entered the hallway. They explained that they were the house cleaners.

While Jay was trying to assure the women there was nothing to worry about, John burst in with the stocking over his face. It took the two ladies a few seconds to absorb the situation before one of them could speak. 'You're not really coppers are you?' she said nervously.

'No ladies, we're not, but don't worry, we're not here to harm you. But until our work is done here, we're going to have to restrain you. So if you don't do anything stupid, you won't get hurt.' John's attempt at reassuring them didn't do much to relax them.

They sat the two women down on chairs and tied them up, while John tried to pacify them with his calm voice. 'Now let's get on with our business, so we can all get out of here,' he said once they were securely tied up.

David realised he had no choice but to do what they had instructed him to do. He picked up the phone and tapped in the number.

'Put it on speaker,' John told him.

'Howzit, son?' they heard a voice answer. John immediately recognised the South African accent.

'Listen Dad, I'm in a spot of trouble and I need you to transfer thirteen million pounds to an account number I'm going to give you...'

'Thirteen million pounds! Are you out of your skull, what the heck do you want to do that for?' they heard the father shout.

'Dad, I don't have time to argue, I'm in trouble and if I don't transfer that money I could be in a lot more, so please just do as I say; we've got more than enough to cover it. And don't make it too obvious, take it from different accounts, okay?'

'Okay, but that'll take more time. I'll try to have it done by tomorrow.'

'No Dad, it must be done now, right now!'

'Sounds like you got a gun to your head.'

'In a manner of speaking I have, so just blooming well do it.'

When David hung up, John asked, 'Can you log into the accounts on your computer?'

'Yes I can.'

'Good, fire it up, so we can see it happening.'

'There's another car pulled up at the back gate,' they heard Tam's voice on the walkie talkie.

'What the blooming heck's happening here? Another bunch of early birds!' John exclaimed.

'That must be the kitchen fitter; he was also due to start today,' David said.

'The man's walking up to the house,' Tam's voice echoed.

'Right, I'll deal with him,' John said, hurrying out.

'Okay, now I just want the combination of the safe and then we're done with you,' John said when he got back. 'Better still, you go and open it.' He put the gun to David's head and cocked it.

David reluctantly walked over to the safe, applied the combination and opened it. John shoved him aside, reached in and took hold of the bundles of money stacked in neat piles. 'That's twenty eight grand there,' David said.

'That'll do nicely. You just get on with transferring the money, okay?' John said, clutching the bundles to his chest as he walked out to the lounge.

'Now, before we let you ladies go, we'd like to offer you some compensation for what you've been through. I'm giving each of you ten thousand pounds,' John announced, holding up some of the wads he was clutching. 'That's to help you forget this morning's edification, so you don't go running to the police. We can't let you leave for at least half an hour, so I suggest you sit quietly and count your good fortune,' he continued with a reassuring smile. 'Are we understood?'

The two women nodded as enthusiastically as their restrained movements would allow.

'Good, we'll untie you and I want you to try and relax while my friend here looks after you,' John said, pointing at Michael.

'There you are, four million has just gone through and the rest is processing, so we're done,' Jay said as he came out of the study and followed John into the kitchen.

'Don't forget to cut the landline,' John reminded him. 'Let's get the heck out here.'

'I just hope those old ducks don't blooming well go to the police,' Michael said as they drove off.

'No they won't, I gave the cleaners ten grand each, and...'

'You did what? You gave away twenty grand to the cleaners?' Jay shouted. 'What the heck does that leave us?'

'Listen lads, you've got two grand apiece and the big money is yet to come. Don't forget, we get twenty percent of the thirteen million, so you just work out how much that is for each of us.'

CHAPTER 34

THE SMELL OF FEAR

2001

The German was pleased with the outcome. He offered to set up an offshore account, so he could transfer the money and give them a code and password to access the account.

He immediately started talking about the next jobs—apart from Spider in Benidorm, there were three other guys from the Newcastle area who had cheated him out of seven million pounds, all of whom he wanted to be dealt with. If the team was up for it, he said, he wanted them kidnapped and brought to his factory in St. Austell in Cornwall.

The promise of another percentage of seven million pounds had John and his team champing at the bit. They met up at Tam Kelly's place, Oscar's Bar, got their gear together and set off for Newcastle. The three men they were targeting were called James, William and Steven. They only had James' address, because that was where all the transactions had taken place.

John had bought two relatively old cars that wouldn't draw attention to them. He installed a delayed action camera concealed in a shoe box on the back shelf of each of the cars, to record one photo every minute.

James' large semi-detached house was in an upmarket area on the outskirts of Newcastle, and John set up the first car outside the house to record the three men's activities. He parked the other car at the street entrance before joining Jay, Michael and Tam at a local hotel where they had booked in under false names.

Later that evening the team watched the recordings. 'That one must be James,' John said and pointed to a well-dressed, stocky man on the screen that fitted the description the German had given them.

'And that has to be William, that nerdy looking bloke,' Michael cut in as they continued to study the recording.

The third man never appeared on any of the recordings.

They felt it would be too risky to attempt a kidnapping in such a closed neighbourhood, and decided to follow the two men's movements the next day.

The men drove a bright red Porsche and stopped at a small factory on the edge of an industrial estate outside of Newcastle. It looked like the perfect place for a kidnapping, and the team decided to head back there the following week.

Back in Merseyside John set about finding a suitable vehicle. He was told about a man who specialised in modifying vans for bank robbers and drug dealers.

'Oakes's the name, hoax's the game, what can I do yer for?' Bill Oakes asked in a heavy cockney accent when John stepped into the tiny hut that was his office.

'I want a van with a sliding side door, panelled inside, with the walls and rear door windows all blacked out,' John told him.

'Shouldn't be a prob, give me a day or two and I'll see what I can come up wiv,' Bill promised.

Bill was as good as his word, and came up with a long-wheelbase Ford Transit, fitted out as John had requested, together with a fake tax disc and MOT certificate.

The team set off back to Newcastle having equipped themselves with police outfits, handcuffs, duct tape, cable ties, pillow cases, white overalls and slip-on shoes, a shotgun as well as John's 9mm pistol and two baseball bats.

The Porsche pulled up outside the factory and they waited until James and William were inside before driving the van up to the entrance. Using the same tactics as before, they charged in, with Jay dressed in the police uniform, shouting, 'Stay where you are! This is a police raid; place your hands behind your backs!'

With swift, practiced movements the team cuffed both men while Jay explained that they were being arrested as part of an ongoing investigation into VAT fraud. He was so word perfect and authoritative that the team had difficulty suppressing their laughter.

While Michael and Tam held onto the men, John made a quick search of the premises for anything worth taking, but found nothing. 'Right, we're taking you to the police station for questioning. A police team and customs officials will come and search this place and your home. Let's get them out of here,' Jay continued.

'What about my Porsche?' James asked as he and William were marched out to the van.

'Where are the keys?' John demanded.

'In my pocket,' William replied.

John took the keys. 'Right, I'll put them on the bench just inside the door and we'll radio HQ to deal with it when they arrive,' he said.

The two men were hauled into the back of the van and made to sit cross-legged. John and Jay got in and stood either side of them. Tam and Michael sat up front with Tam driving.

As they moved off, James' eyes narrowed with undisguised malice and he said, 'You're not police, are you? Where are you taking us?'

'Shut your mouth, you'll find out soon enough,' John snarled.

'You don't know who you're dealing with; you'll pay for this.'

'It's more like the other way round, you don't know who you're dealing with,' Jay said, reaching up to the shelf above the two men and grabbing hold of one of the baseball bats.

John restrained Jay's hand, fearing that he would be too heavy-handed, and said with a steely glare, 'Leave this to me.' Like a reprimanded child Jay let go of the bat.

'You think you can frighten us with that thing. That's nothing to what will happen to you lot when we get out of here,' James said vehemently.

John had seen that look before and knew what it meant to those who were unlucky enough to be on the receiving end of it. He whacked James with a measured blow to the head. As blood started to flow from the wound opening up on James' forehead, Jay said, 'And you warned me to keep them in one piece!'

'You lot don't know what you're dealing with...' William stuttered and John hit him across the nose and then across the top of his head, and blood started gushing from his nose. He let out a blood-curdling scream.

'I won't tell you to shut your gob again. Open it and you'll get more of this,' John said, caressing the baseball bat. 'I think we should put the hoods on them,' he said to Jay.

'Are you going to kill us?' William sobbed.

'No, we're taking you to the German; he's peed off with you lot for stealing seven million pounds from him and he wants it back.' A smile twisted John's lips as he looked at their agitated faces. 'You thought you could get away with it, like all you thieves, but the thing about luck is, it eventually runs out, and yours ran out today.'

'We can sort it out with the German. It was just a misunderstanding, that's all. When we explain he'll understand, you'll see,' James said, but John could see in his face that he knew it was a useless plea.

'I've had enough of this! Put the hoods on them or I'll beat them to death.' Jay was ready to swing the baseball bat. He grabbed William by the throat and pulled the pillowcase over his head, causing William to lose control of his bowels. This seemed to amuse Jay. 'What the heck is that smell? Aw, have you popped your pants, little boy?

'There's a police car approaching, with lights flashing and siren blaring; you want us to pull off here?' Michael called over the walkie talkie.

'We can hear it. Just keep calm and tell Tam to keep going but don't speed up.' James and William had started to shuffle about when they heard the siren approaching, so Jay held the shotgun to William's head as John shoved the pistol against James' temple.

'Either one of you make a noise or try to get up and it'll be the last move you ever make.'

They all listened anxiously as the police siren got louder, and then slowly diminished into the distance.

After a six hour journey they arrived at the German's factory. Tam hopped out and pulled back the sliding door. The smell immediately overwhelmed him. 'What a stink! How the heck did you manage not to throw up?' he asked, his face ashen.

'We didn't have much choice, did we?' John said, taking in large gulps of fresh air.

'I've seen men scared before, but I've never seen a man crap scared,' Michael chuckled when he joined them.

John spotted a hosepipe attached to a tap near the factory entrance. 'Right, get them out of those stinking clothes and hose them down with this!' he said. 'Then get them into those white overalls, but make sure you keep their heads covered. I'll go and find the German.'

An eerie silence pervaded the factory, where there were no workers to be seen and the machines stood idle. It made John feel uncomfortable. Had he come to the right place? Was it a trap, or was Lloyd betraying the German and in cahoots with Spider? Perhaps it was a set-up to catch them red handed on a charge of kidnapping.

'Ah, you got here at last.' John immediately recognised the German's voice. He was standing in a doorway at the end of the factory with Lloyd next to him.

'Where are those two scheissehauses?' the German asked in his guttural accent. He was smartly dressed again, in a dark blue silk suit blending perfectly with his tie and pale blue shirt.

'Funny you should call them craphouses, one of them was so scared he actually crapped himself,' John said, and they both laughed.

They're still in one piece, I hope,' the German said. 'I've got things to ask them.'

'Oh, they'll be alright, they're just having a shower,' John said casually.

'Very thoughtful of you; sounds like they needed it.' The German guided John into the next room, which may have been a storage area at some point, but was now empty except for a desk with a kettle and cups on it and two swivel chairs in front of the desk.

'When they are ready bring them in one at a time, but make sure you keep their heads covered. I can't wait to see those two snivelling verraters,' the German said, and sat down on one of the swivel chairs.

John and Jay dragged the struggling William into the room, shoved him down on the other chair, bound him to it with duct tape and spun him around to face the German. 'You can remove the hood,' he said.

John pulled the pillowcase off and William began to shake when he saw the German, who took a measured look at his bloodied face and said, 'I want to know what you have done with the seven million pounds you stole from me.'

'We didn't steal seven mill...'

'Shut this snivelling dieb up!' the German shouted, looking across at John.

'Shut up and listen,' John said, and whacked William across the back of his head.

'Things are going to get a lot worse if you don't tell me what I want to know,' the German warned him.

'Look, I don't know where the seven million pounds are. It was something arranged by James and David; you know I don't have anything to do with the bank account...' he pleaded between frightened sobs.

'Get rid of this räuber and bring the other one in,' the German said, anger rising visibly in his face. John and Jay ripped off the duct tape, hauled William up and dragged him out.

'William seems to think you're the one with all the answers,' John said as he and Jay grabbed hold of James.

'Okay, so William says you know where the seven million pounds are and what it's got to do mit that other swindler David,' the German said once James was secured to the chair.

James almost forgot about his fear of the German when he spotted Lloyd. 'What you doing with this lot?' he asked, giving him a puzzled look.

'Never mind about him, tell me where my money is, or you are in deep scheiss,' the German hissed into his face, spittle flying out of his mouth.

John moved over to the table and switched on the kettle, making sure James saw what he was doing. The German eased his chair closer to James. 'You know where the money is and I want it back. If not, you die,' he added menacingly.

'Maybe this will help him remember,' John said, carrying the kettle across and aiming the spout at James' groin. 'If you don't tell us where the money is, I'm going to pour this over your crown jewels and the last time I did that, the man had to change his sex.'

James cried out, 'Okay! I can tell you where the money is, but I can't access it. You'll have to talk to David; he has all the details and codes. I didn't want to get involved in the first place, but David told us you had ripped him off and that you were going to rip us off too, so he said he'd put a few million aside for us. Honest.'

The German's face darkened. 'You expect me to believe that? How is it you got so devious when you were earning so well with me?'

'We believed what David told us! I don't care about the money, you can have it all, I just want to go home,' James pleaded.

'Damn generous of you, since it was my money in the first place, you gauner!' The German turned his attention to John. 'While he tells me the finer details you two get ready to take the two of them to some quiet place and wait to hear from me if these two are telling the truth. If not, you know what to do.'

This was not what John had expected to hear, but he was already too far in to argue or disobey. 'I understand,' he said, and walked out with Jay.

'You know, when you threatened him with the kettle I had my legs clenched together at the thought. I've known you to do some dastardly things in your time, but burn a man's nuts off with boiling water! Have you really done that?' Jay asked once they were outside,

'No, of course not,' John said, smiling in amusement. 'In any case, when I switched the kettle on, I immediately switched it off again, so there was no boiling water in it.'

'Well it convinced me, and it certainly convinced him,' Jay said.

When they got back to where Michael and Tam were holding William, they put the cuffs on him and took him to the van.

'Where are we going?' Michael asked.

'I don't know yet, depends on what happens in there.'

A few minutes later Lloyd came out holding onto James' handcuffed wrists. 'You can take him now,' he said, shoving him forward and turning to look at John. 'The German wants a quick word.'

'I want you to take them somewhere in the countryside where you can't be seen and wait for my phone call, because if the information he's given me is rubbish, I want you to dispose of them, understood?' the German said firmly.

John felt his blood run cold. The man was talking murder. Kidnapping was one thing, but murder!

The German noticed the flicker of doubt on John's face. 'What's the matter, you not up to it?' he asked, his voice icy cold.

'No problem,' John quickly assured him. 'It's just that, well, you're paying us to kidnap them, you never mentioned anything about...'

'Okay, if you have to do it, I'll double your fee; does that make you feel better?' the German said with an air of condescension.

It really is the root of all evil, John thought, *when big money can so easily change who you are.*

It was getting dark by the time they got into open country. 'This looks a good spot,' John said when they stopped alongside an open field surrounded by trees.

'Yeah, just a few cows over there, and I don't think they'll go running to the police,' Jay said jovially, trying to ease the tension.

John opened the sliding door of the van. 'Walk them a hundred yards or so into that field and lay them down on the grass,' he said.

'We'll wait here until we get a call from the German.'

'To tell us what?' Michael asked, a worried frown between his brows.

'If they live or die,' John said impassively.

The answer caught Tam by surprise. 'You mean he wants us to kill them?' he asked, a shiver of apprehension running down his spine.

'Oh no, please don't kill us, we've done what he asked,' William whimpered.

'No, you won't kill us, you're thugs but you're not murderers!' James called out with a quivering voice.

'If the German says you'll die, you'll die, so keep your mouths shut or I might be tempted to do it anyway,' John warned, and gave James a whack over the head with the Browning.

Just then John's mobile rang. 'You'd better start praying, because if the German tells me you've given him a load of crap, it's all over,' he said. A wry smile broke on his face as he took the call. 'Okay, we have to wait, they're still checking out everything. We'll know in about ten minutes,'

'Yeah well, whatever, I'll have nothing to do with any killing.' Tam sounded adamant.

John looked at him sharply. 'Tam, whether you like it or not, you're involved just as much as we are and there's no way around it if you want to earn any money. If we have to get rid of them, so be it.'

It was an agonising ten minutes, the scenario of what he might have to do playing like an endless loop in John's mind. He checked the Browning, cocking and uncocking it, simply for something to do. He had an overwhelming urge to go ahead and do what he felt he was going to be told to do, and damn the consequences. It gave him an exhilarating feeling that he had never felt before.

'Do you want to shoot both of them or can I have a pop?' Jay asked, caressing the shotgun he was holding, jerking John out of his revelry.

'No, the shotgun will be too messy. One bullet to the head will be quick and clean; leave it to me,' John said, his resolve returning.

The mobile started ringing. John took a deep breath, his pulse speeding up as he answered, the rest of them watching his face to try and read the outcome. His face remained implacable until the call ended and then eased into a smile.

'It's your lucky day; the German says you can go. You seem to have given him what he wanted. So here's the thing, we're going to leave you here and be on our way. We'll take the handcuffs off, but leave the hoods on. You wait here for a good fifteen minutes. Don't risk leaving before then, because we could just be waiting to see if you do, and then you'll get a bullet, okay?'

Back in the van the tension was over. 'Now we've got a percentage of twenty million to split between us. That's what I call a good day's work,' Jay said reflectively as the team drove into the night.

CHAPTER 35

CRIME DOESN'T ALWAYS PAY

John reacted with a jolt when his mobile started ringing. 'Where are you?' he heard Lloyd's voice ask.

'Having a celebratory drink with the boys; a game of pool and talking about what we're going to do with the money.'

'Can you go somewhere quiet? I need to tell you something,' Lloyd said, and John thought he sensed tension in the voice. He walked out of the pool room at Oscar's.

'Right, I can hear you better now. So when's the money coming through?' John hoped that was what Lloyd was ringing about.

There was a long pause. 'There's been a problem...'

'What blooming problem? We've done our bit and we want our money.'

'That's the problem, the German can't make the payment; he's...'

A chill swept over John as the words penetrated his brain. 'He's what?'

'Been arrested. The place is all locked up, his cars are all standing in the driveway and they're going to seize all his assets, so he can't do anything. I've been caught too; he owes me hundreds of thousands.'

'He owes us millions! We risked our lives! I was even prepared to kill for the kraut! I have to come and see you, Lloyd. I'm not sure I trust what you're telling me.'

'I have to go,' Lloyd said, and before John could say anything more, Lloyd's phone clicked off.

John stared at the voiceless phone, feeling as if he had been dealt a physical blow. Random thoughts flooded his brain and welled up like bile in his throat, almost choking him. *I should have known, these people are crooks. How am I going to tell them it was all for nothing?*

'Come on John, it's your turn, I've played three shots for you while you've been telling Jenny what you're going to do for her with your money,' Michael said, holding out the pool cue.

John didn't take the cue, and the look on his face began to unnerve Michael. 'What's the matter, John?' he asked.

'That was Lloyd. The German has been arrested and we're not going to get our money.'

The three men stared at him as if unable to process what he had just said. 'Is this some kind of wind up?' Jay asked angrily.

'No, Lloyd's just told me the German is in custody and they're going to seize all his assets.' The words hung over them like a heavy cloud, confusion and uncertainty written all over their faces.

'This is a rip-off!' Tam exploded.

'Yeah, we're being ripped off! How do we know he's been arrested? He could have buggered off back to Germany for all we know,' Michael said vindictively.

'I'll kill that German if it's the last thing I do, and Lloyd is gonna get it too!' Jay was seized by a sense of outrage. He snapped the cue over his knee and hurled it to the floor. 'Come on, let's go and find them and sort them out!'

'Know anyone who wants to buy a helicopter?'

'Are you still taking the Mickey??' Jay said, pressing his gun against Lloyd's forehead where he lay pinned to the ground. 'We want to know where our money is and where that traitor of a German is.'

'That's what I was trying to do when you charged in here, ready to blow my head off,' Lloyd said.

'What do you mean, that's what you were trying to do? It looked to me like you were trying to do a runner.' John said, his eyes narrowing.

'I was looking for the paperwork for his helicopter. I've got the keys and I know which hangar it's in. It belongs to one of the companies I set up for the German. It's worth a few million and if we can sell it quick I'm happy to split the proceeds with you.'

'Oh yeah, would you have been willing to do that if we hadn't come looking for you?' John asked.

'Yes, I was going to get in touch with you when I got everything together. The helicopter is the only thing the Customs will hopefully not be able to get their hands on. If you let me up and point that gun somewhere else, I can explain more.' There was a spark of fear in Lloyd's eyes.

'Let him up,' John said. Jay and Michael released their grip on Lloyd and hauled him to his feet.

'So explain,' John said, his eyes fixed expectantly on Lloyd. 'Just remember, people mess with me at their own risk.'

'I'm not messing with you. The German has been arrested and is in Birmingham's Winson Green prison. He's being charged with VAT fraud as well as James' and William's kidnapping.'

The team exchanged alarmed glances. 'He's a dead man if names us!' Tam said. 'Because once that genie is out of the bottle it's impossible to put it back.'

'No, I don't think he will. It would only implicate him more and link him to other frauds; besides, he doesn't know your real names or where you're from,' Lloyd assured them.

'I hope you're right,' Michael uttered.

'I've been caught out just as you lot have and I'd like to get my money back too, which is why I can only think of selling the 'copter. As I said, it's worth a few mill, so do you guys know anyone who wants to buy it?'

'Oh yeah, someone was only asking me the other day if I knew where he could buy a helicopter. Are you kidding? I wouldn't have a clue. How about you guys?' John asked, turning to the others.

'You know the guy you bought the van from, maybe he might know someone,' Jay suggested with a hapless shrug.

'No, it's not like selling a car. Trying to flog a helicopter could raise a lot of suspicion and a lot of questions. No, I think we'd better leave well alone.'

'The only thing I can suggest is that I try and sell the 'copter and you lot go after Spider. I was over there about four weeks ago, and while I was there Spider showed me a hold-all stuffed with euros and pounds. He told me there was about a hundred grand just in that bag alone and then there's still the shoe boxes, so I reckon there must be well over a million in cash. It's all yours if you want to go for it. If I just manage to get a million for the helicopter I'll be happy and I'll disappear out of the country,' Lloyd suggested.

CHAPTER 36

FLY TO CATCH A SPIDER

2002

They had been in Benidorm for four days and had met up with Big Jimmy McQuade, a Scouser running the doors at some of the biggest clubs there. Jimmy was into running drugs and arms and Jay knew him through his army connections. He was a big brute of a man and good to have on one's side. Jimmy managed to get hold of a couple of stun guns, but they weren't Taser guns and needed to be pressed against the victim's body to be effective. He was also hoping to have a pistol and ammo for them in a couple of days. John asked if he could get hold of four Spanish police uniforms, which Jimmy assured him wouldn't be a problem.

John telephoned Lloyd to find out what the situation was with the German, and Lloyd said he was still on remand and awaiting trial with every prospect of going down for a very long stretch. Lloyd asked how things were going with Spider and John told him everything was on course, they were just waiting for a gun.

Lloyd gave a little laugh. 'You don't need to wait, Spider keeps a gun, a Smith and Wesson, and I think it's a 357 Magnum. He keeps it in a cubbyhole at the front door. You can grab it once you're in there.'

With the problem of the gun resolved, the next obstacle was the two Rhodesian Ridgebacks that roamed Spider's grounds. Jay arranged for some heavy tranquilisers which they would lace into a couple of juicy steaks to throw over the fence. John decided to do one more day of surveillance, with all of them walking around like holidaymakers having a good time. They stopped at a local supermarket to buy some drinks, and while Jay queued up at the cash machine John stood to one side. To his surprise Spider walked in and brushed right past him, causing him to freeze for a moment.

You can't take him down here, not in front of all these witnesses; we're not armed, we haven't even got the stun guns, John reasoned with himself as he waited anxiously for Jay to complete the transaction.

'What the heck's the matter?' Jay asked, giving John a puzzled look as soon as they were out of the supermarket.

'Spider, he's in there.'

'Great, let's get him!' Jay exclaimed, spinning on his heels, ready to charge back inside.

John grabbed his arm and held him back. 'No, we can't, there are too many people around; we can't risk it. We'll do it tomorrow, and after that we can charter a blooming plane to fly back if we need to.'

With everything set they put on the police uniforms, keeping them covered with coats as they got in the car and drove off. Adrenaline was pumping and every muscle in their bodies strained when they pulled up outside the villa.

'This is it guys,' John said. 'Should be as easy as taking candy from a baby,' he added with a chuckle. But the chuckle stuck in his throat when he saw a minibus pull up outside the villa and a whole family of men, women and children, all Eastern European in appearance, pile out. The gates opened and Spider came out to greet them and usher them inside.

'I don't believe it! What the heck is this?' Tam exclaimed. 'After all our careful surveillance!'

'What the devil do we do now?' Jay stared in total disbelief at the unfolding scene.

'There's nothing we can do,' John said, starting the engine and driving off.

'You mean we've done all this for diddly squat?' Michael exclaimed.

John could see his own confusion reflected in their eyes. Of all the things he expected to happen today, this was certainly not one of them.

'No, not necessarily. We know all we need to know about him and we'll just have to come back and do it another time,' John said, sounding more convinced than he felt.

'Why can't we do it tomorrow?' Tam asked.

'Because if we do, we'll miss our flights,' Jay cut in.

'But then we'll have more than enough money to pay for our own fares,' Michael interjected.

'Yes we would, but we've just seen a family arrive and we have no idea how long they're staying, and we're running out of money. The machine has swallowed Jay's card, so if we miss the flight we'll be well and truly stranded,' John explained.

'It's not fair, there's no justice in this world,' Jay moped.

CHAPTER 37

HAVE THEY STILL GOT THE STOMACH FOR IT?

2003

Christmas had come and gone and it was February 2003 before John had got enough money together from working the door at Oscar's to pay for a trip back to Spain. This time the plan was that he and Jay would fly directly to Benidorm, do a recce to make sure Spider was still at the villa and that nobody else was there. Once they were satisfied, they would phone Tam and Michael to come out.

After John and Jay had booked into a cheap hotel, they went out to find an equally cheap restaurant for a meal. They found a small place that specialised in paella and shared a dish to keep the cost down. When they got back to the hotel and settled down for the night, Jay got the shakes.

'What's the matter Jay? The food wasn't that bad, was it?' John quipped.

'I don't know, I feel terrible,' he said, leaping off the bed and rushing to the bathroom.

John heard him retching, wondering what the heck could have caused it. Jay emerged from the bathroom, his face drained of colour and his body shaking. He stumbled back to his bed and collapsed on it. John went to help him and realised he was shivering with fever. He pulled the duvet from under the prostrate Jay and covered him, not bothering to get him to undress.

In the morning Jay's condition was even worse. He was in no state to go anywhere, so John went off to do a recce of Spider's place while Jay stayed in bed.

This time there were no visitors. The only other person John saw coming and going was a pretty young woman who he guessed was Spider's girlfriend. *Well, if we have to take her down as well, so be it*, he thought as he watched her walking down to the supermarket. He made his way to an abandoned building site next to Spider's villa. Walking around with a clipboard, pretending to be doing a survey, he retrieved one of the stun guns and a small truncheon they had stashed there on the previous trip.

On his way back to the hotel John developed a queasy feeling in his stomach, and by the time he got to the room, he was shaking like Jay had the previous day. He dumped the stun gun and truncheon in the nearest hold-all as an icy feeling enveloped him.

For three days John and Jay were unable to move from their beds, sometimes almost lapsing into unconsciousness, and by day three they knew they had to get to a chemist. After getting dressed with great difficulty, they both headed down to reception. The porter looked at them suspiciously, thinking they were high on drugs, but explained that there was a chemist about a quarter of a mile away.

The pharmacist looked at them in the same way the porter had. With neither able to speak Spanish it was difficult to explain what they were suffering from. In an attempt to get rid of them, the pharmacist offered some medication, which they took without knowing what it was. They tried to hail a taxi, but the driver took one look at them and drove on. They made their way back to the hotel, supporting each other like a couple of junkies in need of a fix.

'I don't think I'm going to make it back to the hotel,' Jay said, stopping to take a rest. Just then he spotted a travel agency across the road, turned to John and said, 'It's no good, we can't stay here; we need to get back home. The way I feel, I could die here.'

'Yeah, I'm beginning to feel the same, let's go and see if we can change our flights.' The travel agent seemed to take sympathy on them and arranged a flight for the next day at a small extra fee.

'Are you alright?' the stewardess asked as she walked down the aisle to check that all seatbelts were fastened.

'Yeah, it's just that, well, we sort of splashed out on our last night and had a load too much to drink and now we're paying the price. I've got the hangover of all hangovers and he's no better. We'll be alright once we've slept it off,' John said, trying to control the shaking as best he could.

The stewardess studied them carefully for a moment, considering whether they were a health risk to other passengers. 'If you need a blanket, let me know,' she said kindly.

'Yes please, a blanket would be great,' Jay said.

They slept through the entire flight and the stewardess had to wake them to bring their seats back to the upright position and fasten their seatbelts. Incredibly, as the plane made its final approach to Heathrow they started to feel better. It was as though they had travelled through a void and been cleansed of their ailments.

By the time they had gone through Customs all the symptoms of their sickness had disappeared. 'I don't know about you, but I'm starving; I haven't eaten a single thing for four days,' Jay said.

'I haven't eaten for the last three days either,' John said, as they quickened their pace to the nearest burger bar.

'I don't know how the heck we're going to explain this to Michael and Tam,' Jay said, biting into his double cheeseburger. 'They'll never believe a word of what happened to us.'

'We're going to have to convince them somehow, or neither of them will want to come out with us next time,' John said, dipping a chip into the ketchup.

'Will there be a next time? We've screwed up twice and it's cost us a lot of money. Can we afford it again?'

'We can't afford not to, not with all that cash just lying there for the taking. We have to go back,' John said, and he wondered if Jenny would believe him. A sense of foreboding tightened in his chest.

CHAPTER 38

DOORSTEP PROTOCOL

'So okay, what the heck happened?' Tam asked angrily, when the four of them got together in the pool room at Oscar's the day after John and Jay's return from Spain.

'We don't really know, it's a total blooming mystery,' Jay said, deciding which cue to choose from the rack. 'We arrived, found a cheap hotel and went out for a meal. We shared a dish of paella and everything was fine until we got back to the hotel and I started to feel queasy. I was as sick as a dog. It felt like my gut was being forced up my throat or being pulled out of my arse.'

'I was still fine at that point,' John continued. 'So the next morning I went to recce Spider's place and everything looked good there. All I needed was for Jay to recover.'

'The problem was I didn't recover; I got to the point where I could hardly get to the bog, never mind taking Spider down,' Jay continued.

'And that night I also went down with the lurgy and we both spent the next three days banged up in the hotel like a couple of junkies with cold turkey' John said.

'So when did the miracle take place?' Michael asked his voice heavy with sarcasm.

'We slept all the way back on the plane and when we woke up as the plane came down at Heathrow we both felt better. By the time we'd cleared Customs, the symptoms had gone,' Jay told him.

'And if you think that was a miracle and God was looking after us, I think it was the other way around—God was looking after Spider,' John cut in grudgingly.

'Talking about miracles,' Jay said, 'how's this for a laugh? When I got home and unpacked I found the blooming stun gun and a truncheon lying on top of my clothes. I walked right through Customs without knowing I was carrying them and nobody stopped me.'

'Sorry, that must have been my fault,' John explained. 'When I got back from the recce, I was feeling so sick I just dumped them in the nearest hold-all. And then I forgot about them. One good thing is we've got a damn good weapon for when we need it.'

'So what do we do now?' Tam asked, wanting to get back to Spider and the cash in the shoe boxes.

'We go straight back there, kick the door in, get him and sod anybody else who happens to be there. We've done the recce, so let's just go for it,' Michael's manner was brusque as he hit the cue ball too hard and sent the red bouncing off the table.

'Hang on, let's think this through. We have to hope for the best, but plan for the worst. The uniforms and stun guns are still safely hidden on the building site, so we won't have a problem with that, but we've got to get enough money together for the four of us—this time enough to stay longer if we have to wait for anybody to leave,' John reasoned.

'So how long is it going to take to get the money together?' Michael was becoming a little irritable.

'There might just be a way to get the money quickly, if you guys are up for it,' Tam surprised them by saying. 'I've got a problem you guys might be able to solve for me. But it involves my girlfriend, Jan.'

'So let's hear it.'

'Jan and I are moving in together as soon as her divorce from John Johnson comes through. He's a nasty piece of work; he used to beat her up. He was one of those on-course bookies, that was until he cheated on a heavy bet with a group of gypsies who I gather are still looking for him. Then he set himself up as a property developer and that's where the problem started. Jan lent him ninety grand to buy a house to renovate and then sell on at a profit.'

'Wow! I didn't know she had that kind of money,' Jay said.

'She's a smart girl; always taken care of her money. She wasn't very keen to lend it to him, but he said if she didn't he'd obstruct the divorce, so she kind of had no choice.

'Wish I had a woman like that,' Jay said, laughing at his own humour.

Tam continued, 'Anyway, he bought the house, did it up and sold it, but never gave her back anything. I also tried to get him to pay back the money, but he turned really nasty. Told me it was none of my business and if I didn't keep my nose out of it he and his heavies would come and break my legs and smash up the club.'

'No way! Someone should sort him out,' Michael said.

'I wish someone would,' Tam's voice dropped. 'I can't fight this one on my own; he's not the type you can beat up and expect to be left in peace. I'm constantly worrying that he's going to come in here and carry out his threat.'

John inhaled deeply, wishing he knew what to say, for if he offered to help, it would mean breaking their protocol. *You don't do anything personal, you don't deal with civilians and you don't crap on your own doorstep,* he reminded himself.

'You want us to sort him out?' Jay spoke up before John had a chance to come to any decision.

'You realise, if we got involved in this, it would mean breaking protocol?' John cut in.

'I realise that, that's why I hesitated telling you. I know Jan would be so grateful to get her money back, I'm sure she would happily pay a reward.'

'Listen, I don't care about blooming protocol, I'm off back to South Africa as soon as we get the money from Spider. So if sorting that skelm out is going to get us the money to go to Spain, I'm all for it,' Michael said with conviction.

'I don't know,' John said hesitantly. 'It's a rule I've always stuck to.'

'I agree with Michael, let's do what we have to do, the rules can come later,' Jay spoke up, an air of excitement in his voice. 'It's going to make getting back to Spain a damn lot sooner.'

'So are you two happy to do something about this?' John asked, looking from Jay to Michael.

'Yes, Tam's one of us and we all have something to gain from it,' Michael agreed happily.

'I agree, no rules are made that can't be broken and the sooner we get back to Spain the better,' Jay said firmly.

'Right then, Tam you need to stay out of it from now on. You're too close to the situation and the least you know the better. Oh, I've heard from Lloyd that the German has gone down for seven years, and Customs seized the chopper before Lloyd could sell it, so he's had his legs cut from under him,' John informed them.

It was decided that Jay and Michael would do a recce of Johnson's flat, and to their surprise it was much easier to gain access than they had hoped. The wood of one of the window frames was rotting, so it was easy to force the latch and climb in. They found no money or safe anywhere, so they climbed back out and eased the latch back, leaving no sign that they had been there.

John tailed Johnson for two weeks and noted that he rarely received any visitors. Every night after closing the office he would get into his Jaguar with blacked out windows, drive back to his flat and stay home for the night. The only change to his routine was on Fridays. Then he would get home, reappear after half an hour having changed his clothes, get into his car and drive to his girlfriend's house, where he would pick her up and go to a nearby restaurant before spending the night at her house.

Because John could have easily been recognised in this area, it was agreed Jay and Michael would do the hit and John would wait in the car around the corner, ready to drive them off when the job was done. Armed with the stun gun and the truncheon they set off, John driving, Jay in the passenger seat and Michael in the back holding the stun gun and truncheon. John dropped them outside the apartment block and drove off to position himself where he could watch for Johnson's arrival.

Jay eased back the loose fitting latch, raised the window and they both climbed in. Once inside they hid in the walk-in wardrobe in the main bedroom to wait for John's message that the Jag was on its way.

Once John spotted the Jaguar, he drove around the corner and sent the text message.

'He's arrived,' Jay whispered to Michael as he covered his face with a balaclava. Michael followed suit.

They heard the key turn in the lock, the door open and close and waited until the footsteps were coming towards them. They leapt out of the wardrobe, with Jay aiming the stun gun at the target. But they both froze when they heard a high-pitched scream and found themselves staring at a terrified woman.

Michael moved swiftly towards her and put his finger to his lips, indicating for her to be quiet. 'Don't scream and you won't get hurt,' he whispered with meaning.

'Who are you and what are you doing here?' Jay asked, lowering the stun gun.

'Who the blazes are you and what do you want?' she demanded, ignoring his question.

'I want to know who you are and what you're doing here,' Jay said, and raised the stun gun to her head.

'I'm Diane, John Johnson's fiancée. I just came to collect his suit; he's working late and we're going out to dinner,' she explained, a look of terror still on her face. 'What are you going to do to me now?' she asked.

'Keep your eye on her,' Jay told Michael, and went to the other room to call John.

'Another cock-up—it's not him, it's his tart come to pick up a suit. What do you want us to do now?'

'Get out of there as quick as you can. Spin her some line that you're friends of the gypsies who've come to collect the twenty grand he owes them,' John said.

Having done what John suggested, the two men shoved the woman into the walk-in wardrobe and closed the doors without locking them. Then they climbed out of the window and carefully eased the latch back so as not to leave any sign of forced entry.

'Talk about expecting the unexpected, how the heck did that happen?' Michael said, disbelief and exasperation sounding in his voice as he slid into the back seat of the car.

John gave a deep sigh, his face matching the others' expressions. 'In the whole week that I did my observation, I never once saw anyone come to his place,' he said.

'Maybe we should have held onto her and forced him to come to the house,' Jay reflected. 'I bet she's been straight on the phone to him; we should have smashed her phone up.'

'No, we're going to have to work out another plan of action,' John said.

John stood in the phone box and took a series of long breaths to steady his nerves, then he practiced the Irish accent several times before lifting the receiver and tapping in the number.

'Hello,' a male voice answered.

'John Johnson?' John asked.

'Who's this?'

In his best Irish accent John said, 'I'm one of the fellows you ripped off for twenty grand and we want our money. You can't steal from us and get away with it. We sent some people around to warn you, I do hope you've taken their advice seriously and you're getting the money together. I'll phone you again in a week's time to tell you where to drop it off. We know where you live and where you work, where your ex and your kids live; we know who your girlfriend is and where she lives, so have the money ready. You won't like the consequences if you don't.' He replaced the receiver before Johnson could say anything.

John smiled as he came out of the phone box, pleased with his efforts, feeling he had scared him enough. But he had in fact scared him more than he hoped to; so much so that Johnson went to the police and reported the raid on his house and the threatening phone call.

This proved to be the undoing of all their plans. Breaking the protocol, dealing with civilians and messing on their own doorstep was about to come back to haunt them.

CHAPTER 39

ENTRAPMENT

It was now coming to the end of 2003. On Friday 31 October, a few days after his thirty-seventh birthday, John got up feeling in a jubilant mood, believing he had scared Johnson enough to come up with the money and that they would soon be able to plan the trip back to Spain. While making breakfast for Jenny and the kids, he planned to go out and buy some fireworks for bonfire night, and his mind drifted back to when Flemmo took him to the village of Oxton and showed him a series of tunnels that ran under the church. He had told him all about Guy Fawkes and the gunpowder plot, and why they lit bonfires to celebrate his capture.

He was brought back sharply to reality when the phone rang. He hoped it was Tam calling to tell him Johnson had agreed to pay back Jan's money. 'Hi Tam!' he said, snatching up the receiver, but discovered his mistake when a toneless voice said, 'Mr. Lawson?'

'Who's this?' John asked, not recognising the voice.

'This is Detective Sergeant Cowden from Musselburgh police station. I was wondering if you would be kind enough to come to the station for an informal chat to help with some enquiries regarding certain threats that are alleged to have been made against a Mr. Kelly. I believe you are acquainted with him.'

John's breathing eased. *Thank heavens, at least it's nothing to do with the threats we've made to Johnson*, he thought.

'If I can be of help sergeant, when would you like me to come?' John said in a polite and cooperative manner.

'Today, if that's convenient sir,' Cowden said, his voice adopting a friendlier tone.

'Bit difficult today, I'm doing an early shift,' John said, thinking he ought to tell Tam about the call before going to the station.

'No problem sir, how would tomorrow morning suit you, say ten o'clock?' Cowden suggested.

'Fine, sergeant, I'll be there at ten o'clock sharp,' John agreed.

'Thank you for your cooperation sir,' the sergeant said, maintaining his friendly tone.

John stared at the phone for a long moment, then heard Jenny's voice asking, 'Who was that?'

'The police can be such idiots. That was a detective from Musselburgh police station, wanting me to help them about some threats made to Tam Kelly and Jan,' John said nonchalantly.

'So why do the police think you can help?' Jenny asked, nervous at any mention of the police.

'Because they're always running around like headless chickens; couldn't find a needle in a haystack if it was stuck up their own backsides,' John said, almost chuckling at his own humour.

'When are you seeing the police?' Tam asked, feeling a little uneasy as he sat with John in his office at Oscar's.

John noticed the worried look on Tam's face. 'Don't worry, they obviously have no idea about Johnson. Ironically it seems someone has made a complaint about the threats he's been making to you; maybe Jan did.'

'She hasn't mentioned anything about it.'

'Maybe one of her friends has. Anyway, I'm going to wait until I know what the police have got on Johnson before I phone him and tell him where to drop the money,' John said, looking Tam in the eye. 'There's nothing to worry about, the police are too busy policing law abiding citizens to have time to bother with criminals like us. I'll just tell them how upset and worried you are about the threats and about your and Jan's safety.'

'Just be careful what you say; don't say any more than you have to,' Tam cautioned him.

John parked his Range Rover in Musselburgh High Street and walked the short distance to the police station, looking forward to pretending to be a law abiding citizen helping the police to protect the public against criminals.

'Good of you to come, Mr. Lawson,' Detective Sergeant Cowden said with a smile, facing John across the table from him in the small interviewing room.

'Anything to help the police, detective,' John said with slight arrogance in his voice.

'We're making enquiries about allegations of hostage taking and demands for money, and we wondered if you knew anything about it,' Cowden said, his large eyes searching John's face for a reaction. 'Do you know a Mr. John Johnson?'

'I thought you invited me here to help you with enquiries regarding Mr. Kelly,' John said, doing his best not to look confused.

'We'll come to him later. Do you know a Mr. Johnson?' Cowden persisted.

'No, I don't,' John said firmly.

Cowden gave him an I-know-you're-lying look. 'Are you sure you don't know a Mr. Johnson?' he repeated, emphasising the name.

'I've told you I don't know him,' John repeated, thinking it was technically true, as he had never actually met the man.

'Really? Well, here's something I'd like you to think about. After Mr. Johnson had come to us with his allegations, we set up a recorder to monitor the calls to both his home and his office, and guess what?'

'What?' John asked, his eyebrows rising into an innocent grin.

'We got a recording of your voice,' Cowden said, a look of triumph on his face.

John's eyebrows lowered into a frown. 'You can't have. I've never made any calls to a man I don't know.'

The look of triumph stayed on the sergeant's face as he said, 'You see, we're very lucky these days in that we have the services of an expert speech analyst and he compared your voice with the voice making the threats, and guess what.'

John almost said, 'He couldn't possibly know it was me, I spoke with an Irish accent,' but checked himself and just said. 'What?'

'They match. Your attempts at an Irish accent were not that good and what was interesting is that your voice has certain resonances that are unique and helped to define it. The analyst found there was a blend of South African, Scouse and of course Scottish traits in your accent.'

'You're making it up! I've never heard such rubbish. I come here to help you and you're trying to trap me into something I know nothing about. I'm out of here,' John exclaimed angrily, leaping to his feet.

'SIT DOWN!' Cowden shouted.

John grudgingly sat down and glared back at the sergeant, whose smile had become much broader. Just then a constable tapped on the door and beckoned Cowden, who went over and spoke to him and then hurried off, leaving the constable to watch over John.

'What the devil is that?' Jenny exclaimed, jumping out of her chair where she was watching television with the children, when she heard an incessant hammering on the front door, as if someone was trying to break it down.

It was the police, and when Jenny opened the front door she was roughly pushed aside. They stormed in shouting 'POLICE!! POLICE!! This is a raid, everyone remain where they are!' Jenny screamed as the police started moving through the house, searching every room.

'How many people are in the house?' the uniformed officer asked Jenny.

'Just me and the three children. Would you please tell me what's going on?' she bravely demanded, trying to control her anger.

'We have a warrant to search the house,' he informed her, producing it from his breast pocket.

'I don't understand. Why don't you talk to my husband?; he's at the police station right now,' she said, a confused look on her face.

'Indeed he is, and I suspect he'll be helping us for some time. Do you have the keys to the garage?' the officer asked, determined to get on with the search.

'They're in the kitchen drawer, I'll get them for you,' Jenny said, walking off to the kitchen, the officer following close behind her.

She followed him back out into the lounge where the children were staring through the window, the red and blue colours of the police lights reflecting on their faces. It was as if the circus had come to town—six or seven police cars and vans surrounding the immediate area of the house, lights flashing and all the neighbours out to goggle at what was going on.

Cowden's face was beaming when he walked back into the room where John sat waiting.

'We've just searched your car, and we...'

'You searched my car? You have no right to search my car without my permission,' John retorted angrily.

'Yes we have, and we're also searching your house.'

'You have no right to search my house either! I know my rights. You need a search warrant to enter my property. I'll blooming sue you!' John's face was a mask of anger.

'We have a search warrant,' Cowden said, and watched his expression change.

John could hear his own breathing. 'You've set me up; this wasn't about me helping you with your enquiries, this was to get me here and keep me here while my property was being searched, you dirty scumbags!'

'I'd be careful with my choice of language if I were you. You're helping us with our enquiries, but I can't say you're being particularly cooperative. However, since the Range Rover can be considered part of your property, it was quite in order for us to search it and guess what we found.'

'My spare tyre's flat.' John smirked, but the smile on his face did not match the anxiety in his eyes.

'That too. But what would you be doing with a powerful stun gun and a truncheon in the boot of your car? I wonder.'

'I know nothing about a stun gun or a truncheon; you lot must have planted it,' John said contemptuously.

'I bet they've got your fingerprints all over them.'

'I bet they haven't,' John said confidently, remembering that he always wore gloves when he handled the stun gun or the truncheon. But he shifted uneasily in his seat as he realised the gloves were also hidden in the boot.

At that moment the constable tapped lightly on the door again and gestured to Cowden, who got up to hear what he had to say, his smile widening as he listened. John was drumming his fingers on the table when Cowden came back and said, 'They've just finished searching your house. Quite a house, by all accounts, which makes me wonder how the likes of you can afford to live like that on a doorman's salary, or a bouncer or whatever you guys like to call yourselves. Anyway, guess what they found.'

'I'm tired of these guessing games,' John said arrogantly. 'Why don't you just tell me, so I can get out of here and get home to my wife?'

'You're not going anywhere Mr. Lawson; we found a tray of cartridges in your garage. What would you be needing with them, I wonder, and where are you hiding the gun to fire them?' the detective asked with an unwavering stare.

John said nothing, his flickering eyes showing the first signs of fear. If he had known there was going to be a raid he would have hidden those cartridges where he had buried the Browning, in the wooded area next to Cockenzie Power Station near Musselburgh.

'We've got you bang to rights Lawson, so make it easy on yourself and tell us the truth, because we're also interviewing a Mr. Thomas Kelly, who we know you work for.'

'Yea, the man you supposedly wanted me to help with your enquiries,' John quipped, managing to keep his composure.

'Well, we had to get you in here somehow,' Cowden said unapologetically.

John gave a sharp intake of breath. His eyes narrowed with disguised malice and he said, 'Okay, so I threatened Johnson, but it was only a threat, I never intended to hurt him. Thomas Kelly had nothing to do with it, I was working alone. I heard the guy had ripped off my mate's girlfriend and thought I'd scare him into handing over some of it,' he added in an attempt to protect the Jay, Tam and Michael.

John and Tam Kelly were arrested and charged with kidnapping and attempted extortion, and John was also charged with possession of firearms. After a few days in HMP Edinburgh, they got bail and were released until their case was ready to come to court. They both headed home in solemn silence at the prospect.

CHAPTER 40

HAIL THE HERO

2004

John leapt to his feet when he heard Jenny's car pull up, and rushed out into the hallway to open the front door for her. He stood in the doorway, his heart pounding, as he watched her slam the car door with more force than necessary. She was trying hard to ignore the curtains twitching in the neighbours' windows.

She fixed a steady gaze on John and brushed past him. He followed her into the lounge and tried to embrace her. 'Don't touch me!' she said, shrinking back from him. 'Have you any idea what it's been like? Police cars swarming all over the place, men searching every room, cupboard and drawer, even the garage. What were they looking for?' It sounded more like an order than a question.

This was the moment of truth. With guilt hammering at his conscience he said, 'They found some bullets in the garage.'

'Bullets!!' Jenny exclaimed. 'Are you completely crazy, what if the kids had found them?'

'They couldn't have, they were well hidden,' he said meekly, and watched her slump down into an armchair.

'Not well enough apparently, because the police didn't take long finding them,' she said scornfully. 'What else did they find?'

'Nothing else,' he lied, knowing what the reaction would be if he told her about the stun gun and the truncheon.

'Have you any idea what it was like with all the neighbours coming out and gawking at what was going on? I can't go anywhere now without someone staring or pointing at me,' she said, her cheeks red with anger.

'I'm sorry, I didn't mean for this to happen,' he started, not sure what more to say.

'What did you expect would happen? Did you think you could just go on doing what you're doing and it wouldn't catch up with you? I've lived in fear of this happening every time you've gone off somewhere debt collecting. So tell me what terrible things you've done this time.'

'Depends what you consider terrible,' he replied, and Jenny could see the conflicting emotions on his face.

'Don't bandy words with me,' she cut across him. 'Didn't it ever occur to you that at some point your luck would run out? Weren't you ever afraid of being caught?'

'Yes, but that was part of it. I'm sorry, I should have been more honest with you,' he dropped his voice in acquiescence.

'Yes, you damn well should have! You're so arrogant you think everyone else is stupid. Look what you said about the police, not capable of finding a needle in a haystack if it was... I won't even repeat the rest of it. Well, it turns out they're a bit smarter than you, aren't they?'

'It must have been scary for you and the kids, I'm sorry.'

'How could you have been so thoughtless, so reckless?' Jenny was almost incandescent with rage.

'I thought what I was doing was to protect you and the kids. To have money to buy all the things you deserve...'

'That's your problem—you think money is the answer to everything. Well, it's not; look where it's got you, us. You realise we won't be able to live here any longer. We're going to have to sell the house and find somewhere else to live where nobody knows us.'

When they put the house on the market it was valued at £193,000—a full £100,000 more than they had paid for it three years earlier. It sold faster than they had anticipated, and they found a four-bedroomed ground floor maisonette in Pinkie Road, Musselburgh. It was in a pretty bad state, but the price of £110,000 left them with more than enough money to completely refurbish it. John took £10,000 of the money that had been deposited into their joint account at the Bank of Scotland and put it into his own account at the Halifax across the road.

Still on bail, waiting for his trial date to be announced, John was determined to keep his nose clean and stay out of trouble. While working the door at Oscar's he befriended Andy Warburton, who he had recruited to work alongside him. Andy lived in the Gorgie area of Edinburgh, and didn't have a driver's licence, so in the early hours of the morning, after Oscar's had closed, John would give him a lift home. At that time of the morning the streets were relatively deserted.

On a Sunday in March, around two thirty in the morning, John and Andy turned into Dalry Road as usual, passing the row of tenement buildings with a variety of shops occupying the ground floors. They carried on past the graveyard, and approaching the petrol station they noticed smoke billowing from one of the shops. Two people were frantically hammering on a door between the shops, which was the main entrance to the flats above. They were pressing all the buzzers and shouting up at the windows.

'What the heck's going on there?' John asked as he pulled the Range Rover to an abrupt stop.

'Looks like the nursing agency is on fire,' Andy said as they leapt out.

They looked up at the windows immediately above and saw people poking their heads out and shouting down at the two men to go away and stop making a nuisance of themselves.

'What's going on here?' John asked one of the men.

'The Scott Nursing Centre is on fire and the idiots upstairs aren't taking any notice. They think we're a couple of drunks. They're going to die if we don't get them out,' the man said.

John immediately started kicking at the entrance door to the flats, and with Andy's help it soon gave way. They tore up the stairs and started banging on the doors, shouting for everyone to get out. Smoke was beginning to pour into the communal stairwell, and the flames seemed to follow them as they climbed up to the second floor, still banging on the doors.

People started hurrying down the stairs. By the time John and Andy got to the fifth floor it seemed as if everybody had managed to get out safely. John hammered on the last door, but nobody answered. He banged again, and looking over the balcony and saw black smoke obscuring the entrance. *Got to get out of here before the smoke kills us*, he thought, but kept on banging until the door finally opened and an elderly man appeared, wearing only a pyjama top. 'What's the matter?' he asked, his voice sleepy and his eyes bleary.

'You've got to get out, the place is on fire!' John shouted.

It felt like forever before the man understood what he was saying. 'I need to have a pee and find my bottoms,' he said, and turned and ambled back into the flat.

'We need to get you out of here! Is there anyone else in the flat?' John asked, becoming exasperated at the man's inability to understand the seriousness of the situation.

'I think my wife heard the commotion and she's looking for her cat,' the man replied with no sense of urgency.

When he heard sirens approaching, John said to Andy, 'I think I'll have to barricade us in the flat, put some wet towels around the gaps and open the windows. You go down and tell the firemen I'm up here with these two elderly people.' Andy pulled his jumper over his nose and made his way back down the stairs.

As John was about to barricade the door, a man came rushing up the stairs. 'I'm Jonathan Torrance. I live down on the next floor. We've got to get them out now, it's too risky for anyone to stay here, the building could collapse,' he said in a strained voice.

'It's going to be very risky,' John said, looking down the stairwell at the smoke billowing up towards them. 'If I carry the man, do you think you could help the lady?'

'Sure, but the sooner the better,' Jonathan said, following John into the flat.

John, weighing a good eighteen stone, had no problem lifting the man onto his shoulders in a firemen's lift and carrying him out of the flat. Jonathan took hold of the woman's hand, led her out and picked her up while she kept protesting about her cat.

The descent was perilous. Every step had to be carefully judged. With only one free hand to guide him, John knew one slip could send him and the man tumbling to the bottom. Almost blinded by the smoke, he felt his way along the wall.

By the time they got downstairs John was gasping for air, feeling he would faint if he didn't get to fresh air quickly. As he reached the front door, he saw a haze of light through the thick darkness and the silhouette of a fire-fighter, and for a split second he had a flashback of watching his father driving away through a haze of exhaust fumes after visiting them at Gran's house with that woman.

'You're a very brave man. These people would have died if you hadn't brought them out. Good job you lived near them,' one of the firemen said as he helped John out.

'I don't live here, my friend and I were just passing and we saw the smoke...' John explained, taking in deep gulps of fresh air.

'You mean you just stopped and went into the burning building to rescue people? You're even braver than I thought. Not many people would have done that,' he said with a sense of admiration.

'It wasn't only me, there's my mate Andy and another guy who said his name was Jonathan,' John told him.

'Right, I'll have word with them and leave you with the medics,' the fireman said, and walked off to talk to the others.

'Hail the hero!' the customers joked, patting John on the back as they came through the door at Oscar's. It had become a regular thing since the story appeared in the newspapers. John loved it. It made him feel good that for once he had saved someone's life instead of threatening it, and it temporarily distracted his worries about the upcoming trial.

But the period of euphoria quickly evaporated when he got a frantic call from a tearful Jenny who had gone to buy new curtains and was told the debit card had been rejected.

'It doesn't make sense, there's over twelve grand in that account,' John said, just as puzzled as she was.

'Well, you'd better go and sort it out with the bank. I'm embarrassed enough not being able to pay for a few damn curtains,' she said in frustration.

'Okay. In the meantime I'll draw some cash for you from the other account,' John said, trying to pacify her.

'I'm sorry sir, this account is frozen,' the bank teller told him, his face implacable.

'What do you mean it's frozen?' John asked angrily, trying to control his temper.

'I'm afraid it is sir. Do you have any other accounts with us that you can draw from?'

'You must be joking! All I wanted was a couple of hundred,' John said with a fatalistic shrug of his shoulders.

'Sorry we can't be of assistance sir,' the bank teller said, forcing an apologetic smile.

'I'm afraid you are now subject to the Proceeds of Crime Act. I'm surprised you haven't been notified,' Mr. McAlister, John's solicitor, informed him when he called at his office to find out what the problem was.

'What exactly does the Proceeds of Crime Act mean?' John asked disconsolately.

'In effect it means the Procurator Fiscal Service, through the Assets Recovery Agency, have seized all the assets that they consider you've benefitted from through criminal activities. It entails a restraint order that prohibits you from dealing with anything you own—your house, cars, furnishings, everything they consider of value. It allows the PFS to recover anything they consider as property obtained through your unlawful activities or which you intend to use in an unlawful way. This includes seizing your bank accounts so as to prevent any movement of money or possible money laundering,' McAlister explained in his matter of fact manner.

'How can they do that?'

'Well, it would appear that the police came to the conclusion you were living well beyond your means in terms of what you are reportedly earning as a doorman.'

'But that doesn't make sense! We sold the house because we couldn't afford to live there anymore.'

'Unfortunately that doesn't explain where you got the money to buy the house in the first place,' McAlister pointed out.

'Does that mean we have no access to our money?' John said, desperation beginning to wash over him.

'To that money, no, but they will allow you to keep the money you and your wife are currently earning to pay essential bills.'

'How generous of them.'

'Not really. They've issued a demand for you to pay back £100,000 in reparation of your ill-gotten gains, shall we say.'

'That's rubbish! They can't prove how I made that money.'

'They don't have to; the onus is on you to prove how you did. So I suggest you start trying to sort out your affairs before they sell the house from under you.'

'They can do that?' John said, overwhelmed by this news.

'Once they've got their hooks into you, they can do almost anything.'

After the meeting John walked along Musselburgh High Street past the police station where he'd been arrested. He noticed a man climb onto one of the benches at the bus stop and start to preach, holding a Bible in his hand. 'You are all going to face God one day! You are going to face the final judgment! Now is the time to repent!'

John turned to walk on, and couldn't believe his eyes when he spotted a wallet lying in the gutter. In his practised way he swiftly moved over, snatched the wallet up surreptitiously, shoved it into his pocket and hurried off to a darkened doorway.

His excitement quickly evaporated when he discovered the wallet only contained a gospel tract, which read:

1. If this was a real wallet, packed with real money, would you: A. Keep it? B. Take it to the police? C. Give some of the money to the poor?
2. You have been underpaid for years. There's a big mistake in your pay cheque to your advantage, would you: A. Tell the boss? B. Keep quiet? C. Give some to a church?
3. If telling a white lie would save a friend's job, would you: A. Tell the truth? B. Act dumb? C. Lie?
4. Do you consider yourself to be a 'good' person? A. Yes. B. No.
5. Have you ever told a lie for any reason (including 'fibs' and 'white lies')? Be honest. A. Yes. B. No.
6. Have you ever stolen anything, irrespective of its value? (Listen to your conscience.) A. Yes. B. No.
7. Would you consider a person who admits to being a liar and a thief to be a 'good' person? A. Yes. B. No.
8. Who do you think will enter Heaven? A. Those who say they are good when they are not. B. Liars and thieves. C. Those whom God has forgiven and cleansed of sin.
9. Do you realise that the Bible warns that thieves, liars, fornicators, idolaters (those who create a god to suit themselves), adulterers and the covetous will not enter the Kingdom of Heaven? A. Yes. B. No.
10. Do you know that God so loved the world that He gave his only begotten Son, that whoever believes in Him should not perish but have everlasting life? A. Yes. B. No.

Please repent today and place your trust in Jesus alone for your salvation. God will grant you everlasting life. Then read your Bible daily and obey it.

John shoved the wallet and the tract back in his pocket and started to laugh as he made his way home. *Well, looks like I'm headed for hell on top of everything else*, he thought to himself.

It was a tough ten months waiting for the trial date, and John and Jenny's marriage was being tested to the limit, with the pressure mounting as the day approached.

'Why is my trial taking place here?' John asked, sitting across the small table from his solicitor Mr. McAlister and Mr. Gilbert Rawlings QC in the interviewing room of the Dunfermline Sheriff Court in Fife. Mr. Rawlings, his Advocate, was dressed in a silk gown over his business suit, but not wearing a wig, in line with Scottish court tradition. He reminded John of Cecil Watkins, although this man was thinning on top, so there was no dandruff problem. His face was severe, but John wondered if it wasn't just part of his act as Queen's Council.

Gilbert Rawlings drew in a deep breath as he studied John, before looking down at his notes and back up at John's face again. 'As far as I can gather they have chosen to try you here to avoid complications with the trial of your colleagues, Thomas Kelly, Jason Davies and Michael Chamberlain, which is due to be held in Edinburgh in a couple of months' time. It seems the police started building a case against the three of them after forensic investigation of the sim card in your phone revealed incriminating evidence against them. They also found text messages to Jason Davies and Michael Chamberlain at the time of the crime. Triangulation of phone mast positions placed them firmly in the frame. CCTV footage of the route you drove to Johnson's flat and images of Chamberlain and Davies getting off the train at Edinburgh's Waverley Station on the day of the crime all add weight to their guilt. So it's clear to me they want you to be tried and convicted before that trial comes up.'

'It seems they're determined to get us all. They're more devious than I thought.' John sighed reflectively.

'They can be when they want to, and they certainly are in this case,' Rawlings said. 'As you are probably aware, the jury's verdict is by majority vote, so I hope I can appeal to their good nature, show them you have been working regularly, with no reports of any misdemeanours. And of course you have the police commendation and meritorious award for your bravery in the fire escapade, which should help. When you get to court I want you to behave as though you are a reformed man who has renounced his criminal activities. I might just manage to split them, then who knows? We might even get a not proven verdict, or the judge might order a retrial.'

'Then I guess there's still hope,' John said, not convinced at all.

'The good news is they've agreed to drop the stun gun charge on the basis that the search of your car was illegal because it was parked on the High Street and therefore not covered by the warrant to search your house. Also, the tray of bullets turned out to be blanks, as you obviously knew. So the only admissible evidence would be the voice recordings of you making the threats.'

'I should have practiced my Irish accent a bit more,' John scoffed with a shrug of his shoulders.

'You go into court with that attitude and I tell you now, the jury will return a guilty verdict and the judge will throw the book at you. So be smart for once and play the reformed citizen,' Rawlings rebuked him.

'You have been found guilty of attempted extortion,' the judge pronounced after the jury had given their verdict. 'I have taken into account all the facts of this case. Mr. Johnson has admitted he owed certain monies to his ex-wife and you have admitted your part in the matter, although you had originally pleaded not guilty to the charge. However, one cannot ignore the seriousness of the threat, plus the fact you solicited two men to carry out the threat. One has to wonder what would have happened had Mr. Johnson turned up instead of the young lady. I have also taken into account that no one was hurt physically and that you are to receive a commendation and meritorious award for your bravery in rescuing people from a blazing fire. That is commendable, but that also demonstrates your tendency to be impulsive and reckless in that you don't consider the consequences of your actions. I am going to release you on bail for a period of four weeks in order to obtain psychological and family reports. On receipt of those reports you will be summoned back to this court to be sentenced. I should advise you however, that you can expect a lengthy custodial sentence.'

CHAPTER 41

DOWN FOR A THIRD TIME

John had been in Glenochil prison near Stirling for six weeks when he was told his solicitor was coming to see him. McAlister explained that the cases against Jay, Michael and Tam were coming up in the High Court and that John had been made a compellable witness.

'Compellable witness? What's that?' John wanted to know.

'It's where the Court has the right to force you to give evidence or face the Court's displeasure should you refuse,' McAlister explained in a serious tone, trying to make sure that John understood the consequences.

But John's immediate reaction was, 'No way will I give evidence against them.'

'If you refuse, you could be charged with contempt of court,' McAlister warned.

John remained steadfast. 'I was always told, never open your mouth about anyone unless you intend to benefit by it, and I certainly don't intend to benefit by giving evidence against my friends.'

In the High Court John was led from the holding cells to the witness waiting room, his mind playing havoc over what McAlister had said. Would he be able to defy the court and stick to the villains' code that you don't welch on your fellow villains?

'Right Lawson, your turn,' the court official said.

They ushered him through a door and before he'd gathered himself he was standing in a witness box on an elevated platform surrounded by high rails. When his eyes had adjusted to the bright lights, he looked around and saw everyone in the courtroom staring at him, including Tam, Jay and Michael. He averted his glance and looked towards the judge.

The clerk of the court came forward, handed John a Bible and said, 'Repeat after me: I swear by Almighty God that I will tell the truth, the whole truth and nothing but the truth.'

John remained motionless, his body tense and his voice measured as he said, 'I don't need to do that, as I won't be giving evidence.'

'Mr Lawson, you are a compellable witness and as such you are here to give evidence in this trial...'

'I didn't ask to come here and I don't want to be here. I am not prepared to be a witness. I've had my trial, I've been sentenced and that's the end of it as far as I'm concerned, so you can stick your evidence up your...'

'Mr Lawson!' the judge banged his gavel heavily on the bench. 'You are in contempt of this court and if you continue this behaviour and refuse to give evidence I will have no alternative but to...'

Again John interrupted the judge. 'You can do what you like. I'm not giving evidence.'

'Very well, I hold you in contempt of court. I will deal with you later. Take him down,' the judge ordered, his face red, his voice thick with anger as he banged the gavel with a resounding thud.

John was taken to the holding cells to await the long drive back to Glenochil. He later discovered that as a result of his refusal to testify, Tam had been released due to a lack of evidence, but Jay and Michael had been found guilty, as the evidence was heavily stacked against them. Jay got five years and Michael four.

John was pleased that his actions had got Tam off, but he was shocked to hear rumours that Jay and Michael felt he had stitched them up; that he had in some way implicated them and done a deal with the police to let Tam go free.

Four weeks later John was once again in the sweatbox, being taken from Glenochil to Edinburgh. Contempt of court is not a criminal offence, and therefore such cases are held in a Civil Court and not the High Court. As John stood facing the judge, he looked across the courtroom and saw Jenny sitting in the public benches. He smiled at her, but before he could measure her reaction the judge spoke up. 'Mr Lawson, you have been charged with contempt of court and you need to understand that in doing so you have interfered with the court's ability to administer justice to those who are accused of breaking the law and brought before it. Contempt of court is a serious offence and if we were to let it go unpunished, the courts would cease to function effectively. As a consequence the punishment must reflect the seriousness of your refusal to give evidence when summoned to do so. Your disrespectful conduct leaves me no alternative but to impose a custodial sentence that takes into account your language and your behaviour. I therefore sentence you to fifteen months imprisonment, the sentence to run consecutively with your current prison term, in that when you have finished serving that term you will then begin to serve the second term of fifteen months. Take him down,' the judge pronounced.

John looked across at Jenny, her face flushed and furious, and he thought he saw hatred in her usually beautiful sparkling eyes. She shook her head at him as if to say, 'How much more do the children and I have to suffer because of your arrogance and stupidity?' It made him feel sick, for he knew at that moment his marriage was all but over.

CHAPTER 42

SETTLING IN

They say the first few months of a prison sentence, while one is adjusting to the routine, are the hardest. As Alfie had told him on his first stretch inside, 'One fing I've learnt, is yer av ta try not ta fink of what's appening on the outside. Yer world until yer done yer time is prison, and the bleedin' day ta day routines yer just av ta get used ta. Yer start finking about anyfink else and it'll start ta drive yer bleedin' crazy. Do yer bird and that way yer survive.'

It had held him in good stead; he'd knuckled down, kept his nose clean and accepted he was banged up for the next two and a half years at least. The only thing that constantly nagged at his conscience were his kids and Jenny.

Christmas and New Year had come and gone and life was settling back into the daily routine of prison life, but John was determined not to let it get him down. He would survive whatever it took. He got the job of cleaner in the prison library, and joined the art class, where he discovered he had a passion for clay modelling—making all sorts of models, putting them into the kiln and firing them, then painting them.

While doing his daily cleaning chores in the library he was approached by a stocky Nigerian who had the broadest smile John had ever seen. 'Do you have any books on religion?' he asked John, his voice polite and respectful.

John was taken by surprise by both his manner and the fact that he was interested in religion. 'Haven't got a clue mate, no one ever asked before. You a Christian?'

'Yes, I'm a Christian. I believe in the Lord; He's all powerful and He's delivered me from my sins,' the Nigerian said, his wide grin stretching even wider.

This was not the answer John had expected. 'If the Lord is so powerful, why hasn't He delivered you from this hellhole?' he said, and continued dusting the shelves.

'Unfortunately I fell from the path of righteousness and I slipped into the devil's wicked ways.'

'Really? So it was the devil, huh? That's a new one on me, mate,' John said sarcastically. 'So what were the wicked ways that brought you to this hellhole?'

'I got involved in credit card fraud and now I must pay. Justice must be served, as it will be served on Judgement Day before the Lord. But know one thing my friend, I've already been set free by Jesus,' the Nigerian said, ignoring John's sarcasm.

'I don't know about Him setting you free, but the law sure as heck won't. The only time they'll set you free is when you've done your time, mate.'

'I'm in God's hands and I'm happy.'

'Well good luck mate, as long as it keeps you smiling, but to me there's something childish about believing that there's somebody up there with supernatural powers. Going from being a villain to holier than thou only happens in books and you've obviously been reading too many of them,' John said, sweeping his arm around, indicating the array of books on the shelves.

'The only book I read is the Bible and books to do with religion,' the Nigerian said demurely.

'I'd rather read a book about the Krays or gangland. Anyway, what's your name? I've seen you walking around the exercise yard, but you don't seem to mix with anybody.'

'My name's Tony and I come from Africa; Nigeria to be precise.'

'I once lived in Africa; South Africa actually.'

'Not a good place for a black man to live.'

'No, I guess not. Certainly not when I was there.'

'Why did you leave?'

'My father abandoned us. It's a long story and I'd better not go into it now, the screws will be along any minute and they won't like to see us talking. Maybe I'll catch up with you in the exercise yard,' John suggested, anxious not to get into trouble and lose his privileges.

'Of course, I mustn't stop you working,' Tony said and sauntered off.

When John would meet up with Tony in the exercise yard Tony would always say, 'Hello my friend, and how are you today?'

'I'm fine, thank you,' John would reply politely, and hope they could have a conversation that didn't deal with religion.

Tony had a quiet, approachable demeanour. He never swore and tended to keep to himself. He wasn't on drugs, never scrounged or tried to borrow anything from anybody. Every Monday the prisoners were handed a canteen sheet on which they could order things they wanted—tobacco, sweets or toiletries, within the limits of the money they had earned from the jobs they were doing. Their orders were then delivered to their cells on the Friday. It was inevitable that some of the prisoners would use up what they had been given well before the next Friday and then go on the scrounge.

'You know what day it is today my friend?' Tony asked as they walked around the exercise yard.

'Of course I know what day it is, it's Thursday, it comes after Wednesday and before Friday,' John said in his sarcastic manner.

'No my friend, it's not Thursday today, it's Christian Fellowship day,' Tony said in his usual gentle way.

'Tony, you tell me this every Thursday and I tell you the same thing. I'm not interested. If it was a Villains' Fellowship day I'd be more interested,' John said derisively. 'If you want to believe in all that rubbish, that's up to you, but don't expect me to. I've seen what religion did to my grandmother. She believed in God, but it didn't stop her from getting mugged. Where was your God then? I also saw what it did in South Africa—men would go to church and pray for goodness and their sins to be forgiven, but as soon as they came out of church, they'd strike out at the first black man they saw. So don't talk to me about religion.'

'That's not God's doing, that's the devil's work, John,' Tony insisted. 'I'll pray for you tonight my friend, and hope God sends His blessing upon you.'

Vadim was a quiet man, a gentle Russian who spoke very good English. John learned in conversation that he had got the nickname of 'Vlad the Impaler'. He was over six feet tall, with dark hair and sharp features.

'What did you do to get a name like that, if you don't mind me asking?' John asked when he and Vlad struck up a conversation.

'You may ask. I had a very successful business that arranged for the children of wealthy Russian families to obtain places in some of Britain's most prestigious public schools. We did all the paperwork, visas, travel and accommodation arrangements and saw to their wellbeing and safety while they were studying here,' Vlad explained.

'So what happened that you ended up in here?' John was curious why a man so well educated would be locked up amongst villains.

'I was driving to a meeting in Scotland, with my mind on what I was going to discuss. I wasn't familiar with the narrow roads and I clipped the kerb. The car went into a spin and hit an oncoming car, which spun out of control, down an embankment and crashed into a fence. The driver and the passenger, two elderly people, were killed. The passenger was impaled on the fence, hence the nickname. I got five years for causing death by dangerous driving. I'd never been in trouble before, never even been in a police station, let alone a prison. And I've lost the business, of course.'

'With luck you'll only do two and half years,' John said, trying to offer some consolation.

'Yes, with luck, but I'm worried about some of the hardliners, the ones that stuck the nickname on me. They can cut up rough when they want to and I wouldn't fancy my chances against them,' Vlad said mournfully.

'Listen, if you get any trouble from anyone, you let me know because I'm more than well equipped to deal with them. Besides, the way I feel sometimes, I'd like to vent my frustration on some of those scumbags,' John offered, puffing himself up to his full size to let Vlad know he was quite capable of doing what he said.

'Thanks, that makes me feel better. So what are you in for?'

'Kidnapping and extortion, but I made one mistake.'

'What was that?'

'I got caught.'

'I think I'm going to like you,' Vlad said, offering John his hand.

After his talk with Vlad, John walked back to his cell and accidentally bumped into an inmate coming from the opposite direction. He glanced at him, apologised and walked on.

'Oi, you!' the inmate called after him.

John stopped and looked around, 'What?' he asked innocently, not wanting to get into any argument. And in any case, the man was huge, carrying some twenty stone of muscle.

'You just barged into me,' the inmate said.

'Yes, and I said sorry,' John said with an apologetic smile, but the inmate's stare made him feel uneasy.

'You looking for trouble?' the man challenged.

'I'm not looking for anything, just making my way back to my cell, no big deal,' John said, and turned to walk on.

'You'd better start showing some respect man, or else.'

John stopped in his tracks and turned back, the hairs on the back of his neck starting to rise. 'Or else what?' he asked, anger flaring up in him.

'You'll find out if you don't show respect the next time you walk past me.'

John said nothing, just turned and carried on along the corridor.

'I saw you having a few angry words with that body builder; McLean, I think his name is,' Vlad said to John at suppertime that evening.

'Yeah, ignorant idiot thinks he owns the place. Another moron looking for trouble,' John replied.

'Yeah, he treats his cellmate like a slave. Some poor young guy,' Vlad told him.

'Yeah, his name's Vaughan; the kid arrived the same day as me. What's he in for again?' John wanted to know.

'A bit like me really, death by dangerous driving. Crashed his car and his girlfriend got killed. McLean makes him clean the cell, clean his shoes and do his ironing, and if he refuses, McLean threatens to beat him up. If the screws know, they don't care, so the poor guy really suffers.' There was pity in Vlad's voice.

'Maybe when I bump into the guy again I should have a word with him,' John said as they got up from the table.

'I don't know of any easy way to say this, but I want a divorce,' Jenny said as she sat facing John across the table in the family visiting room. 'I can't take it anymore; my whole world is falling apart. I can't touch the bank accounts, there's the constant threat of the house being taken away, there's nothing left of our marriage. I think it's best if we parted.'

John saw the sorrow in her eyes. He tried to give her an understanding smile, but it didn't hide the anxiety on his face. 'I've been expecting this; I've let you and the kids down so badly. I don't blame you. If this is what you want, I won't contest it.'

'Thanks. I don't think I could stand it if we had to fight. There's been enough unhappiness and the children have also suffered. I won't stop you from seeing them, and I'll still bring them to see you.'

'What will you tell them?'

'I'll tell them we're separating, but we're still good friends and they'll still see their daddy whenever they want to.'

'I'm sorry it's come to this...'

'It's no good being sorry, it's too late for that. Getting four years was bad enough, but you couldn't stop there, you had to go and get yourself done for contempt of court without even considering the consequences. You're going to be inside for nearly three years.'

John knew everything she had said was true. 'I'll tell the kids the same, and you know I'll always be there for them, and for you. Please call them over so I can give them a hug before the visit ends.'

Jenny called the children over from the play area. John cuddled each one of them, the thought of their family unit falling apart tearing at his insides, misery settling in his chest like lead and reflecting in his eyes.

In his cell after the visit, John wept for what seemed like hours. The knowledge that he had ruined everything and broken his children's hearts almost suffocated him, and he wondered if he would ever be able to undo it.

In jail trouble often comes without warning, as happened when John was walking along the passage to meet up with Vlad. He heard a commotion coming from one of the cells further along the landing. He immediately knew it was McLean when he heard him shout at someone to clean the floor or he'd kick his head in. Still upset about Jenny's visit, John became enraged.

As Vaughan rushed out of the cell to get a mop, John dashed in, charged at McLean, shoving him hard against the cell wall and gripping him by the throat. 'I don't care how big you are mate, but if you ever threaten that young lad again, I'll break your jaw.' McLean had been caught unawares, and just as he gathered all his strength to push John off him, John smartly stepped back. McLean's momentum carried him forward and gave John the opportunity to swipe his legs out from under him. McLean crashed to the floor and John grabbed his shirt, his face a mask of anger. As he raised his fist to smash it into McLean's face, something stopped him. It was as if a powerful force was clutching his wrist and restraining him. He released his grip and lowered his arm. 'Make sure next time you pick on someone your own size. And be careful when you pass me on the landing. I might just get upset, and you will definitely not like me when I'm upset.'

Arran's birthday was coming up, and John was suffering pangs of guilt about not being there for him. Jenny brought them for a visit on the Saturday. While the children were in the playroom, she said to John, 'You'll never believe what Arran did last week. There was a book fair at school and the kids were allowed to choose a book each to take home.' There was an edge of nervousness in her voice.

I suppose he chose a book about gangsters, John thought, looking at her apprehensively.

'He took a book called *When Parents Separate*,' Jenny said, and saw the shock on John's face as he looked across to where Arran was playing. 'And here we've been thinking we're protecting them from the truth.' she continued.

Tears ran down John's face and he turned his head so as not to let the children see him cry. 'Kids grow up so quickly these days. It would be interesting to know what he expected to find in the book that we haven't already told him,' he finally said. 'I suppose it's time to tell them the truth. It'll come out one way or another in any case.'

'Well, they know you're in prison, they're here now, for goodness sake,' she said, struggling to keep her voice calm. 'But what about the reason why you're here and why I can't live with it anymore? I don't know how to explain that,' she said, shaking her head in despair.

'Do you want me to tell them?' he asked in an attempt to redeem himself.

'No, this is something I'm going to have to do. This is not the right place and I have to choose the right time too,' she said, turning her head to hide her tears.

CHAPTER 43

IF A WICKED MAN

2005

Tony the Nigerian tried for four months to persuade John to come to the Christian fellowship gatherings, but John always refused. On one particular Sunday morning he happened to mention the nice coffee, cakes and biscuits that are served there, and John's ears pricked up. *Hmm*, he thought to himself, *might be the perfect opportunity to fill my pockets while they're praying.*

'Hello John, glad you decided to come, my friend, you'll enjoy tonight,' Tony said with his usual broad smile.

John's attention was drawn to a man who was going around embracing and welcoming all the inmates. He stiffened when the man approach him.

'Welcome brother,' the pastor said with a beaming smile, his arms outstretched to embrace John.

John instinctively took a step back and put his hands up. 'I'm not your brother and I don't like anyone embracing me, particularly in prison,' he said, looking at the pastor with hostile eyes.

'My apologies, you're new here. May I welcome you to our gathering. My name is Duncan Strathdee, I'm a pastor...'

'Well, you don't look like one,' John interrupted him. The man was dressed in a white T-shirt, jeans and trainers.

'It's not how a man is dressed, but what's in his soul that matters,' the pastor said, unphased by John's aggression.

I'm more interested in what's in my stomach, John thought as he looked across at the table laid out with plates of biscuits and cakes, tea bags and sachets of Nescafé. He looked around at the other inmates, and was surprised to see many of the hardened criminals serving life sentences for murder, bank robberies and drug dealing. What surprised him even more was that they seemed so relaxed and friendly towards each other. It gave him a strange feeling.

'Right everybody!' the pastor called out, 'Shall we take a seat and begin?'

They all moved across to a group of chairs set out in a circle, with one chair set apart and a guitar resting against it. John held back, wondering why he had allowed himself to be talked into coming. Then he looked across at the food, and he remembered why. He reluctantly moved to the circle of chairs and sat down.

'Right guys, tonight were gonnae start by saying the Lord's Prayer,' the pastor announced.

The group bowed their heads, closed their eyes and began to pray; all except John, who sat looking around and shifting uncomfortably in his seat at the realisation that he was stuck, whether he liked it or not. After the prayer one of the inmates handed out laminated song sheets. *The prayers are bad enough, but singing hymns as well! This is beyond a joke. I thought we'd just be sitting around drinking tea and coffee and eating nice cakes*, he thought miserably. He watched as the pastor picked up the guitar and started strumming it as if he was a rock star. The inmates joined in, clapping their hands to the rhythm, a blues beat developing as they started singing.

Open the eyes of my heart, Lord,
open the eyes of my heart.
I want to see you, I want to see you,
see you high and lifted up,
shining in the light of your glory.
Pour out your power and love
as we cry Holy, Holy, Holy.

As he sat staring at the words, John felt his aggression slowly starting to slip away, and being replaced by a sense of warmth. It enveloped him, but at the same time guilt was hammering at his conscience. It was like nothing he had experienced before, and it scared him. Panic welled up inside him and made him shiver. It was as if his lifelong way of thinking was being challenged, plunged into uncertainty, as if his world was shifting. He tried to hold himself together as a blanket of sadness fell over him and indecision crept up on him. What was happening? Was the devil putting him to the test? Was this a contest between good and evil? Tears started rolling down his cheeks.

He lifted the song sheet to his face in an attempt to cover the shame he felt. What was it that made him react like this? This stupid, ridiculous way. He started feeling angry about it, and some of his aggression came back. He lowered the song sheet, wiped away the tears with the back of his hand and started feeling a little better.

'Are you alright, my friend?' Tony asked, having seen the troubled look on his face. John glared at him, trying to regain his composure, annoyed that Tony might have noticed his tears.

'I'm fine,' he said defiantly. 'I just don't understand all this stuff. You're all singing away as if there's no tomorrow, but there is a tomorrow, and the day after that there'll be another and another, all in this same crapty place. Which makes me wonder if there is a God and if there is, why does He let these things happen?'

'You have to have faith, my friend, only then can you hope to find the answers.'

'Faith in what? Why is there all this evil in the world? If there's a God, why does He make people suffer, destroy human lives, allow people like us to do the things we do?'

'Those are questions the greatest human minds have been struggling with since man was created,' the pastor intervened, as he came across to join the conversation. 'Life in itself creates all manner of problems. We think we know how life should be, but things have a way of changing, things we can't control.'

'And God is supposed to be all powerful?' John cut in.

'You're not the first one to ask these questions, John. Almost everyone wants to know why there's so much pain and suffering in the world.'

'And what is your answer to that?'

'Okay, let's remove God from the equation, for the sake of argument. So if there were no God, the same question would remain—Why is there so much pain and suffering in the world?'

'And?'

'Because of man. Because of us. You see, John, the pain and suffering are caused by man and the free will that God gave him. There's much we can't control in life,' the pastor said reverently.

When John got back to his cell, he lay on the bunk, his head buzzing with what had happened to him. What was it about the hymn that affected him so, was it the words or the music, and why had it made him cry? The thought made him cringe. There's a song that says 'Big Girls Don't Cry', so how much more should big boys or big, tough men not cry.

John tossed and turned all night, unable to blank out his troubled thoughts. Every time he closed his eyes, he saw the sign that hung outside the Charles Thompson mission:

'It is appointed unto men to die once and after this the judgement'

Sometime in the early hours of the morning he saw his grandmother waving her finger at him, saying, 'What will it profit a man if he gains the whole world, but loses his soul?'

No sooner had that image gone when another would come—the wallet he had picked up, with all the questions in it:

Do you believe you are good enough to get to heaven?
Have you ever told a lie?
Have you ever taken something that didn't belong to you?
Have you ever used God's name in vain?
Have you ever committed adultery?

For the first time in his life it troubled him that his answers to all but the first question would be 'Yes'.

The following day John could hardly open his eyes for the early morning head count. He wasn't in the mood for breakfast or anything else, for that matter—he was still struggling with his thoughts, angry that he had allowed himself to be drawn into something so alien to him, so against everything he believed in, or rather everything he didn't believe in.

'Good morning John, how are you today?' Tony asked as he appeared in the cell doorway.

'If you don't mind, I'd rather be on my own,' John said.

'I brought you something my friend,' Tony said, and produced a Bible from behind his back.

John's mind flashed back to when the officer of the court had held out a Bible for him to swear on. 'I told someone else what they could with their Bible, including a judge, so don't tempt me to say the same to you.'

'No, my friend, you need this. I saw how you reacted last night. I saw you trying to hide your tears from the rest of us.'

'I wasn't crying,' John retorted angrily.

'There is no shame in crying. It takes a brave man to cry,' Tony said gently.

John reluctantly took the Bible, threw it onto his bunk and walked out to go and work in the library.

Because of staff shortages, Fridays were early bang-up days. This meant that all prisoners would have their evening meal at four o'clock, have their canteen orders delivered and be back in their cells by five o'clock, where they remained locked up until eight o'clock the next morning.

The prison was as quiet as it could be, with the humming sounds of inmates talking, moaning, fidgeting about in their cells, and generally settling down for the night. John had never felt as lonely as he did at that moment. It was going to be a long solitary night. He sighed out loud, in an effort to clear the confusion, the anger, the sorrow and hatred, combined with the awkward feeling of love running riot in his mind. He needed something to make him feel whole again, make him feel part of something, but the problem was he no longer knew what that something was. Was he unable to understand what he had encountered, or didn't he want to understand it? Or was he just too scared to allow himself to understand?

He looked at the Bible that was now lying on his bedside locker, and reached out to pick it up. He felt the soft leather binding, opened it and began to thumb through the pages, not knowing where to look or what to look for. He had never really read a Bible, other than at Sunday school one time, very long ago; and he hated it, because he had been forced to go.

Midway through he stopped thumbing and cursorily glanced at the page—Ezekiel chapter eighteen. His eye caught verse twenty seven, and a feeling of warmth started enveloping him, much like being covered by a soft cloth, as he read:

> *'But if a wicked man turns away from the wickedness he has committed and does what is just and right, he will save his life. Because he considers all the offenses he has committed and turns away from them, he will surely live; he will not die.*
> *Yet the house of Israel says, "The way of the Lord is not just." Are my ways unjust O house of Israel? Is it not your ways that are unjust? Therefore, O house of Israel, I will judge you, each one according to his ways declares the Sovereign LORD.*
> *Repent! Turn away from all your offenses; then sin will not be your downfall.*
> *Rid yourselves of all the offenses you have committed, and get a new heart and a new spirit. Why will you die, O house of Israel? For I take no pleasure in the death of anyone, declares the Sovereign LORD. Repent and live!'*

The words 'If a wicked man' cut deep into him, for he knew he was a wicked man. As he lay there, the words 'wicked man' kept flashing before his eyes. Then the flashes stopped, and he said to himself, *It didn't say* I *was a wicked man, it said* if *a wicked man.'* It made him reach for the Bible again. He picked it up and found that it was still open at the same page.

Not quite understanding why, he slipped off the bed and came to rest on his knees. He wanted to say something, wanted to pray as he had seen others do, but he didn't know what to say or who to say it to. *Who is this God? Why am I so affected by Him? What does He want from me?* One question after the other screeched through his head.

The images of some of the terrible things he had done—the kidnappings, the beatings, the robberies, the readiness to kill—played like a film through his mind. He stayed on his knees for a long time, afraid that the feelings he was experiencing would disappear before he knew what they meant. He didn't want that, he wanted them to stay so that he could try to understand, because with it all he had never felt so good, so uplifted, as his heart beat with a new enlightenment.

The more he studied the words, the more questions they evoked, which made him anxious for Thursday to come around so he could ask the pastor for answers, for a way to get this new heart and new spirit.

As they gathered in the chapel on the Thursday evening, Duncan warily approached John, not trying to embrace him as he had before, but he was surprised when John spread out his arms, ready to embrace the pastor.

'Welcome brother,' the pastor said. 'I'm pleased to see you're more relaxed, ready to embrace the spirit of the Lord.'

'I think I am, Duncan, but I have so many questions.'

'Then ask and I will try to answer them.'

'Where do I find this new heart, this spirit of the Lord you preach about?'

'Why do you want a new heart and a new spirit?'

'Because I think there *is* a God, He is real and I *am* going to stand before Him on judgement day. I think there is a heaven and a hell and I'm heading for hell if I don't do something about my life.'

The pastor studied John for a moment, and a compassionate smile eased onto his face. 'The first thing is to admit to God that you're a sinner. All of us have sinned against God, some more than others, but a sin is a sin.'

'I want to make good, and when I get out of prison I want to help people, I want to do some charity work or something.'

The pastor's eyes narrowed. 'John, you can't buy your way out of sin, you can't earn forgiveness. As you found out in your own court case, the judge couldn't be bribed by the fact that you had rescued a couple of elderly people from a fire. If that judge had let you off because of that, he would have failed in his duty to uphold the law. It's the same way with God; you can't bribe Him either. You can't redeem yourself in the eyes of the Lord because you've done some good deeds. That's simply not enough.'

'So what do I have to do?'

'The first thing is that you have to be truthful. You've probably heard the word repent many times. To repent is a very real thing. It means more than just saying you're sorry; regret without repentance is worthless.'

'What do you mean by that?' John didn't quite understand.

'Ask yourself how many times your children have told you they're sorry about something they'd done, but they've gone on doing it. It means they're not really sorry for what they've done, just sorry they got caught. Repentance means actually turning away from what's wrong in God's eyes and doing your best to not go there again. Then you must put your faith and trust in Jesus Christ, because He says, 'I am the way and the truth and the life and no-one comes to the Father but through Me.'

'Forgive me Pastor, it might sound easy, but what does He actually mean by that?'

'God realised that humanity has a problem, and the problem is sin. The Bible says the wages of sin is death. That's why we realise our need for a Saviour when we go through our list of sins. God sent Jesus to earth; Jesus lived without sin and was the perfect sacrifice that God needed. He willingly laid down his life for you and me. Jesus went to the cross and God allowed it to happen. God allowed Jesus to be crushed for our iniquity, He allowed his Son to die on the cross so that justice could be served and God's wrath was poured out on Him instead of on you and me. Jesus took the hit for you, John; your fine was paid by Christ on the cross. He bled and died for you and after three days God raised Him from the dead, defeating death itself. God declared that all who sin will die, both physically and spiritually. This is the fate of all mankind. But then in His grace and mercy, He provided a way out of this dilemma, by shedding the blood of his only Son on the cross. Unlike the judge in your court, God will not punish you; all you have to do is to repent of your sins and put your faith in Jesus, and you will be saved, if you are willing.'

'Tell me more about being saved,' John asked.

'You can be saved from the sins that would lead you to an eternity separated from God; in hell. John 3:16 says, "For God so loved the world that He gave his only begotten son Jesus Christ that whosoever believes in Him shall not perish but have eternal life." If you want to repent and you put your faith in Christ, I promise you John, God will give you a new heart and spirit when you turn away from your sins and you surrender your life to Jesus.'

'So I can only be redeemed because of what Jesus did? I can't earn this new heart and new spirit, it's only given by God when I repent and trust in Jesus, right?'

'Exactly. But it's more than just saying a quick prayer; it's so much more. It's giving up on your self-reliance and putting all your trust in Jesus. You have to be willing to surrender to Him, to let His Gospel change you. Call out to God with a sincere heart and let Him start the work in you that He started in me many years ago.'

When John got back to his cell he was overcome by what the pastor had said. He fell down onto his bed, and images of the terrible things he had done rolled out before him like an endless series of slides, ultimately driving him to floods of tears.

With these images came the realisation that he, John, had in his way also been responsible for Jesus being nailed to the cross, and the pain of this knowledge became almost unbearable. How could Jesus have given his life for someone who cursed His Name and spat in His face? John fell to his knees.

'Jesus, please forgive me for the sins I've committed and the people I've hurt. I'm so sorry for what I've done. I want to turn away from all of that now; I want You to be my Lord. I believe in my heart that God raised You from the dead and You are alive to this day and I surrender my life to You. Make me yours, do with me as You will,' John prayed out loud, tears streaming down his cheeks.

How long he remained on his knees he could not remember and didn't care, for he was overcome with such a feeling of relief and well-being that he felt no pain, just a tremendous sense of joy. He knew that he was being changed in a way he could never have imagined.

CHAPTER 44

A NEW CREATION

When John woke up the following morning, everything felt different to him—the prison, the cell, everything. It felt as if an overpowering sense of peace and gentleness pervaded the air. When his cell door opened, John walked out a different person, a man at peace with himself.

'You look cheerful this morning, Lawson,' the wing officer quipped as John strode purposefully past him.

'I've found something that I think is making me happy.'

'As long as we don't have to start searching your cell for drugs, I'm pleased for you,' the officer said with a smile as he watched John head off for breakfast.

Later that day he was doing his daily chores in the library and had just finished cleaning one of the classrooms when Michael Chamberlain appeared in the doorway. 'Hello John,' he said with an expressionless face.

'Michael!' John exclaimed. 'What a surprise!'

'Why are you surprised? You're the reason I'm here,' Michael said, this time with clear hostility.

John felt the weight of his anger like a physical blow and winced inwardly. 'We need to talk,' he said.

'Damn right, we do,' Michael retorted.

'Look, I've heard rumours that you think I stitched you up...'

'You did; you did a deal with the Procurator Fiscal to get Tam Kelly off and get yourself a reduced sentence.'

'You've got to be joking! I got an extra fifteen months for refusing to give evidence!'

'Good on you, but how come Tam was released the very day you came to court?'

'Look, they had me bang to rights, they had recordings of my voice making the threats, they had the sim cards from my phones, they had us all on CCTV—you arriving at the station, everything. They had all the evidence they needed and if I hadn't put my hand up I would have received a much longer sentence. Okay, I know I dropped you and Jay in it by pleading guilty, but remember, you and Jay dropped yourselves in it too by denying you were in Edinburgh that day when they had you both on CCTV. You did the crime just like me and now you gotta do the time just like me. I'd like to know what you would have done!'

Michael simply stared at John; a long, hard stare.

'You tell me, Michael, who got the longest sentence, eh? You got four and Jay got five years, but in the end I got five years and three months. And has either of you been hit with the Proceeds of Crime Act?'

'No, I haven't.'

'Well I have, and I'm going to lose my house, my cars, my bank accounts have been seized and I'm about to lose my wife. So you tell me who came out worst on the so-called deal.'

'Yeah well, I've lost Cara as well. She's gone and run off back to South Africa. But when you put it like that I guess you didn't get off so lightly, but you shouldn't have put your hands up in the first place.'

'Maybe you're right, but it's something we have to live with and we can stay friends or become enemies and I wouldn't want that, because I now have a new heart and a new spirit; I've become a Christian.'

Michael stared at him in stunned amazement. 'You a Christian? When the heck did that happen?'

'Only recently, since I've been going to Bible classes. I'm a different person, Michael. I'm beginning to feel at peace with myself and it's wonderful.'

'You're serious, aren't you? So what about Spider, you still on for that when we get out?' Michael asked, still staring at John in amazement.

'No, I'm a changed man. I'm never going back to crime. That life is behind me. All I want to do is know God more, know His ways and serve Him.'

'You're serious.'

'Yes I am, and I'd love you to come to the Christian Fellowship meetings,' John heard himself saying.

'Well, I don't think I'll ever become a Christian. As you know, I'm into Apache Shamanism, but I think it'd be interesting to come; if nothing else, to see how it has affected you.'

John's mother thought she had noticed a change in him during her last visit. He appeared more relaxed and he didn't seem to be so angry. It gave her hope that the strict regime of prison was beginning to have an effect on him and she prayed it would continue. The prayer was answered when John rang her. There was the usual silence as she listened to the recorded message, 'The phone call you are about to receive is from an inmate of Her Majesty's Prison, Glenochil. Please hang up now if you do not wish to receive this call.' Then her son's gentle voice.

'Hi Mum, how are you all?'Jose noticed that he had called her 'Mum' instead of the usual 'Ma'.

'All fine, how are you?' she asked casually.

'Fine Mum... Mum, I've...'

'You seemed more relaxed on the last visit,' Josie interrupted him. 'Maybe prison is teaching you a few things at last.'

'I don't know about prison, but you're right, I am a lot more relaxed.'

'I'm pleased to hear that; so what has brought it about?'

'I've found peace, Mum. I've become a Christian.' He heard a sharp intake of breath and then silence. 'Mum, are you there?' he asked, 'Mum, are you there? My card is going to run out soon.'

'Sorry son,' her voice came back, and he realised she was crying. 'I've been praying for this day and I've never given up hope. I can tell you now, after my first visit, I telephoned Pastor Strathdee and told him about you and we prayed together that you would be guided to God.'

The surprise at what she was saying travelled through his body to his face and he was pleased she couldn't see it. 'Then your prayers have been answered, because someone found me and led me to the Bible study. I've found God and surrendered myself to Him to do with as He will.'

John heard the happiness in his mother's voice. 'I've got my son back! Praise the Lord! You know, I visited the Logos Hope ship in Liverpool last week, and I met George Verwer, the founder of O.M. Ministries. He's got such faith. I bought you a book while I was there; it's called *Taming the Tiger*. I'll post it to you tomorrow.' *Please mother, don't start Bible-bashing me, let me do it my way in my own time*, John thought silently, but said, 'I'll call again next week, Mum. Take care of yourself and love to everyone, God bless,' he said, also struggling to control his emotions as he replaced the receiver.

The change in John was noticed by the authorities as well, and they started allowing him to move around more freely, trusting him with tasks that they would not have entrusted to him before. One such task was to collect cleaning materials and other supplies from the main stores, which meant he had to go out into the prison yard to help unload the deliveries.

On one such a day as John stood waiting with the civilian in charge for the truck to draw up, he did a double take as the driver scrambled out of the cab. 'Kenny!' he shouted in surprise.

It was his cousin, Auntie Betty and Uncle Tommy's son. 'What's going on John, what are you doing here?' he asked as they stood staring at each other.

'What do you think I'm doing here? This is a prison and I'm in it. Don't you recognise the uniform?'

'Nobody told me you were in prison. Does your Ma know? Do my Ma and Da know?'

'Yes, they know, but we decided to keep it quiet to prevent pressure on the rest of the family.'

'And what about Jenny and the kids?'

'Jenny is divorcing me, and I can't say I blame her...'

'Lawson, there's no talking to drivers! There's work to be done, so get the barrow!' one of the screws called out.

'Give my love to the family,' John managed to say before moving off. As he started unloading the supplies he glanced up at Kenny sitting in the cab, staring straight ahead with a bemused expression on his face. *I guess now everyone will know*, John thought, and continued offloading the provisions.

'Lawson, after breakfast get your gear together and wait in your cell, you're being moved,' the wing officer told him as John made his way to the canteen.

'Where are they moving me to, boss?' John asked.

'Wait and see; just make sure you're ready,' the officer said with a smile.

John was relieved when they told him he was being moved to the newly built wing, and he was even more relieved when he saw it. Compared to D Wing it was a palace. The cells were clean and neat, each fitted with a toilet, sink, a much more comfortable bunk and even a television set. At the end of the central landing there was a shower block and recreation room with a pool table and table tennis table, as well as a separate gym with running machines and fitness equipment. John was allocated his own cell which overlooked the exercise yard and football pitch. It had a lovely view over the Ochil Hills, all the way to the William Wallace Monument that stood tall and proud overlooking the place of Scotland's victory over the English in the Battle of Stirling Bridge. John could even see Stirling Castle, where several Scottish kings and queens had been crowned, including Mary Queen of Scots. Being able to gaze at the landscape through the barred window gave John a new sense of contentment, his faith having gifted him with freedom from the anger and pain of the past. In the book of Luke he found a verse that summed it up:

> *'The spirit of the Lord is upon me, because He has anointed me to preach the gospel to the poor; He has sent me to heal the broken-hearted, to proclaim liberty to the captives and recovery of sight to the blind. To set at liberty those who are oppressed.'*

By August 2005 John had been in prison for just over a year and was a completely changed man, preaching the Gospel to any prisoner who cared to listen, although many avoided him, turning away whenever they saw him, thinking he was mad or on some kind of drug. But John remained determined; after every rejection he would repeat a verse from Paul's second letter to the Corinthians to himself:

> *'To the one we are the aroma of death leading to death, and to the other the aroma of life leading to life. And who is sufficient for these things? For we are not, as so many, peddling the word of God; but as of sincerity, but as from God, we speak in the sight of God in Christ.'*

On a visit with the children, Jenny handed John a letter that she had been given permission to bring in. A broad smile spread over his face as he read the contents. There was one letter from the police stating he had been awarded a meritorious award for bravery in saving two elderly people's lives and another letter from The Society for the Protection of Life from Fire, awarding him a commendation for his bravery in rescuing nine people and carrying two elderly people to safety. The ceremony was to take place on the 21st of November at the Gallery in Fettes College.

'Fettes College, that's where Tony Blair went, isn't it? Doesn't say much for the college though. How the blazes do they expect me to attend when I'm banged up here in any case?' John said, looking up at Jenny.

'Surely they'll let you out to receive the awards. I mean, they can't be that strict, especially now that you've changed your ways and become a Christian.'

'I guess I can ask.'

'Show them the letters. You should have seen the kids' reaction when they saw them. They are so proud of you; they want to be there when you receive the awards,' Jenny said, and he didn't miss the hint of pride in her voice.

'I'll see what I can do. I'd love the kids to be there, to be proud of what their dad has done and what he's become.' John had to suppress the emotions welling up in him.

'I'm told the Governor, Kate Donegal, is due to visit the library on Monday, so I might get a chance to ask her.'

While getting on with his chores, John waited nervously for the Governor to appear so that he could try and have a word with her. Once she came within striking distance, John ventured, 'Excuse me Governor, may I have a quick word with you, please?'

She stopped and looked at John, almost as if to say, 'How dare you address me?' But John carried right on. 'I received these letters, Governor, and I wondered if I might be granted permission to attend the award ceremony; I think it will be really good for my future.'

The Governor took the letters and studied them. 'This is wonderful Lawson, congratulations,' she said.

'Thank you Ma'am.'

'However, you're a long term prisoner in a high security prison. For you to attend we would have to arrange for a private security van to transport you to and from the event and assign a prison officer to escort you. Also, you need to know that as a high security prisoner you will be handcuffed and remain handcuffed throughout. That might cause you some embarrassment, particularly if your family were to attend,' she explained in a formal but not unfriendly manner.

'I understand Governor, but I would still like to put in an application to attend if I may.'

'Very well, I'll see what I can do. But I don't want to raise your hopes,' she said before moving on.

CHAPTER 45

CASTLE HUNTLY

The morning began well, as did every morning; there was no better feeling now than waking up to God. But this day wasn't to be blessed, it seemed. John was called to the wing office and handed a letter informing him that his application had been denied.

He walked back to the library, disappointed, but taking solace in the words he had read in the Bible the previous evening—*'Be anxious for nothing, but in everything by prayer and supplication, with thanksgiving, let your requests be made known to God.'*

Later that day his solicitor Mr. McAlister came to visit him. 'The Asset Recovery Agency has finally agreed on the final sum and you'll be pleased to hear they've settled on forty grand...'

'Forty grand!' John exclaimed, 'What makes you think I'd be pleased to give away forty grand?'

'You seem to forget they wanted a hundred to begin with, so on the face of it I think you've got a good deal,' McAlister reminded him. He placed some paperwork on the small table of the private visiting room.

'And when do we have to pay that?'

'If the court is satisfied that you need time to pay, it will allow you up to six months, plus a further possible six months if you can show exceptional reason for an extension. So that means in effect we could delay the selling of the house...'

'If I were to take full responsibility for the money, could we avoid selling the house?' John asked. He couldn't bear the thought of Jenny and the children having to move out of the house they had so lovingly refurbished, all because of his stupidity. 'I'm the criminal; I'm the only one who should be punished.'

'Unfortunately the law doesn't see it that way. They look at who else might have benefitted from the proceeds of your criminal acts. They feel the house was purchased with the proceeds of your criminal activities and as a consequence your wife is considered equally culpable and therefore she cannot be exempt. As I was saying, I'll endeavour to give Mrs. Lawson time to find suitable alternative accommodation, but I should warn you, twelve months is the limit. After that interest will be charged and that could push the cost up considerably,' McAlister explained.

'The longer we can give Jenny to find something suitable, the better. I'll take full responsibility for the outstanding amount once the house has been sold,' John said in a sad voice.

As he made his way to his cell after the evening meal, John decided to check the notice board to see if there was mail for him, which there was. He approached the wing officer. 'I see my name is on the board; is there mail for me boss?' he asked.

'Yes Lawson, there's a letter and a parcel,' the officer said. John took them and hurried off to his cell. First he opened the letter, guessing that the parcel was a Bible from his mother. The letter was from Jenny's solicitors outlining details of the divorce proceedings, which did nothing to lift his spirits, so he turned his attention to the parcel. It wasn't a Bible, but a book entitled *Taming the Tiger* by Tony Anthony. The words 'From the Depths of Hell to the Heights of Glory' were emblazoned at the bottom of the front cover.

John was so taken by the book that he read it in two nights. He loved the part where Michael Wright goes to visit Tony Anthony in Nicosia's notorious Central Prison and Tony asks, in a not too friendly manner, what made Michael want to come and visit him. Michael simply answers that he believes God sent him to tell him about Jesus.

It reminded John of how the Nigerian Tony had sought him out and led him to Jesus. By the time John had read the book a second time he was determined to make contact with Tony Anthony when he was released, to tell him how much the book had inspired him. John even gave the book to a Muslim inmate named Bash, in the hope it would inspire him to think about Christ in a different way. The book had done much to encourage him in his faith and he was beginning to feel better about himself and his belief.

The change in John had convinced the authorities that he could be moved to an open prison, and in November 2005 he was taken to Castle Huntly. 'It's a holiday camp compared to this, but you deserve it, Lawson, you've kept your nose clean and stayed out of trouble,' the wing officer told him. But as much as he looked forward to the change, John knew he was going to miss the comfort of his little cell as well as the new friends he'd made, including Vlad and Michael, of course. Most of all he was going to miss the Bible classes.

Bash had been sent to Castle Huntly two weeks earlier, so at least there would be someone there he knew. Five other prisoners were being transferred with him, two of which he was pleased to see, Rooney and Vaughan. They were taken down to reception, signed out, handcuffed and loaded into the prison van—the sweat box—and driven out of Glenochil prison.

To see the outside world after thirteen months of brick walls and barbed wire was breathtaking, albeit through bars.

After a three hour drive they turned into the prison drive leading to the North Gate entrance. It was a simple barrier between what looked like two Gothic towers. The barrier was raised without much preamble and as they drove on the castle on the hill became visible. There were open fields and woods, with no apparent walls surrounding them. The van pulled up at reception, and they were led into a clean, modern building. A senior prison officer approached them, looked at his watch and said. 'It's almost lunchtime, so the other prisoners will be heading for the dining hall. I suggest you go and have a look around the place, see where everything is, then go to the dining hall, have something to eat and be back here at one thirty, right?'

Nobody moved, stunned by the fact that they could just get up and walk around. 'Go on, off you go,' the officer said with an amused smile.

John walked out with Rooney and Vaughan and they stared in amazement at the vast open grounds, the manicured lawns, the trees with their leaves in the last of their autumn shades, the greenhouses and long plastic hothouses containing all sorts of plants and vegetables.

'One could walk out of here and you wouldn't even need to scale a wall, 'cos there aren't any,' John said as they sat down on the grass, touching it as if they had never seen anything like it before.

'Only an idiot would think of absconding from here, that's why there are no walls or barbed wire. You get caught and they bang you back up and you lose your remission; not worth it,' Rooney said, as he pulled out a handful of grass and smelled it.

The dining hall was clean and well furnished and there was a good selection of appetising food. The three men, having selected what they wanted, took their meals to a table and tucked into the best meal they had ever had in a prison.

'Better than some of the meals I've had outside,' Rooney joked.

Back at reception the prison officer said, 'Right, I guess you all know the prison rules. Although this is an open prison, the same rules apply, and appropriate action will be taken if you break them. So, no mobile phones, no drugs. You will be subjected to urine tests and anyone failing a test will be punished and immediately sent back to a closed prison. You've no doubt seen there are no walls or barbed wire and you are free to move around within the precincts of the prison, but don't think you can just walk out, because you'll be caught and you'll lose all your remission and may have your sentence extended.'

John was assigned to Room 12, as the wing officer referred to it, and issued with a key. The 'room' looked as if it had been furnished from Ikea, with a television, a desk and a table with a kettle and the other paraphernalia for making tea and coffee. In the far corner was a separate toilet, which pleased John immensely. His only disappointment was that there was a bunk bed, the top of which had bedding laid out on it, clearly occupied by another prisoner. By four o'clock he had collected his bedding and made up the bottom bunk, when he heard a key turning in the lock and the door flying open.

'Hi pal, Shaun's the name, drugs' the game, welcome,' Shaun announced as he sauntered in.

John looked at Shaun and all his fears of sharing a cell were realised. He was a big guy, overweight and bloated. He had greasy black hair, a pale complexion and displayed a row of rotten teeth when he smiled—the hallmarks of drug addiction.

'So what are you in for?' Shaun asked the standard question that every prisoner asks a new inmate.

John gave him as brief an answer as possible.

'You want to chase the dragon, mate?' Shaun offered.

'No thanks, I don't touch the stuff,' John was quick to answer.

'Want a smoke?'

'Don't smoke either,' John replied curtly.

'You some kind of goody two shoes, pal?

'No, far from it, but I've become a Christian, mate. Jesus has changed me and He can set you...'

'Aye, aye, aye I've heard all that before, pal. I'm not interested in your Jesus, but if you change your mind, there's plenty of drugs around,' Shaun said. 'I can score you a bag for a tenner and I can get you a mobile phone if you want,' he offered, lighting a cigarette and blowing out large clouds of smoke.

John knew he had to do something, and made his way to the wing office. 'Sorry boss, but you've put me in with a smoker. I don't smoke, never have. I need to move or you need to move him, please' he said to the wing officer.

'There's nothing I can do about it, that's the cell you've been assigned to and that's the end of it, so make the best of it.' The officer was unperturbed.

On his way back to his cell, John noticed a small lounge area and to his amazement he spotted his Muslim friend, Abdul Bashir, sitting on a sofa. Bash looked in a terrible state, rocking back and forth and staring blankly into space. His eyes were sunken, his body frail and thin, and his light brown skin looked grey.

John sat down beside him. 'Bash? What's going on? What's happened to you?'

Bash stopped rocking and slowly turned his head, his eyes blinking while his drug-fuelled brain struggled to recognise John.

'It's me, John, don't you recognise me?'

'John, John,' he said when at last his eyes had focussed and there was a glint of recognition. 'Sorry man, I'm on the smack, I'm on the hard stuff and I can't get off it.'

John remembered Bash telling him that his sister had run off with a drug dealer, and Bash had gone and kidnapped her to get her away from him and the drugs, which is why he finished up in jail. 'So what happened for you to become hooked on drugs, mate?'

'I don't know John, this place is boring and I haven't got any friends like I had with you in Glenochil. They stuck me in with a serious user and I just gave in one night when he kept on offering me the stuff for free. I was feeling lost, and the drugs stop you from feeling, and before you know it you can't do without them.'

That night was the worst night of John's entire prison sentence. His cellmate was in and out of the cell scoring drugs and using the toilet without closing the door. The stench coming from the toilet, combined with clouds of cigarette smoke soon had John in a fury. He wanted to grab Shaun, shove him against the wall and beat the daylights out of him, but something held him back. He lay back on his bunk, closed his eyes and prayed that God would find him a way out of his dilemma. Shaun arrived back the following morning, looking rather angry with himself.

'What you doing back here, aren't you supposed be at work?' John asked.

'I've been sacked, and I've been told to move,' Shaun said, and started gathering up his belongings.

John felt as if his prayers had been answered. As soon as Shaun had left he started cleaning up the cell, opening the windows and unpacking his meagre belongings. He came across the invitations to the award ceremony, which he suddenly realised was to take place the following Monday—three days away. Surely, now that he was in an open prison, he would be allowed to go?

The wing officer studied the letters and looked up. 'You see Lawson, you have to have been here for at least a week before we can assess if you're suitable to be allowed out, and you only arrived yesterday. I doubt that this will be approved.'

'Please boss, this is a big thing for me and it could really help me with my future when I'm released,' John pleaded.

'I'll take these letters up to the castle and see what I can do, but don't hold out too much hope,' the officer said.

CHAPTER 46

IF THEY ONLY KNEW

Once again John's prayers were answered, and he was let out of prison for the award ceremony.

John and Jenny met up with Daniel at the Dreghorn army barracks, where he was now stationed. He looked splendid in his army uniform, and together the three of them entered the gallery at Fettes College. Uniformed police officers, members of the fire brigade as well as members of the public were seated in rows of chairs. The Lord Mayor of Edinburgh, the Chief Constable, Chief Fire Officer and other dignitaries were seated at a table at the end of the gallery. Members of the press were moving around talking to people and taking photographs. They were ushered to their seats and were just in time for the Lord Mayor's address.

'Ladies and Gentlemen, I would like to welcome you to this award ceremony to honour both members of the emergency services and members of the public who have gone beyond the call of duty and shown exemplary courage in putting their own lives at risk to save others.'

John looked around warily, by now quite over-awed by the situation. He felt a hot flush of panic, felt his strength drain away, and he wondered if any of the police had recognised him. The Lord Mayor's words became a blur as he continued to scan the policemen's faces.

The Lord Mayor rambled on until finally the Master of Ceremonies announced the names of those to be honoured. One award after the other was handed out until Daniel suddenly nudged him—his name had been called out. John got to his feet and made his way to the front.

'Mr Lawson is to receive a meritorious award for his bravery in saving the lives of nine people from a burning building, personally rescuing two elderly people from the top of the building at great risk to his own life and also alerting the other residents of the building to the dangers with the help of his friend Andrew Warburton who, although not present, is also to receive a meritorious award.'

The Chief Constable handed John the framed award and as they shook hands and posed, the cameras clicked away. The Master of Ceremonies then announced,

'Mr Lawson also receives a commendation from the Preservation of Life Society for his actions in the same incident.' The Chief Fire Officer presented John with the award, and once again they shook hands and posed for the photographers.

With the ceremony over, everyone was invited to enjoy light refreshments, but John took a quick glance at his watch, knowing he had to get back to the flat, change out of his suit and have Jenny drive him back to prison.

'Won't you join us Mr Lawson? That was a very courageous thing you did. Do come and have a drink,' one of the police officers invited.

'Thank you, but unfortunately I can't stay, I have to go.'

'Back to work?'

'In a way, yes.'

'You mean to say your boss wouldn't give you time off for such a special occasion?'

'Well, I'm with Her Majesty's services at the moment and I really have to dash back,' John said sheepishly.

'Anyway then, well done. I just wish there were more public spirited citizens like you, instead of the increasing number of criminals we have to deal with these days. Keep up the good work,' the officer said, shaking John's hand.

CHAPTER 47

FREEDOM INSIDE

2006

The best perk of being in an open prison was the monthly home visits. John was thrilled to be able to spend Christmas with Daniel, Siobhan, Arran and Lewis, but after they had opened their presents he was quite taken aback when Jenny told him she would be spending the rest of the day with her new boyfriend, Kenny. At least John had the pleasure of watching the younger children enjoy their presents, but what really interested him was the present he had given Daniel—a Bible protected by a metal casing, designed specifically for military personnel to carry with them into battle. As Daniel flicked through the pages, he looked up with a smile and said, 'This is going to be very useful to take with me to Iraq.'

'What did you just say?' John was stunned.

'Sorry Dad, I was going to tell you. Our battalion is being sent to Iraq at the end of January for a six month tour.'

'You see, there is God working His miracles again. He must have guided me to buy you that Bible,' John said, as the shock on his face eased into a reassuring smile. 'Hold on to it and keep it with you always, son. I believe it will give you strength when you need it.'

'And it will remind me of you, Dad, and that you'll be praying for me,' Daniel said, giving the Bible a gentle rub.

'I'll pray every day that Jesus brings you home safely, and the rest of the men with you.'

On New Year's Eve he popped down to Oscar's to wish Tam a happy New Year. He stayed for just one drink and then headed out the door. But it was the wrong moment. Grant, the new bouncer, was finding it difficult to hold back a drunken crowd of youths, and while he was trying to deal with two of them, another one sneaked up behind him and raised a beer bottle, ready to smash it over his head. John acted instinctively and shoved Grant out of the way, inadvertently placing himself in line with the bottle, which caught him squarely on the head. The bottle didn't break, and John was able to disarm the man. Many in the crowd recognised John, and knew his reputation, so they quickly turned and ran off. Grant thanked John profusely, shook his hand and said, 'If I can ever return the favour, you let me know, okay?'

John returned to Castle Huntly on the 2nd of January and soon settled back into the prison routine. He decided to join the Bible study group and during one of the discussion sessions he told the group about the book, *Taming the Tiger*.

Not long thereafter he couldn't believe his eyes when he spotted a poster at reception, announcing that Tony Anthony, the author of *Taming the Tiger*, would be visiting the prison to share his story. This was the man whose words had so moved him that he had pledged to seek him out when he got out of prison, and here he was, coming to this very prison. John couldn't wait to phone his mother and tell her the news.

'You see son, how God has connected everything? These things don't just happen, it's not just a coincidence, it's a God incidence,' she said with great passion in her voice. 'God works in mysterious ways, always remember that,' she added.

Tony Anthony's visit had a profound effect on John, adding to his resolve to re-shape his life with God's help. But as Tony clearly stated, 'Prison takes many shapes and forms and you don't have to be behind bars to be imprisoned. Many of you were in a prison before you ever came here, a prison of violence, of addiction to stuff you look at on the internet, a prison of anger or self abuse and much more, from which only Jesus can truly set you free.'

After the talk John rushed up to shake Tony's hand. He told him he had read his book and what an impact it had had on him. Tony seemed pleased, and invited John to make contact when he was released from prison. His parting words to John were, 'Remember, everyone suffers in life at some point, but Jesus will see you through.'

John often thought of these words when he struggled to find courage or to understand the changes that were taking place within him. He also found strength in Jesus' words that anyone who is in Christ, is '... a new creation; old things have passed away'. By now John knew that once he was released from prison, he would go out and share with others what Jesus had done for him.

Daniel was serving the second half of his tour of Iraq and John spent many nights praying for God's protection over his son. It was tough being in prison knowing Daniel was in a war zone, but at the same time he felt a great sense of peace as he sat reading his Bible, believing God would protect him.

John and two other prisoners, Matt and Dave, were allowed to do community work at an old people's day care centre in Dundee. They were taken by bus into the city centre and dropped off at their various places of work. John was happy about the opportunity to do some good, and it also kept his mind occupied, which made the days pass quicker.

Life was even better when Daniel returned safely from Iraq and was stationed back in Edinburgh, which meant he could visit John and they could meet up on the days John was allowed out; particularly on Sundays, when they visited the Perth Christian Centre.

John heard rumours that Jay was being transferred to Huntly Castle and that he had told everybody he was going to make John pay for selling him and Michael down the river. Not long after that Johns spotted Jay in the reception area with a group of heavies, and he knew no matter what his own feelings were, he had to face Jay and sort things out.

'We need to talk,' he said to Jay. 'I suggest we go to my cell.'

Jay was caught unawares. He knew John to be a violent man and capable of doing him more harm than vice versa. He was sure that one wrong word or move would be enough to set John off. 'It's okay, John, I don't bear any grudges. It's all in the past, so let's forget it,' he said, while his companions stared at him in surprise at his apparent surrender.

'No Jay,' John said. 'I suggest we go to my cell to talk, not fight.' Realising he had no choice, Jay followed John, with the others looking on.

Once in his cell, John said, 'Listen Jay, I've heard that you think I did a deal and stitched you and Michael up.' He held up his hand when it looked as if Jay was about to protest. 'Let me tell you, if I did, I made the worst deal in history. Not only did I get four years, but I got another fifteen months for refusing to give evidence against you. All my assets were seized and I've lost my wife, so you tell me who's come off worse in all of this.' There was no anger in John's voice, just a quiet dignity.

Jay took a long measured look at John. 'Sorry, I didn't know that.'

'No you didn't, and another thing, you'll be out of here long before me.'

'Yes I guess I will, so I suggest we forget about it and put it behind us.'

'Fine by me, but you've made a rod for your own back,' John told him.

'Why is that?'

'Well, you've announced to everyone you were going to do me in, so you could lose face if we don't handle this properly.'

'So what do you suggest?'

'We keep our distance in here and you tell everybody you're going to wait until you can get me on the outside,' John suggested.

'Okay, sorted. But there's another thing I want to sort out with you. We've spent so much time and money on it, I hope you're still up for going back to Spain and getting our hands on Spider's money,' Jay said.

'No Jay, I'm not, I'm done with all that. I've changed, I'm a Christian now.'

Jay shook his head as if he was hearing wrongly. 'Are you serious? This is not one of your cons to get early release, is it? What do they call them—"prison Christians"'?

'No, it's no con; I've become a servant of Jesus. That is what I want to be now. It only happened once I'd let go of my past and died to myself.'

Jay shook his head again. 'I don't know what to say.'

'Then say nothing, but remember, Jesus changed me, which means he can do that for you too. So when he knocks on your door Jay, you must be willing to open it.'

'Yeah well, another time maybe, but I can't handle that now. I find it all a bit cranky. If it makes you happy, then fine, but watch out for some of the guys who came in with me; a couple of them are loose cannons and they'd love to have a pop at you. They think you're some kind of fruit cake,' Jay warned.

CHAPTER 48

IT IS FINISHED

2007

John was due for release in October 2006 on his first sentence, but he still had to serve the civil conviction for contempt of court. Thus only seven and a half months later, on the 17th of May 2007, he was finally released on parole from Castle Huntly prison, walking out with his belongings stuffed in a black plastic bag.

Tam Kelly was waiting for him with a welcoming smile. 'How does it feel to be free?' he asked as he opened the boot of his BMW and unceremoniously tossed John's plastic bag in.

'I've been free for quite some time now,' John said.

Tam gazed at him, a puzzled expression on his face. 'I don't understand; you've only just been released,' he said.

'You forget, Tam, I was set free by Jesus; I told you I'm a Christian now.'

'Oh yes sorry, I forgot. I thought that was just for the prison authorities and that once you got out...'

'The only thing I know is that I knew nothing until I found God, and Tam, until then I was nothing,' John said with a warm tone in his voice.

'Right, well, we'd better get you to the probation office so they can sort you out, and when we've got you settled, come over to the club and we'll have a celebration drink.'

'Tam, you're not listening to me, I'm not into that anymore, I must follow my belief now.'

'Which I guess means you're not interested in going after Spider's money either?' Tam said despairingly.

'No I'm not, we've been through that already and I haven't changed my mind.'

'Well, maybe when you've been back outside in the real world for some time you'll change your mind,' Tam said wistfully, as they drove away from the prison.

John didn't look back. To him the past was behind and he was on a journey into the future.

The future didn't get off to a very good start—the room he was allocated by the local Council was a small bedsit in a run-down block of flats near the Musselburgh racecourse, mainly occupied by down-and-outs, junkies and alcoholics. The familiar acrid smell of unsanitary conditions was just as bad as, if not worse than he'd experienced in prison.

Well, at least I'm in the right place to share the Gospel with lost souls, John thought as he dropped his black bag on the floor and slumped down on the narrow bed.

However, with none of his prison friends to talk to and feeling completely alone, his new home felt more like a prison than Huntly Castle had. Alone with his thoughts his mind drifted to the nice flat he and Jenny had shared, the new furniture, his Range Rover, his motorbike, money in the bank—the £40,000 from his share of the profits of the house sale—but fortunately Jenny had enough money left to rent a new house in Prestonpans. He lowered his head into his hands and prayed.

'How are things going, you settled in alright?' Tam asked as John walked into Oscar's.

'Not really; I've been given a miserable little bedsit in a block of flats that quite frankly should be knocked down. I was wondering if you knew of anyone who might have a flat to rent.'

It turned out that Grant, the bouncer John had helped out of trouble some months earlier, was looking for someone to take over the lease of his flat, as he was on his way to Canada.

At 11 Graham Street John stood on the pavement looking up at the modern, grey stone apartment block with its large windows, and he wondered for a moment if Tam had given him the wrong address, but he hadn't. The apartment was well beyond John's expectations, with floor to ceiling windows that provided a panoramic view of the Edinburgh skyline. It was well furnished throughout, with a fully equipped kitchen.

Grant was hoping to get back some of the money he had spent on the flat, but John was quick to explain, 'Look, I've just come out of prison and there's no way I can afford any of this, much as I'd love to. The flat is fantastic, but it's well beyond me.'

'I owe you John, you saved me from being smashed over the head, so as long as you take over the rent, you can start paying me for the furniture when you're back on your feet. And if you can't, well, then don't worry about it.'

After Grant had gone, John sat down on the black leather sofa and looked out at Arthur's Seat, the extinct volcano that dominates the city skyline directly in front of him, with Edinburgh Castle in the distance. The only movement across the sky was an occasional bird or plane. He had despaired at the thought of being stuck in that terrible bedsit, but as he looked up to heaven he realised his prayers had been answered again, and God had done more than he had asked for or could ever have imagined.

A week later Grant popped in to see how John was doing, and surprised him with a proposition. 'I know you're short of money, John, so I've got something that might interest you.' John looked at him expectantly, ready to listen to anything he had to offer. 'There's a job I'm thinking of doing with a couple of mates, which will give me a nice big wedge to go to Canada with. With your track record I was wondering if you'd be interested in coming in with us.'

'What exactly is the job?' John asked, beginning to doubt the reply.

'There's this guy who owns a scrap yard who's reported to have about £200,000 stashed away in a safe. If you're willing to do the surveillance work so we can work out the best time to make the hit, and then be ready with the getaway car, you could earn yourself a nice fifty grand,' Grant explained.

'Sorry Grant, I'm not interested, I'm a Christian and I've turned away from crime. God is my saviour now, not money.'

Grant studied his impassive face and narrowed his eyes as he said. 'I don't believe this; you really mean this stuff, don't you? It's amazing what prison does to some people, but I never thought it would change a hard man like you.'

John smiled gently. 'It wasn't prison that changed me, it was God, and I've given myself to Him. Let me give you an example: Remember at the club when I pushed you out of the way and took the hit for you, that bottle that was meant for you?'

'Of course, that's why I was happy for you to have the flat.'

'Well, Jesus took the hit for me when He sacrificed Himself on the cross and my sins nailed Him to the wood. He paid the price for me, Grant. He gave His life for me and there's no greater love than that. I owe Him in a much bigger way than you said you owe me.'

'Well, I didn't expect to hear all this, but as I said, there's fifty grand in it for you. It's a lot of money John, and you're skint, so think hard, because you won't get another chance like this,' Grant said, before turning and walking out.

John slumped down on the sofa, his mind spinning. Fifty grand was a lot of money and it could set him up for the future. He got to his feet, crossed to the window and stared out at the skyline before raising his eyes to heaven and praying for an answer. Leaning wearily against the glass with his eyes closed he seemed to hear a quiet voice say, *'But those who desire to be rich fall into temptation and a snare, and into many foolish and harmful lusts which drown men into destruction and perdition.'*

He slowly opened his eyes, studied his worried reflection in the window and saw the question etched on his face, 'Am I really a new creation? Have I truly been given a new heart and new spirit?'

The words 'If A Wicked Man' sprang to mind once more, and John breathed a sigh of relief as he began to comprehend what they truly meant. The violence, the kidnappings, the beatings, the sex clubs, the blood on his hands, had all been wiped clean. There was that voice again, this time even louder: '**IT IS FINISHED**.'

Wiping the tears from his eyes with both hands, he heard himself say to his reflection, *'Believe your beliefs and doubt your doubts, for with God all things are possible,'* and it made him feel good, cleansed, knowing in that moment of temptation that he had truly turned his back on the past, let go of what he had been and that his future was now in God's hands.

The following week John joined a local church and so began another chapter in his life that would take him to over twenty countries to date to speak to millions of people about how Jesus Christ had changed his life.

ABOUT THE AUTHOR

John Lawson lives in East Sussex with his wife Carolyn and her two children, Mya and Brandon. He has worked in a full time voluntary capacity since his release from prison in 2007. John has spoken in some of the toughest prisons on the planet in over 25 countries as well as schools, colleges, universities, youth clubs and church events. He also trains and equips Christians all over the world to share their faith. He maintains a good relationship with Jenny and his children; Daniel, Siobhan, Arran and Lewis, who are all grown up now.

You can e-mail John directly at john@escapeministries.co.uk
www.escapeministries.co.uk

John Sealey lives in Essex with his wife Shelley. Since retiring from the film industry as editor, producer and director, John has written several books, with many more in the pipeline. He is also working on several screenplays, including that of If a Wicked Man.

You can e-mail John Sealey at johnswritersblog@gmail.com

ENDORSEMENTS

There are those who argue that hardened criminals and gangsters are irredeemable—that we should simply lock them up and throw away the keys. They are wrong. I have visited many prisons over the past few years, and worked with some pretty tough characters through prison charity organisations. In doing so I have met a number of men like John whose lives have been challenged and turned around in prison by the same message and dramatic encounter that he experienced. In that sense John's story is not unique, but it is nonetheless a truly powerful account of a life changed by the seemingly impossible.

—**MAJOR GENERAL TIM CROSS**, CBE

I was groomed as a Mafia Prince in 'Little Chicago' and grew up to become an enforcer in the underworld of the Mob before switching sides to become a crooked cop and a bent politician. I was embroiled in a world of corruption, even planning murder to become a 'made man in the Mafia' before being sent to the State Penitentiary.

If A Wicked Man is a book I can easily relate to. I was captivated, as I saw elements of my own life in many of the pages. The story of how the breakdown of a marriage can turn a quiet and polite son into a violent and dangerous criminal is a reflection of the lost and fatherless generation of today. Social deprivation and the destruction of family life can have profound effects on our children, which may only surface years later.

The love of money and a cold heart can drive violent men like us to take by force what we feel society owes us. Taking the law into your own hands is a recipe for disaster with dire consequences for all involved. This book will take the reader on a journey where they will love, hate, empathise, laugh and cry with John Lawson as he rises through the ranks of serious crime before the police finally catch up with him. While serving five years in a Scottish prison for attempted extortion, a dramatic encounter took place that revolutionised John's life and changed him forever. His account of events is brutally honest, deadly serious and yet strangely funny at times.

This is a compelling story of a wicked and violent man that will take you on an emotional rollercoaster with an unexpected twist that will leave you challenged.

—**ROCCO MORELLI**, AUTHOR OF *FORGETTA 'BOUT IT*,
WWW.ROCCOMORELLI.ORG

We have all made mistakes at one time or another, and struggled to overcome them, but for some people it can become a lifestyle. John Lawson was a man who had profiteered on the weakness, fear and vice of others. Vividly told, this frank account of a life of twists and turns is a captivating and at times shocking insight into another world where there are no rules, no remorse and no regrets.

This is the true story of how one man, immersed in a world of crime and violence, found a turning point in his life in the most unlikely of places—his prison cell. It was a radical change that forced him to admit for the first time in his life that he was lost and headed for destruction. Nothing fundamental is easy, but this story proves that change is possible, even for those written off by society.

If A Wicked Man is told faithfully, in simple language and with no excuses. Read it, and believe that there is always hope.

—**ANNE PERRY**, BEST SELLING AUTHOR

WHAT JOHN IS DOING NOW

Update on John Lawson

I am thankful to you for reading my life story which only really began after I surrendered my life to Christ. I can vividly remember the sense of freedom I felt behind bars which has stayed with me ever since. When I was released from prison I had a burning desire to share my faith, I did not know how to go about it, but I tried in my clumsy way to share the Gospel with anyone I came across. As I read the Bible I was aware of the need for fellowship, but I was getting caught up in trying to build my life again and I never looked for a church straight away. A few months later my mother reminded me of the importance of finding a church and I realised that I was growing cold in my faith. I still believed but some of the fire was going out as I tried in my own effort to rebuild my life. I was fortunate to find a good church in Edinburgh where I began to grow in faith and discipleship and yet there was something missing. Hardly anyone at church wanted to go out and share their faith, I could not understand this and began to feel increasingly frustrated. After a year of church life I realised that I could not remain silent, I could not keep my mouth shut about Jesus. I contacted Tony Anthony, the author of a book I read in prison after I had read more about his ministry which is now called Great Commission Society. He invited me to visit him at an evangelism training conference in London and a week later we met. I learned things at that conference that confirmed the importance of sharing The Gospel and at the end of the meeting Tony invited me to join the ministry and a few weeks later I went on my first mission: Three weeks in Moldova and then over the border to Ukraine for another three weeks. It was fantastic to go on mission and reach tens of thousands for Jesus. It was quite an odd feeling at first to stand before strangers and share the terrible things I had done in my life, but it felt amazing to share the most important part...The Gospel.

At the time of the book being written, I have been blessed to share the Gospel and teach Christians to do the same in many countries to hundreds of thousands of people. I have visited some of the toughest prisons on the planet as well as schools, universities, community centres, and churches. I have also taught in Bible colleges and Christian conferences in the following countries: England, Scotland, Ireland, Wales, Austria, Belgium, France, French Guiana, Germany, Guatemala, India, Moldova, New Zealand, Nigeria, Poland, Romania, Singapore, South Africa, Switzerland, Ukraine, and Zambia with many more lined up.

Jesus Christ has rebuilt my life in many ways and continues to do so today. If I can serve your church or ministry in any way, then please do feel free to get in touch.

CPSIA information can be obtained
at www.ICGtesting.com
Printed in the USA
LVHW022316061222
734486LV00005B/487

9 781610 362252